WOMEN WHO KILL
PROFILES OF FEMALE SERIAL KILLERS

Women Who Kill
Profiles of Female Serial Killers
Carol Anne Davis

First published in Great Britain in 2001 by
Allison & Busby Limited
Suite 111, Bon Marche Centre
241-251 Ferndale Road
Brixton, London SW9 8BJ
http://www.allisonandbusby.ltd.uk
Reprinted 2001
Copyright © 2001 by CAROL ANNE DAVIS

A catalogue record for this book is available from the British Library

ISBN 0 7490 0535 1

Printed and bound in Spain by
Liberdúplex, s. l. Barcelona

CAROL ANNE DAVIS was born in Dundee, moved to Edinburgh in her twenties and now lives in southern England. She left school at fifteen and was everything from an artist's model to an editorial assistant before going to university. Her Master of the Arts degree included criminology and was followed by a postgraduate diploma in Adult & Community Education.

She has been a full time writer since graduating. Her crime novels *Shrouded* (1997), *Safe As Houses* (1999) and *Noise Abatement* (2000) have been described as chillingly realistic for their portrayals of dangerous sex and death.

For Ian

Contents

Acknowledgements

Researching a book that involves so much suffering and death takes its toll - and there were times when I saw nothing but hatred and weakness in the world. But the many people who gave freely of their time and knowledge helped restore me to a more balanced view.

I'm very grateful to the Rev Peter Timms who agreed to meet me and answer my questions. Peter is a former prison governor and an experienced counsellor. He is also the man who Myra Hindley confessed to about her role in the murders of Keith Bennett and Pauline Reade.

I'd also like to thank Robert Adams, Professor of Human Services Development at the University of Lincolnshire and Humberside for allowing me to interview him. Robert has been a prison officer and the deputy and acting governor of a young offenders institution. He also spent seven years as the director of a community programme keeping young offenders out of institutions and is the author of the compassionate and detailed book *The Abuses Of Punishment.*

It is easier to get detailed information on certain cases if you contact someone in the country where that crime occurred. To this end, thanks are due to true crime reviewer Lisa DuMond for providing additional information on several of the American cases. Lisa is a science fiction writer and author of the novel *Darkers*, but here she kept strictly to the facts. Thanks also to Australian policeman Ron McKay for giving me up to date information on the Catherine Birnie case.

Closer to home, thanks to Chameleon TV, the British producers of the Moors Murders programmes, for providing videotape and transcripts of this three part series. Thanks also to Channel 5 who aired the series and helped me obtain the information I required.

I'm equally grateful to EPOCH for sending me their materials. If they can help stop adults hitting children then we might grow into a society without violent adults. They are a small charity who deserve to make giant steps.

Finally, my grateful thanks to Allison & Busby's Publishing Director David Shelley who suggested I write this book.

Preface

Why does a young woman lure teenagers into her car then participate in their extensive rape and torture? What makes a nurse lethally inject the healthy babies in her care? Women, statistically, aren't a deadly breed - females comprise only two percent of the world's serial killers. But when the distaff side *does* commit multiple murders, they can be as cruel and compassionless as the male.

Chapters one to thirteen profile such female serial killers, with each being given her own detailed chapter. Catherine Wood and Gwen Graham share a chapter - but have their early lives separately profiled - as they killed as a team.

Most crime books jump from past to present and back again but I've worked hard to put events into chronological order so that the reader can see how the woman changes in personality and in criminality as her life unfolds.

The first two profiles are historical ones, notably Anna Zwanziger the mass poisoner who was born in 1760 and Jeanne Weber the strangler who was born in 1875. They show many of the serial killing patterns we see today - the predatory targeting of a victim and a willingness to wait till the coast is clear before offering violence. These cases also show that female serial killers aren't a modern phenomenon brought about by video nasties, violent computer games or television.

The other cases are much more contemporary, with the killers mainly active in the eighties. Though America produces many of the killers featured there are also cases from Britain, Australia and Canada plus those previously mentioned which are set respectively in Bavaria and France.

Chapter fourteen examines the classifications that female serial killers fall into - for example, the Profit Killer, the Revenge Killer or the whimsically-named Angel Of Death.

When selecting which female serial killers to profile, I concentrated mainly on the Thrill Killer cases as these are the most fascinating and also the hardest to understand. After all, most of us can empathise with a Profit Killer desiring wealth, even though we personally wouldn't murder for it. Similarly, we can comprehend the *motivation* of a Revenge Killer, who wreaks suffering and death on her unfortunate foes. But the female Thrill Killer who lures innocent people to hours or even days of suffering is much more difficult for the layperson to fathom, especially when she commits these murders again and again.

Chapter fifteen looks at how these women are often erroneously regarded by the courts as helpless pawns who murdered for love or because they were terrorised into it. It also looks at those rare instances where women are more harshly treated because of their sex.

If these findings seem in part contradictory it's because they are - one aspect of a case will depict the woman as the victim of her team killing partner, whilst in another instance she'll demonstrate that she's the sadistic one, the one in charge.

All too often, when the evidence is partially contradictory like this, the writer leaves out the facts which don't suit his or her cause. This makes for a simplified read - and it may please the casual reader who can then say 'oh, she was mad' or 'she was bad' or 'she was a clear victim.' But he will be responding to a biased interpretation of the case rather than the truth.

The final chapter looks at theories about why women kill with such brutality and at how we might change our world to make it a non-violent and desirable place.

I

CANDLE IN THE WIND

The nomadic misery of Anna Maria Zwanziger

Anna was born in Nuremberg in 1760 to a couple named Schonleben who ran an inn. In her formative years she had some security but both of her parents died by the time she was five, leaving her doubly orphaned. The pretty, intelligent child was then foisted on to various relatives.

It was doubtless an unhappy time - we know that, even today, stepchildren are often treated less well than natural children are, with all the attendant problems that abuse or a simple lack of love can bring.

The next five years passed in this way and then ten-year-old Anna was rescued by one of her richer guardians. He ensured that she was well read and educated, and imbued her with a love of good literature that would last the rest of her increasingly harrowing life.

The teenager had some stability during the years of being educated in the merchant's home but when she was just fifteen he introduced her to a man more than twice her age and insisted she marry him. Her new suitor was an alcoholic solicitor called Zwanziger who was over thirty years old. Anna pleaded with her guardian that she had no feelings for this man, but he was determined and the marriage went ahead.

Two suicide attempts

It was a disaster from the start. Her husband spent all of his time away from home - when he was there he was downing cheap wine by the bottle. Anna was left alone to read the heavily dramatised and often woeful novels and plays of the day. She gave birth to two children - and one of them, her daughter, would spend time in prison as an adult for swindling and theft.

Anna herself was given to periods of increasing melancholy and twice attempted to take her own life. Psychologists say that most people who attempt suicide really want to kill someone else, in Anna's case probably her penurious husband or a relative who had abused her. But for now her aggression was simply turned in on herself.

When her suicide attempts failed, Anna regrouped her defences and searched for a means to survive. Her husband kept spending all of the family purse and begging her not to leave him, so she took to prostitution to support her brood. At this time she was still an attractive woman who looked and sounded genteel. It was important to her to maintain a sense of status so she only slept with refined gentlemen and maintained an air of discretion. Anna was one of the successful upmarket escort girls of her day.

When she was thirty-three, her husband died leaving her even more penniless. She had various jobs and at one stage gave birth to an illegitimate child which died in a children's home. Increasingly unstable, she began to drift from one housekeeping and cooking job to the next. She became pregnant by another man who then left her. She had a miscarriage and thereafter attempted to drown herself. Her later life took on the pattern of men either ignoring her or leaving her and she flickered from one delusional relationship to another, as fragile as a candle in the wind.

Theft

Eventually at age forty-four Anna got a job as a domestic in Weimar but she ran off with one of her employer's diamond rings, presumably an attempt to find financial refuge in a world that offered no social security. She then went to live with her grown up daughter and son-in-law. But her employer advertised her theft in the local paper, destroying any good name that Anna might have clung on to, and when the son-in-law saw the advert he threw her out.

Anna now determined to find herself a second husband who could offer her some stability. When a Bavarian judge, who was separated from his wife, took her on as a housekeeper/cook, she saw him as a potential candidate. Anna tempted the wife back into the marital home then duly poisoned her by putting large doses of arsenic - which was widely available at the time - into her drinks. Arsenic is a particularly cruel poison whose symptoms include severe stomach inflammation, vomiting, bloody diarrhoea and extreme weakness, occasionally including temporarily paralysis.

The later stages can include convulsions and coma. Poor Mrs Glaser died within three days, suffering an agonizing death.

Many of the Glaser's guests also suffered from stomach complaints after eating Anna's meals. When the newly widowed Judge Glaser still showed no sexual interest in her and expressed concern at how ill his dinner guests were becoming, she left his employ and became the housekeeper of another legal professional instead.

But this new employer, Judge Grohmann, already had a fiancee and had no intention of replacing her with the thin and sallow Anna. Rebuffed again, the woman put arsenic in his tea. He too died in terrible pain but as he had suffered from gout his death was put down to natural causes and Anna was free to kill again. More sympathetic sources suggest that Anna genuinely liked Grohmann and believed the arsenic would help cure his illness, for it was used in small amounts for medicinal purposes. Other sources say that she killed him out of jealousy after his marriage banns were read out.

The latter is more likely, for poisoners seem to become addicted very quickly to their cruel powders, and she would later refer to arsenic as her truest friend. It's also true that the poisoner takes a childish glee in administering her toxic substances and controlling the outcome. It would have pleased Anna to know that Grohmann would never live to consummate the marriage with his young fiancee. Criminologists believe that there is a psycho-sexual motive behind many poisonings, and it may well have aroused the reluctantly-celibate Anna to watch the man writhing in agony.

Her next choice of employer was a magistrate, Gebhard. It's known that serial killers are often drawn to police and legal circles - Ted Bundy studied law, Ken Bianchi frequented police hangouts and pretended to be a policeman, Tim Harris was a state trooper who carried out his fantasies of hanging women and Dennis Nilsen was a probationary policeman for almost a year. Female serial killers also share this interest. Karla Homolka, profiled later, wanted to be a detective and Myra Hindley, also profiled, actually applied to join the police.

Magistrate Gebhard wanted a nurse as his sick wife had just given birth. Anna again believed that the magistrate wanted a sexual relationship with her so she killed his wife with her beloved arsenic. As Mrs Gebhard's health failed, she accused the new nurse of poisoning her, stating that her food tasted strange. Sadly no one believed her and she too died in terrible pain.

Once again Anna waited for signs of desire from her newly widowed employer - and once again she was disappointed. Now she went into an arsenic-fuelled frenzy, poisoning anyone who visited the Gebhard's household. She also poisoned Gebhard's servants who all disliked her and when she was questioned about the pain that everyone was in she said that she must have over-spiced the meals. When Gebhard found a white silt at the bottom of his brandy glass he asked her to leave, little realising the revenge she would exact.

Further deaths

Going to the kitchen, she put large amounts of arsenic in the coffee, salt and sugar jars. (Some sources say that she just poisoned the salt - but the salient fact is that she poisoned a foodstuff she knew would be used daily by everyone in the household.) She also gave the baby a sweet or a biscuit as she left the house and it too became violently ill.

Realising that a mass poisoning had taken place, the magistrate had the kitchen ingredients tested and white arsenic was found, a substance that is conveniently almost tasteless. The law now wanted to talk to Anna Zwanziger but the cook from hell had disappeared...

For the next few weeks the murderess travelled around seeking a place to live and work. Her son-in-law, now separated from his wife, refused to accommodate her and she moved back to Nuremberg. In October 1809 she was arrested there with a packet of arsenic in her pocket. Still she continued to deny everything, even trying to blame Judge Glaser for his own wife's death. She - like many of the other female killers featured in this book - was a plausible witness, able to answer all of the prosecutions questions convincingly. The trial dragged on for months.

Then the police exhumed the bodies of Fran Glaser and Judge Grohmann and found arsenic in their systems. (If arsenic has been used over some time it remains in parts of the victim's body, including the hair and fingernails.) Anna then screamed out in court that she had killed them all and would have killed more if given the chance. When asked how she could cause such suffering to her acquaintances, she said that she couldn't bear to look at their healthy, happy faces and wanted to see them writhe in pain. She added that if undetected she would have gone on poisoning men, women and children indiscriminately for many years, that she had a compulsion to kill. It was the law's turn to take a life and she was beheaded by the sword in 1811.

Typology

Anna Zwanziger doesn't qualify as a Black Widow style of killer because Black Widows mainly kill people with whom they have a strong personal relationship. Conversely, Anna deliberately poisoned many strangers who came to dine at her employer's house.

She at first fits into the Profit typology, in that she hoped to profit from a first wife's death by becoming the second wife.

Later, she moved into the Revenge category, injuring or killing those who refused to become sexually intimate with her or who simply enjoyed a zest for life that she herself now lacked. Her motivation seems similar to that of the spree killer who decides that he hates life but will injure and annihilate as many others as possible before he shoots himself. The only thing that distinguishes her from other Revenge Killers is that they usually claim their first victim in their twenties whereas Anna was twice as old.

Was she a Question Of Sanity case as some criminologists suggest? It seems doubtful. After all, she took care to hide her poison in substances where it wouldn't be detected. She left the area after poisoning the salt canister. And when brought to trial she denied the crimes for six whole months, only admitting to them when incontrovertible evidence was found in the bodies. (She might not have known that such forensic tests were possible as the method had only been perfected four years before.)

When she at last admitted some of the poisonings - she was tried for the deaths of two women and a child - Anna was quite clear about her motives. She had hated the health and happiness of those around her, which contrasted starkly with her own faded looks. Misery likes company and Anna set about making everyone around her as miserable as she possibly could.

Anna Zwanziger was dealt a bad hand in life, losing her mother and father and then being passed around like a parcel between her indifferent relatives. Her route from educated teenager to young prostitute to menial housekeeper understandably engendered further distress and bitterness. But she lost the sympathy that she was entitled to when she turned that rage on innocent bystanders and made them die early and agonising deaths.

2

LOST IN FRANCE
The dissolute life of Jeanne Weber

Jeanne was born in 1875 into a large impoverished family with the surname of Moulinet. Home was an overcrowded dwelling in a small fishing village in Northern France. Jeanne was plain, something which doubtless added to her childhood misery and she had no especial talents other than a native cunning and an innate acting ability.

Astrologers would later note that there was a complete absence of water in her birth chart, supposedly making her much harder and more ruthless than women born under a more balanced sign - but it's more likely that the childhood struggle for food, clothing and affection is what made Jeanne hard.

Waterless signs apparently also find it easier to cut themselves off from their families, something that the teenage Jeanne certainly did. As soon as she turned fourteen she moved to the capital, Paris, hoping to gain her independence and to find work.

A bad marriage

In Paris, Jeanne drifted from job to job, each of them menial. She did this for four years, until she met an equally unhappy alcoholic called Weber. Soon she married him and started joining him in drinking large amounts of the local cheap red wine. Weber, a Parisian, had few prospects and even fewer ambitions, but Jeanne was glad to have him as she knew that she was a physically unattractive woman who held limited appeal for men.

The couple set up home in a tenement slum in the Passage de la Goutte d'Or in Montmartre. There Jeanne gave birth to three children. But two of them died whilst still babies, giving her a further excuse to down bottles of cheap drink. (She would eventually be suspected of killing both these children - only her son Marcel would live to age seven before she took his little life.)

Soon the persuasive Jeanne was babysitting for two children called Lucie Alexandre and Marcel Poyatos. Outwardly she looked like the ideal babysitter, always enquiring after her charges health. Yet both infants died suddenly in her care.

Meanwhile, her three brothers-in-law and their wives all lived in the same Montmartre passageway, for she had married into a family as large as the one she'd been born into. Her young relatives would provide perfect victims for her increasingly bloodthirsty bent.

In March 1905 she agreed to babysit for her eighteen-month-old niece Georgette and two-year-old niece Suzanne whilst their mother went out to do the laundry. Shortly afterwards, a neighbour passing the door heard choking noises and hurried to alert Georgette's mother that her baby was ill. Madame Pierre raced home to find Jeanne massaging little Georgette's chest whilst the child lay on the bed. The little girl had a blue-tinged pallor, foam around her mouth and a tell-tale red mark on her neck.

Madame Pierre tended to the child and she quickly recovered. The woman then returned to her laundering - and when she came home she found the baby dead. No one suspected the distraught Jeanne Weber for a moment so nine days later she was asked to babysit the luckless survivor Suzanne. A few hours later the parents returned to find her dying in circumstances remarkably similar to those of her sibling. The doctor found the devastated Jeanne entirely plausible and put both cases down to convulsions. Jeanne carried on with her babysitting tasks.

The death toll continues

Just two weeks later a further of her charges died. Germaine was the seven-month-old daughter of another of her sisters-in-law. This time the red marks around her throat were credited to diphtheria - and three days later when Jeanne's seven-year-old son Marcel died his death was ascribed as the very same explanation. Other sources suggest that Marcel's death was put down to accidental choking, but the salient point is that foul play was not suspected and Jeanne Weber was able to continue her killing spree. A magistrate would later suggest that Jeanne killed her own son at this stage to take any suspicion away from herself as it made her look as bereaved as her grieving relatives.

Six days passed and then Weber tried to strangle one of her ten-month-old nephews, Maurice. Thankfully his mother came home at that moment, saw Jeanne choking her son, and called the police. The hospital doctor agreed it looked like someone had tried to strangle the baby so Weber went to trial at the Seine Assizes, but succeeded in acting the part of a wronged woman who'd been recently bereaved. More importantly, the most famous expert witness in France, Dr Leon Thoinot, stated that none of the exhumed children's bodies appeared to show marks of strangulation. Thoinot would later co-write a medical journal article about why he believed she was innocent. Seen as a victim of misfortune at a time when children often died of childhood diseases, she was acquitted by a jury in February 1906.

But Weber's own husband believed she was guilty - as did the general public - and he left her. Changing her surname back to Moulinet, she moved to the village of Chambron, setting up home with a man called Sylvain Bavouzet and his three motherless children. He knew of her crimes but was described as a 'sympathetic farmer', albeit one who wanted a housekeeper and a woman to warm his bed.

Released again

He paid a heavy price for inviting Jeanne into his life, for soon she reverted to type and strangled his nine-year-old son Auguste to death. At first - despite the clear bruises on the child's neck - the local doctor recorded the death as being due to convulsions, but when Jeanne Weber's history became known the doctor contacted the police and an autopsy was performed. The medical establishment decided that the boy had died of diphtheria and she was released again.

After a few months of casual employment Jeanne was offered a post at a children's home by a doctor who felt sorry for her. Soon she was choking one of her young charges. Discovered by her employers, she managed to persuade them that there was an innocent explanation for her actions and they dismissed her without reporting her actions to the police. It seems more likely that they wanted to avoid being involved in a scandal -

a hospital would let killing nurse Genene Jones, profiled later, leave with a reference rather than risk her suing them for unfair dismissal.

The prostitute

Homeless and jobless, Jeanne now returned to Paris and began to earn money as a prostitute. It was a demeaning and destitute existence that saw her occasionally arrested for vagrancy. Soon she met up with a lime-burner called Emile Bouchery and the two of them rented a room at an inexpensive inn. Neither of them made much money and Emile would beat her during their drunken arguments.

To make extra cash, Jeanne offered to babysit the owner's children. He was a busy man so readily agreed to this. She would take the little ones into bed with her for warmth and for company whilst Emile was away. The innkeeper was glad of her services - after all, Jeanne just seemed like a woman down on her luck and he had no inkling of her childkilling history.

But all that was about to change. Alerted by screams one night, he caught her strangling his ten-year-old son with a handkerchief. Weber was so caught up in the murder that he had to hit her several times before she released her manic grasp - she was in the throes of a desire that psychologists would later suggest was psycho-sexual. The object of her sadism, the child, who had bitten through his own tongue during the struggle, was dead.

This time she'd been caught in the act and was charged with murder - and found guilty. Judged to be insane, she was sent to an asylum in 1908 and found dead there two years later, having died of convulsions, her hands locked around her own throat. One French source claims she died during a 'crisis of madness' and suggests she contributed to her own death by self-strangulation. But it's hard to know the truth as two French novels were written about Weber's life, causing fiction to fuse with fact.

A sexual motive

The fact that she spent her last years in an asylum has caused some criminologists to put Weber into the 'Question Of Sanity' typology -

but it seems more likely that she was only insane towards the end of her killing spree. After all, she was sane enough to wait until the parents had left the house before she assaulted their children. And she stopped and pretended to be reviving the children if an unexpected witness appeared. Even with the last case, when the child's father was elsewhere in the building, she took care to lock the door and isolate the child from its siblings. All of these actions suggest a rational and calculating mind.

Those criminologists who see her as a Question Of Sanity case state that there was no motive for her crimes. Others suggest that there may have been a sexual motive - witnesses reported that she was sometimes standing over the dying child in a frenzy. Sexual sadism does seem likely in many strangling cases, with killers half choking the victim, letting them breathe a little, then partly asphyxiating them again. In this way, the killer can play with her - or his - victim's life whilst looking into their eyes for a cruelly long time.

A woman who just wanted to snuff out an infant's life quickly, perhaps whilst denying the full implications of her own actions to herself, would suffocate their victim by pressing their head into a pillow. Strangling involves a much more intimate and overtly sadistic approach. It's a power trip - and as an impoverished, unattractive and uneducated woman living in a slum area Jeanne Weber was a woman who would otherwise have had very little power.

Murder would have provided incredibly stimulating moments in an otherwise depressingly drab and uneventful life. It's clear that she sought out many babysitting opportunities to enjoy it. The fact that she killed her relative's children (and her own) and was able to continue to live with them without betraying any guilt or remorse suggests that she was also a psychopath, a person without a conscience. Psychopaths can be ruthless professionals or brilliant embezzlers. Most of them don't kill - but if they do they feel little or no remorse.

Psychopaths also tend to be of above average intelligence, and if they are criminals they plan their murders carefully. They are usually plausible liars, so much so that guilty psychopaths can effortlessly pass lie detector tests. Jeanne seemed to fit the bill as she originally persuaded France's top legal experts that she was innocent and sane so that they protested strongly in her favour. She was also given second and third chances by doctors, relatives and even strangers who knew her history.

In conclusion, it's clear that Jeanne Weber had a bad start in life - born into poverty and with too many siblings around for her to be nurtured. Given her later cruel actions, it's also likely that she was physically abused throughout her miserable childhood. She took to drink very quickly - and it's known that alcoholism is often hereditary, so perhaps there was also the added abuse or neglect that alcoholic parents bring to the home. She left as soon as she could and became involved with a male alcoholic, who clearly had his own problems. Life shrank to an endless round of drinking cheap wine in a squalid baby-filled tenement until...

Partaking in that first murder clearly gave Jeanne Weber a satisfaction she hadn't known before, and she soon plotted to repeat it. A damaged life went on to damage many others, a theme that will rebound throughout this book.

3

MAD ABOUT THE BOY
Myra Hindley's life altering lover

Myra Hindley was born on 23rd July 1942 to a working class couple in Manchester, England. Her mother, Hettie, was a machinist and her father, Bob, an aircraft fitter, often away from home because of the war. She was three years old before he came home permanently - and he would later admit that he never took to her. He wasn't the kind of father who hugged his children or took part in any of their games.

After the war Bob worked as a labourer and would take part in boxing matches to bring in a few more pounds. He spent most of this money in the pub, often going there after work and staying there for the evening. Sometimes Hettie's widowed mother would come round and keep her daughter company, though the two women weren't particularly close.

Bob would sometimes hit Hettie when he came home drunk, and little Myra would cling to his legs in a vain bid to make him stop the violence. Myra's gran would also hit her son-in-law in an effort to stop him hurting Hettie during these wife-beating acts. Bob would also hit Myra during his drunken rages - and as he often worked on building sites he was a powerfully built man.

When Myra's sister Maureen was born in the summer of 1946, Myra was sent to stay with her gran who only lived a few minutes walk away. Strangely, her parents didn't ever take her home again and she was to live with Gran until she was arrested at the age of twenty-three. She wasn't ostracised as there was lots of contact between the two houses, but it must have made the four-year-old feel different from her peers.

From an early age she learned to hide her feelings, and would later write to a journalist: 'I refused to cry when my father was hitting me or when I drove my mother to hit me too.' But she added that she'd cry alone afterwards in her room. She would remain close to her mother throughout her life but despised her distant father. After he was involved in an industrial accident he became even more taciturn and apparently bordered on being a recluse.

At five Myra went to junior school, where one report said she was not very sociable - hardly surprising given that she was living with an older lady. She was also allowed to skip school often as company for her grandmother. Her widowed gran was only in her fifties yet didn't work and apparently didn't see education as important so at home Myra was lacking a positive influence. Her mother, who has been described as delicate and overworked, also abdicated responsibility when it came to giving the questioning child any guidance and it was hard for Myra to learn anything good by watching her parents together as their relationship was so poor.

Myra would later say that she felt like a 'fish out of water' during these primary school years. Superficially she seemed mature for her age - and very soon started to mother younger children in the neighbourhood. She thought her baby sister Maureen, whose name she soon shortened to Mo, was great.

Maureen was waif-like but Myra herself was stockily built, a tomboy who did well at netball and rounders. She also loved writing poetry and her school essays were often praised. But her lack of attendance took its toll and she failed her eleven plus, which prevented her from going on to the superior schools at this time referred to as grammar schools. Instead she went to a Secondary Modern.

Myra's IQ at this stage was deemed to be 109, which is only slightly above average. She'd grown up in a home where education wasn't encouraged, a home without books. Years later she would earn a university degree in prison, for which you normally need an IQ of 120 or more.

By the time she was a teenager, Myra had taken to babysitting the local children and her young charges loved her. She was good at bathing them, playing with them and even teaching the youngest ones how to walk so their parents felt safe leaving her at the helm. She even considered becoming a full time childminder or nursery nurse, either of which could have been her passport to working abroad.

Myra talked about emigrating, a brave step for a working class girl from an area where people rarely travelled - indeed, some of her father's relatives lived within walking distance. And even when offered a new house in a better area, her mother - by then having an affair with a local bus driver - would refuse to move away.

Just before her fifteenth birthday, one of Myra's younger friends, Michael, asked her to go swimming with him. She declined as she was spending the day with another friend so Michael went swimming in the local reservoir alone. He drowned - and when Myra heard of the accident she was desolate. She cried for days and fell into a deep depression that touched his grieving mother and other witnesses. The maternal teenager blamed herself for not going swimming with him. She even collected money for his funeral wreath.

The only outward signs of a desire for control at this stage are reported in Jean Ritchie's detailed book *Myra Hindley: Inside The Mind Of A Murderess*. Ritchie notes that Myra took judo lessons and would hold her opponents down after they begged her to stop. As a result some girls allegedly refused to practice the sport with her.

This unsportsmanlike trait aside, she was like many other teenagers, becoming passionate about religion, trying out the latest fashions, going to dances and dying her hair. She also dated boys, breaking off an engagement to one on the grounds that he was too immature for her. She continued to love children and animals, but felt increasingly, and understandably, bored. She changed her place of employment four times - being sacked from one typing job for poor attendance - and the man that she met at her fourth place of work would forever change her life.

A change of philosophy

By her late teens she was dissatisfied with living in the same drab area, doing the same type of uncreative work, socialising with the same unambitious people. She therefore began to daydream about Ian Brady, the clerk at her new workplace, writing in her diary that she wanted to look after him and that she was in love with him.

The other people who worked at Millwards Ltd, a chemical firm, were friendly but unexceptional. In contrast, Ian spoke German and dressed exotically in black and was well read. Admittedly his taste ran to studies of Nazism but Myra was more interested in nurturing him or marrying him than in more intellectual pursuits. She was an impressionable eighteen-year-old with love to give whilst he was an ostensibly more mature twenty-three.

The fact that she and her father were so estranged may explain her attraction to Ian Brady, at first impressions an aloof and distant man who alternately spoke to her and ignored her. Adults often recreate unsatisfactory childhood patterns, perhaps in the subconscious hope of improving them this time round. Ian was five years older than Myra - and Myra's father had been seven years older than her mother. Ian was also very good looking, and slightly resembled Elvis Presley who Myra adored.

The lover

Ian's father is unknown - his unmarried mother said that he was a Glasgow journalist who died when she was six months pregnant. Ian would later see his illegitimacy as a source of shame, for it was considered a stigma in those unenlightened days.

For the first three months of his life he lived with his mother Maggie (who would later change her name to Peggy) in a slum tenement in the Glasgow Gorbals, being left with whoever she could find whilst she waitressed nights in a tearoom. It was an exhausting life, and when she could no longer cope she placed an advert describing herself as a working widow who needed someone to adopt her child.

A Mrs Sloan took three-month-old Ian on and took him back to the house she shared with her husband, two sons and two daughters. She was a nice woman who suffered from slight deafness - a deafness that would increase over the years and make her relationship with Ian increasingly difficult. Even as a young baby he was much less outgoing than her other children had been.

As a child Ian was intelligent and dominant and - like many working class schoolchildren before him - very bored. He took to burglary whilst still at primary school, presumably as a means to obtain funds (the Sloans were kind and respectable but poor), to feel stimulated and to have status. At sixteen he was put on probation and ordered to rejoin his natural mother Peggy who had remarried and now lived in Manchester.

This was the first time he'd been told that Peggy was his mother - throughout his childhood he'd been told that she was a close family friend.

Due to her move from Glasgow to Manchester he had had only sporadic contact with her for the previous four years.

In Manchester the locals laughed at his Scottish accent and his stepfather threatened to hit him if he got into any more trouble. The man also found him a labouring job in a market. Once again, he felt like an outsider and spent much of his spare time reading in his room. After loading some stolen lead onto a lorry he was charged again and given the harsh sentence of two years in Borstal. By now he was filled with resentment at society and wanted to make others suffer as he had done.

Myra studied the sullenly handsome youth as he gave her dictation in the office they shared together and was exalted every time he took a sly look at her.

The solitary Brady remained alternatively embarrassed and aloof for month after month but eventually kissed her after an office night out then asked her on a date to see a film. One source states that they went to see *Trial At Nuremberg*. Another suggests it was a movie about the life of Jesus but this seems unlikely as the free-thinking Ian had been an atheist from the age of twelve. A third source says that the film was *El Cid*. Whatever his preferred choice, one thing is certain - Myra wildly enthused about it. She had been infatuated with Brady for almost a year and this was her chance to win his love.

Myra had been looking for something to fill her largely pointless life - and now she had found it. She soaked up Ian's philosophy (which was often racist, violent and simplistic) as if she were a sponge. She read every book he gave her, including the true murder story *Compulsion* and other texts about the strong overcoming the weak.

At one stage he literally overcame her by drugging her drink. Semi-conscious, she could remember intense pain and flashing lights. When she came to he admitted that he had put some of her grandmother's sleeping pills in her wine to see how long she'd be sedated. He added that he was thinking of disposing of his sick dog in this way.

Shocked and frightened, Myra went to her friend May Hill and told her some of the details. She was too embarrassed to talk openly about the entire incident so wrote it down for her friend, adding that if something bad happened to her then May was to take the letter to the police. She added that Ian had threatened harm to three other people she knew -

probably her mother, her gran, and Ronnie Sinclair, the boy to whom she had previously been engaged.

Deciding that she had to get away, Myra applied to the NAAFI for a clerical job in Germany. She took the train to London for the interview - and when she came back Ian was waiting for her. He accompanied her home where she told her mother and gran that she'd got the job, but they weren't impressed at the prospects that this offered her. Instead they were very upset at the thought of her moving abroad and she loved them so much she decided to stay. She continued to date Ian, riding pillion on his motorbike. He took her away from the cramped streets of Manchester's Gorton to enjoy picnics and wine on the moors.

Soon she told May to destroy the letter - though May would testify to its content at the trial. By now Myra had clearly decided to comply with whatever this fascinating but very dangerous lover wanted her to do. This included dyeing her hair blonde and parading about in leather boots in the manner of the female Nazi Concentration Camp guard, Irma Grese.

Forging our own identity is part of growing up, and the rage-filled philosophy Ian Brady fed Myra was a million miles away from the 'meet a nice boy and have kids' option spouted by those around her. But his handsome features, soft Scottish voice and autodidactism made him far more attractive than her unambitious family, so Myra started to remould herself as her lover wished.

She had given him her virginity on their second date (she was nineteen) and soon agreed to have anal sex with him, despite the fact that it hurt her. Serial killers and power rapists often prefer forced sodomy and oral sex to vaginal sex as it demeans the victim more.

On other occasions Brady told her to insert a candle into his anus and then to masturbate him. It may be that he was abused as a child - he certainly spent lots of time alone out of doors as a child feeling different and slighted, a demeanour which would have made him vulnerable to paedophile seduction. The candle incident with Myra might have been his way of trying to take control of such homo-erotic actions forced on him as a child or during his Borstal years. He was clearly concerned only with his own internal script, but couldn't fail to note that she didn't seem to mind.

Before long Ian moved into Myra's gran's house permanently, though they told the neighbours that he slept on the settee and was there to confront any burglars. (There had been many burglaries in the area.) In reality they slept together though Ian quickly tired of conventional sex.

Myra would later describe him as 'a powerful personality' and write that she was 'unworldly... a dreamer, a romantic.' Whatever her true motive, she was letting herself be turned into a woman who would do whatever her lover wanted.

Even at this stage she could have been saved. Many youths feel understandably alienated from the families they're born into. Many want something different and temporarily seek it in the occult, in religion, in the music of alienation or in arcane philosophies. Later they move on to find fulfilment in a career, sport or other interest instead.

Given her childhood experiences, we can perhaps understand why the teenage Myra agreed with Brady's *talk* of killing for thrills - because the existentialism of it all made her feel superior to her peers who thought only of boyfriends and bingo. Her talking about murder also pleased Ian, something that she was desperate to do. She even allowed him to carry her about on the moors as practice for when he had a dead body to dispose of - and she took shooting lessons when he fantasized about them robbing a bank. But then she took the step that would cut her off from most human understanding: she helped him realise his murderous plans.

The first victim

The pair had talked for months about abducting someone for Ian to rape, with his insistance that rape was just a state of mind rather than a criminal act. He looked down on most of the uneducated people who surrounded him and wanted to crush them like ants.

In July 1963 Ian asked twenty-one-year-old Myra to get him a child because a child would happily go off with a woman. Myra obligingly parked her van and waited for a likely victim to walk past. Soon she saw sixteen-year-old Pauline Reade, who lived just two doors away from Myra's brother-in-law, David. The teenage David had recently married Myra's little sister Maureen and they would soon produce their first child. Pauline was on her way to a dance a mere half mile away from the home she shared with her mum and dad.

Myra called to Pauline and asked if she'd accompany her on a drive to the moors to look for an expensive lost glove. She promised Pauline some gramophone records as a reward for helping in the search, saying that she had them in the boot of the car. It was a lovely summer night - and Pauline wasn't sure that her friends would be at the dance - so she said she was in no hurry and happily agreed to the change of plan. Myra drove the unsuspecting girl to Saddleworth Moor and Ian followed a discreet distance behind on his motorbike.

We will never know exactly what was said and done to the frightened teenager when the threesome met up - but by the end of the evening she had been raped by Ian Brady and had her throat cut by him. She struggled so hard that he found her difficult to control and would request that Myra procure him a younger and smaller victim next time.

Now he fetched Myra and a spade from the van and led her back to the body. (Her variously reported reactions to this are detailed later in this chapter.) They buried the still warm corpse in a shallow grave. Myra then drove them home and Ian burned his clothes and shoes to destroy any forensic evidence.

Like many criminals, Myra was fascinated by police work - and would now apply to join the force. She went for an interview, which she passed, and was given forms to fill in. Ian joked that it would be useful to have inside information and it was then, she said, that she decided not to take her application further. But she would later date a policeman who came to buy her van, seeing him on nights when Ian was otherwise engaged. Ian went to see his birth mother Peggy every week, but wouldn't let Myra meet her. Even if she drove him to Peggy's house, she had to wait outside in the car. It was yet another subtle form of his sadism, making it clear to her that she wasn't special enough to be introduced as his girlfriend.

The second victim

Four months later Ian decided it was time to kill again. Myra bought the knife. The pair then offered twelve-year-old John Kilbride a lift home from the cinema. He knew not to accept lifts from strangers but thought he was safe because Myra was driving. He, too, was taken to a desolate part of the moor and raped by Ian Brady, who also admitted slapping the boy's buttocks before strangling him. Myra stayed, acting as look-out, in the van.

Brady later told her that he'd wanted to cut the child's throat but that the knife wasn't sharp enough so he strangled him with a thin piece of string. The boy's remains were found in October 1965, two years after his death.

The third victim

Seven months passed before the third death, that of another twelve-year-old, Keith Bennett. He'd gone to spend the night with his grandmother, a regular occurrence. Myra and Ian encountered him before he reached his granshouse, offered him a lift and drove him to the moors. He too was raped by Brady before being strangled. Despite extensive police searches with tracker dogs and specialist equipment, his body has never been found.

The fourth victim

Ten-year-old Lesley Ann Downey died six months later, on Boxing Day 1964. In *Beyond Belief*, his book on the subject, author Emlyn Williams suggests that the day before, Ian had suggested he wanted to commit another murder but that Myra had refused to take part in it. He then packed his suitcase, suggesting the relationship was over, and she relented as she couldn't live without him. He had become her life.

In truth, it's more likely that this incident took place some time after the *first* murder, that of Pauline Reade. At the time Emlyn Williams wrote his book in 1967 he didn't know for sure that Ian was responsible for the disappearance of Pauline Reade and Keith Bennett so - though he mentions both children in the Appendix - his account begins with the murder of John Kilbride.

Given the evidence that was to follow, there was no doubt that they were responsible for Lesley's demise. The ten-year-old had been at the fun fair when she accepted a lift home from the friendly-seeming couple. They took her back to the house (Myra's gran was visiting relatives) and told her to take off her clothes apart from her socks and shoes.

Then they set up a tripod and began to take pornographic photographs of her. They ordered her to stand and sit in various sexually explicit poses, tied her hands together and gagged her with a man's scarf. Ian hoped to sell the photographs on the black market - he had taken previous shots of himself and Myra wearing hoods in similar states of undress.

Ian switched his taperecorder on and this seventeen minute tape would later be played back in court to a shocked jury. Serial killers often make audio or video recording of their victims during their ordeal, using the tapes afterwards as a masturbatory aid.

The tape starts with a scream, unclear voices then another scream. Then Lesley says 'Don't... Please God, help me.' Brady is heard telling her to do as she's told. The little girl says that she has to go home as her mum is expecting her and Myra snaps 'Don't dally.' Lesley says to Myra 'Help me, will you?' When the child refuses to be gagged Myra says 'Shut up or I'll forget myself and hit you one,' then 'Will you stop it? Stop it!' She orders the girl to put the handkerchief back into her mouth.

The child is heard to be retching because the handkerchief is being pushed down her throat. The jurors would later be handed photograph albums of the crime scene to study. Some of the snapshots showed Lesley with a scarf tied tightly around her mouth and with what appears to be the corner of handkerchief sticking out from under it. An observer at the trial suggested that at another stage Ian or Myra had filled the little girl's mouth with cotton wool and gagged her with tape.

Myra says that she was out of the room when Lesley's murder occurred - but Ian was earlier heard on the tape in Myra's presence, threatening to slit the child's throat, so she must have known that the child's death was imminent. He apparently then told Myra to run a bath as he wanted to wash the child clean of any forensic evidence. When she returned to the bedroom the child was dead and had blood on her thighs, indicating that she'd been raped.

Emlyn Williams, who has seen the photographs, said that the child looks subdued. He believes that the abuse heard on the tape took place first and that only then were the photographs taken. He adds that the poses are like ballet poses, only pornographic to the corrupt eye. The child had been told to stretch out her arms in one photograph - he believes that's where the erroneous rumours about her crucifixtion started. When the body was found the innards had been gnawed at by rats and this led to false suggestions that she'd been disembowelled whilst still alive. This misinformation has persisted over the years so that these murders are almost invariably described as torture murders. But Detective Peter Topping said in his autobiography that there's no proof that torture was involved - though, as he rightly adds, gagging and raping a child involves causing tortuous fear and suffering.

With a captive child in the house, Myra couldn't let her gran return at 9pm. It was after eleven before she turned up at her uncle's house to find the old woman asleep in her chair. Myra appeared flushed and out of breath to her relatives. She told them that she couldn't drive her gran home as the weather was too bad. They disagreed as there had only been a flurry of snow but Myra was insistent that they put the old lady up on the bed settee and she'd return for her tomorrow if the roads were clear.

The next day Ian and Myra took Lesley's body to the moor and buried it alongside her clothes and the string of white plastic beads that her brother had given her for Christmas. Ten months later, in October 1965, the body was found by the police who saw an arm sticking eerily through the soil.

The last victim

Edward Evans was Myra and Ian's last victim simply because Ian became arrogant and decided to involve a third party. Like most serial killers he had increased in confidence as his killing spree progressed and may have started to feel above the law, invincible. The unwilling voyeur was Myra's brother-in-law, seventeen-year-old David Smith.

David was enamoured of Ian's talk about robbing banks - and loved to drink and smoke all night with him. He too had been starved of love and education so was hugely interested in the daytrips to the moors offered by his new friend and by the books by the Marquis de Sade that Ian lent him. The two men became close and Ian clearly thought that David could become another Myra, helping him lure more victims to their deaths.

Myra was totally against bringing David Smith in. She didn't like him and didn't particularly trust him. And she hadn't wanted her little sister Maureen to marry him.

Maureen, for her part, was noticing that her adoring older sister Myra had changed. Outwardly she'd grown harder, agreeing with Ian that marriage was meaningless and that motherhood was for fools. But Myra had also become nervous and insisted on sleeping with the lights on when it got too late to go home and she had to share her sister's bed. She also anxiously told a neighbour not to talk about pregnancy in front of Ian as he'd become enraged.

Ian's rage was about to intensify for the very last time. He and Myra went out looking for a victim and eventually met seventeen-year-old Edward Evans outside a bar. The couple asked him back to their house, saying that they were brother and sister. Back home, they found that Myra's gran was in bed so Ian began to ply the boy with drink. Edward was a slim young man who was all dressed up for the evening, an apprentice engineer who was shy with girls.

It's apparent that the three of them had sex - for David Smith had seen Myra dressed up earlier that day, yet when he saw her that night she had on very old clothes so she must have changed sometime after luring Edward back to her gran's house. It would never be known if she was the sexual bait that lured the youth to the house or if Ian was. The bar that Edward had been to was a homosexual haunt and most newspapers automatically assumed that he was homosexual. But when his body was found there was an old letter from a girl in his trouser pocket that clearly meant a great deal to him.

That some sexual acts occurred is not in question. When the teenager's body was discovered his flies were undone and there were dog hairs around his anus and in his underwear. The hairs were believed to have come from the couch where Myra's dogs liked to lie and where the sex presumably took place.

After the threesome, Ian sent Myra away, telling her to collect David Smith by promising him alcohol. When she arrived at his house he was in bed reading with his wife but he dutifully got up and agreed to walk her home.

David Smith entered the lounge to find Ian swinging an axe at Edward's skull. Myra shouted 'Dave, help him. Help him.' Dave froze as Ian battered at the youth's head again and again. When David Smith still didn't help kill the teenager, who continued to gurgle, Ian grabbed an electric flex and tied it tightly around the dying boy's neck.

When Edward Evans was dead, Brady commented to Myra that this particular death was the messiest yet. She had possibly watched her lover bring the axe down on the teenager's skull fourteen times - David Smith would later admit that she might have been in the kitchen when the bulk of the attack took place. Nevertheless, she was not totally immune to the horror of the situation, retching when confronted by a piece of brain tissue on the carpet and refusing to pick it up.

Ian had tired himself out from the night's events and had also hurt one of his ankles during the struggle. The couple said goodnight to the white faced David Smith and he left their house, trying to look nonchalant. Locking the trussed body into a chest in the spare room, Ian and Myra went to bed.

At dawn the next day a terrified Smith, and his wife, Maureen, contacted the police and told them he thought the body was still in the house. A policeman knocked and when Myra opened the door he thought she was thirty-five or older rather than her actual twenty-three. She was already in full makeup and getting ready to go to work. She tried to keep them out of the locked room, explaining that she kept her guns there and that the key was at work. But the police were insistent so Ian gave her permission to unlock the door.

The trussed-up body was found and he was arrested. Myra wasn't, because David Smith had explained to the police that it was Ian who had battered the boy to death with the axe. But Myra insisted on coming down to the station to be near Ian and she stayed there for most of the next five days, mainly talking to a policewoman in the canteen. She talked about her dogs at length, and it was clear that, next to Ian, they received all her love.

Finally the police phoned her mother and insisted that they take her home. At last she realised that Ian wasn't coming back and she went into shock. At his behest, she destroyed some envelopes that may have contained plans for bank robberies or other incriminating evidence. But later the house was sealed off and she had to stay with her mother. As a result, she wasn't able to get the key that would open the left luggage locker at the station which held the incriminating Lesley Ann Downey tape.

The police found the key, opened the locker and soon sifted through its hellish contents. Myra's fingerprints were found on the photographs of the gagged Lesley Ann Downey and Myra's voice was heard telling her to be quiet on the tape. Most of the orders being given came from Ian, and obviously only he could have committed the rape.

Myra was desperate to protect her lover at all costs. Unlike six of the other cases in this book - where after their arrest the Team Killers swiftly turned against each other - she firmly stood by her man.

When Ian was first arrested, she told the police that she had been everywhere that he had been and that he had done nothing on his own.

By the time of the trial the already older-looking Myra had aged visibly. She now denied everything, suggesting they were both innocent. Both entered a plea of not guilty to all three of the murders they were being charged with - those of John Kilbride, Lesley Ann Downey and Edward Evans. Their responsibility for the murders of Pauline Reade and Keith Bennett wasn't yet known. Myra was determined to remain twinned to her beloved Ian, yet if she'd turned against him and become a witness for the prosecution, she would have been released years ago.

The trial

The charges were answered at Chester in the spring of 1966. After much debate, it was agreed that the two of them would be tried together. This wasn't in Myra's best interests, as a female Team Killer who is tried separately from her male co-conspirator tends to get a lesser sentence. Moreover, she had played a lesser part in the murders than her lover did. Both parties representatives had objected to the potential female jurors so they were heard before an all male jury - though the members of the public who queued to see the trial were mainly women.

The court had to erect bullet-proof glass to screen the murderers as so many members of the public expressed a desire to kill them. It was billed as the trial of the century.

The charges related to Edward Evans whose body had been found in their home, to Lesley Ann Downey because they were implicated on the tape which the police had found at a left luggage locker, and to John Kilbride whose body had been discovered as had a notebook in Ian's writing with John's name in it. The police had also uncovered photos of Myra posing on John Kilbride's moorside grave.

Both denied killing the children and lied about their involvement with Lesley Ann Downey, saying that they had just taken pornographic pictures and the tape of her then watched her leave with two men. They had promised each other that they'd show no emotion at the trial, that they wouldn't give society that satisfaction. Nevertheless, as part of the transcript of the tapes was read out, Myra buried her head in her hands and a vein pulsed strongly in her neck.

The seventeen minute tape of Lesley being stripped and sexually abused was played in court, so Myra had to admit to being present. Incredibly she asked the court to believe that she had been listening to the radio or looking out of the window whilst the child was abused in the same room, so hadn't seen most of the abuse. Brady, however, had slipped up earlier using the statement 'we all got dressed' which suggests that Myra took part in the sexual acts. The photographs were all of the child on her own so there was no visible proof of exactly what took place.

The court said that Myra had taken the child upstairs and stripped her and gagged her then brought her back to the downstairs lounge where Brady was waiting with the camera. They verbally tormented the girl and physically fondled her then they took her upstairs to Myra's bedroom, pulled the curtains closed and set up the tripod again.

Ian's testimony played down Myra's part in Lesley's ordeal - and there was no concrete proof that she witnessed the other murders. She stared at him throughout most of the trial and was clearly in love.

The prosecution said that 'the same pairs of hands killed all three of these victims.' In other words, they held the couple to be equally responsible. The defence disagreed, stating that Myra was the servant and Ian the master. After all, she had loved children and animals before meeting him and had been desolate at the death of her young friend Michael. She'd been a puritanical virgin rather than a sexual satyr. Nevertheless, the jury took a mere two hours and fourteen minutes to make up their minds.

The Moors Murderers were both found guilty on 6th May 1966 of the

murder of Edward Evans and Lesley Ann Downey. Brady was also convicted of murdering John Kilbride, whilst Myra was convicted of being an
accessory to this killing. She'd driven the boy to the moor then driven
home without him, so was clearly implicated as an accessory. She swayed
as her sentence was read out.

She was jailed for life for the murders of Edward Evans and Lesley Anne
Downey, with an additional seven year sentence for her part in John
Kilbride's killing. Ian got life for each of the three murders. The death penalty had been abolished earlier that year but if it had still been in use they
would most probably have been hanged.

Myra's main concern, other than for Ian, was for the welfare of her
remaining dog. One dog, Poppet, had been inadvertently killed whilst in
police custody. The police had sent the dog to a vet to have its age determined and this involved examining its teeth under an anaesthetic.
Unfortunately it had a bad reaction to the anaesthetic and died, prompting
Myra to remark that the police were murderers. She was genuinely concerned about her other dog and continued to send a neighbour money to
care for it.

In prison Myra continued to perceive Ian as the love of her life and lived
for his weekly letters. It seems that she still wanted to show herself as
heartless for she wrote 'they call us the Moors Murderers. I didn't murder
any moors, did you?' Though Brady had been anti-marriage and had talked
Myra around to this view, she now hoped that they would be allowed to
marry in jail as married prisoners are allowed more access to each other
than those who are single. She wrote to him 'Freedom without you means
nothing. I've got one interest in life, and that's you.'

In letters to a journalist she would say it was six years before his hold
over her weakened and she told him to stop writing to her. Thereafter she
reverted to her pre-Brady normal frame of mind.

Confession

For the next twenty years, Myra kept quiet about her and Ian's part in the
murders of Pauline Reade and Keith Bennett, though the police were convinced she and Ian were responsible. Then she received a letter from Keith

Bennett's mother which clearly touched her. Keith's mother wanted to know where her son was buried so that she could put her mind at rest and give her son a regular funeral.

In the same time frame, Myra was receiving counselling from the Reverend Peter Timms, the man whom she would finally confess to. I interviewed Peter Timms in May 2000 whilst researching the case.

Peter Timms trained as a marriage guidance councillor in 1963. When he was twenty-two he joined the prison service and later helped run a young offenders establishment. He was Governor of Maidstone Prison between 1975 and 1981. During his last three years there he was also training to be a Methodist minister, a position he still holds. He had extensive experience of counselling outside prisons prior to Myra and has worked with vulnerable groups within the community.

He also has comprehensive experience of lifers, as when he was governor of Maidstone over a hundred of the prisoners were serving a life sentence. In total he has spent twenty-nine years in the prison service and is a kind and altruistic man.

He started to take an interest in Myra's case in the autumn of 1983 and later went to visit her in Cookham Wood prison at the suggestion of her chaplain. Peter lived near the prison at this time so visited her often and slowly she began to open up. Between 1985 and 1986 he counselled her extensively - and finally she admitted that she'd procured Pauline Reade and Keith Bennett for Ian Brady to rape and kill. For twenty years she and Ian had denied playing any part in these deaths but now she told Peter Timms that she wanted to go on the record and make a public confession.

Many books on the Moors Murders report that Myra initially confessed to Detective Chief Superintendent Peter Topping - but this isn't true. She confessed to Peter Timms and then instructed her solicitor, Michael Fisher, to bring in the police. At this stage Detective Topping was called in and several days of talks took place. The three men listened to Myra's confession, and Peter Timms held her hand whilst she cried. Detective Topping admitted in his frank book on the subject that Myra became deeply distraught at remembering the children's deaths and that at times she had to be tranquillised.

The Reverend Timms says Ian Brady's power over Myra was absolute. 'He had authority, was articulate. She'd grown up in a home where educa-

tion wasn't important yet was suddenly being noticed by this knowledgeable assured man.' For the first time there was a world outside local dances
and bingo halls. He was also very good looking, similar to James Dean who
most young girls were infatuated with at that time.

Peter Timms adds that 'there was a competitive element with the other
women in the office,' and 'she became special for the first time in her life
because he asked her out.' Ian read Dostoievsky as his daily diet and she
had probably been challenged by nothing more taxing than a beauty magazine before.

Peter is honest enough to admit that there must have been a 'psycho-
sexual element' in the murders for her, that it appealed to something latent
in her personality. Nevertheless, he adds that when she saw Pauline's body
she became hysterical and Brady slapped her twice and told her to calm
down or 'you'll go into the grave with her.' He was clearly terrified that
she'd go to the police and stayed by her side watching her closely for the
two days after the girl's death. They lived together, went to work together
and spent their days together, so he had many hours in which to influence
her. During this time she allegedly convinced herself that Pauline's murder
was an aberration, that it would never happen again.

Myra admitted to Peter Timms that she was terrified that Ian would finish with her. After one argument he'd roared away on his motorbike leaving her miles from home on a lonely roadside, and she'd been desolate.

The Sloans, Ian's foster family, also witnessed how lost she was without
him. Ian had taken her to Glasgow to meet them all and they thought that
she looked hard and awkward. Yet at the same time it was clear that she
was desperate to be liked. At night she and Ian went to the cinema and
when they returned it was obvious that they'd been arguing. Myra was
shaking and red in the face. Ian went out again on his own, and the family
felt sorry for the sad-eyed young girl who was so totally in his thrall and
so completely in love with him.

For Ian gave her status, a kind of love, grandiose dreams beyond the dull
repetitiveness of a typing job. Without this, Peter Timms believes Myra saw
herself as 'a non person.' She had wanted marriage - but due to Ian's influence she had now renounced marriage. She had wanted children - but had
given her heart to a man who clearly wasn't capable of showing compassion to kids. The first man in her life, her father, had alternately rejected and

beat her - and now she was desperate to hold on to this long term relationship with Ian, this kind of love.

It seems that her desire to help find Pauline and Keith's bodies was now genuine. 'Myra was prepared to be hypnotised... anything to help. That's why she visited the moors,' Peter Timms says. There, despite becoming very distraught and at times disorientated, she was able to remember geographical landmarks that helped the police locate Pauline's body, but Keith's body has never been found.

Asked if there was torture involved in the murders, Peter Timms says no, adding that the tape recording of Lesley's ordeal was indistinct because the tape was hidden under the bed. Myra claims she didn't know it was there. Lesley screams when asked to strip and again when Ian Brady grabs her by the neck to make her take her coat off. The abuse is verbal and sexual. Someone incarcerated with Ian Brady would later say that the girl's fingers had been cut off with lawn shears - and this also fuelled the rumours of gross abuses. But none of the bodies showed signs of torture and all of the fingers were intact.

Peter Timms explains that after their arrests Ian and Myra made a pact to look coldly at the police camera, to show no sign of emotion. It was important to Ian that they seem to be above society, filled with disdain. Later, when he was photographed without his knowledge looking thoughtful in the back of a police car, he was furious and wanted to kill the photographer.

Asked about his initial impression of Myra, Peter says he was surprised at 'how normal she was.' He had also met her mother 'a nice old lady, worn down by the burden of what happened.' Everyone who knows Myra's mother has referred to her as a hard worker. Unlike most people involved in the case, Hettie Hindley has never gone to the press and sold her story. She could have made a great deal of money but instead resides in an old folks home in relative penury.

Myra has remained close to her mother and Peter Timms says Myra sees her as 'an anchor to her selfhood - to her being.' Her mother has supported her since the trial and has often visited her in prison. Her sister Maureen visited a couple of times, divorced David Smith and remarried, but ultimately died young of a brain hemorrhage. Myra's parents divorced shortly after the trial. Her father never once visited her and is now dead.

Ian's version of the story

A friend of someone who I interviewed has visited Ian Brady for years. Brady has been diagnosed as schizophrenic and is locked up in a high security hospital. He is seriously underweight as he often refuses to eat for fear that the staff are trying to poison him. (Prisoners food is, indeed, often adulterated by other prisoners, either in the kitchens or enroute to the serving place.) At various periods he has refused sustenance altogether as he claims he wants to die.

He is apparently enraged that he has lost his hold on Myra - and one of his visitors believes his one purpose for staying alive is to keep Myra in prison until she dies.

For years Ian maintained that Myra played no part in the actual murders - and this seems likely, given his need to control every situation. He probably didn't want a witness when he was sodomising the male children. He was high dominance and she was medium dominance, so he saw her as his inferior, expected her to do what she was told.

But in the eighties he would tell a journalist that Myra helped carry out the sexual assault on Pauline and also inflicted injuries on the sixteen-year-old's face. He would also add that Myra strangled Lesley with a length of nylon cord.

However, Ian also told Detective Chief Superintendent Topping of another five murders of adults that he'd committed, and police investigation later found that one of those murders was the work of someone else and that another was more likely a suicide. His part in all five of the alleged murders proved unlikely. Either a mixture of time and mental illness had confused the solitary Scotsman or he simply invented his involvement in the hope of feeling in control of his life again.

Detective Topping interviewed both Myra and Ian extensively and found her to be the more credible interviewee who genuinely wanted to help find the bodies. She was, indeed, willing to be hypnotised in case it would help her remember further details of the gravesites. She agreed to do it, her medical adviser agreed she could do it, and Detective Peter Topping found a skilled hypnotherapist who wanted to do it - but the Home Office repeatedly turned the request down.

Ian, like Myra, went back up to the moors with the police and looked for familiar landmarks. He was less visibly distressed than she was during visits there, but also less helpful. He told Peter Topping that he felt ashamed of his actions and could not bear to think about what he'd done.

Denial

Myra has also admitted to feelings of shame and remorse. She seems to have blocked out the picture of the deaths: leastways when a relative died, Myra said that it was the first time she'd seen a dead body, forgetting that she'd seen the corpse of Pauline Reade. Freed from Brady's influence, she returned to normal - and has apparently rebuilt her past vision of herself so that it resembles a more normal one.

Though considered to have a hard side, Myra Hindley is not without her demons. She still opts to sleep with the light on, has occasionally been hospitalised for severe depression and is said to fear death. Yet for some years she has smoked forty cigarettes a day and refused to exercise, despite the fact that she has angina and brittle bones.

In 1999 she was hospitalised after collapsing in her cell and asked doctors to let her die if she lapsed into a vegetative state. Prison visitors report that if she doesn't change to less destructive habits she is likely to die before her sixtieth year.

The tabloids have suggested that this chainsmoking is either a death wish or a last desperate attempt to make herself seem so frail that she is released on compassionate grounds. Peter Timms sees it merely as a means of reducing boredom. 'What else is there to do in prison?' the former prison governor says with disarming honesty.

Personality

So what kind of personality starts off caring for children but is eventually persuaded to lure them into a car so that her lover can murder them? Some journalists have called her a psychopath but psychopathy seems unlikely in a woman who loved her mother and gran and the children she babysat. Psychopaths cannot form strong and lasting bonds with anyone.

Psychologists claimed at the time of the murders that she had a hysterical personality - the term used nowadays is histrionic. That is, someone who is over-emotional yet emotionally shallow, who is gullible and very susceptible to suggestion, a human sponge. This makes more sense as Myra presented herself as anti-social to Ian Brady when he wanted to use another anti-social personality. He wanted to dominate so she pleased him by pointing out the terror in the victim's eyes. But no one acts wholly to please another person so she must have derived satisfaction from the acts herself. It's been said that the female serial killer kills a version of herself, a version she wishes to disassociate from - and Myra helped kill impoverished working class children who were on their own.

The theory of violentization (for more on this please see chapter sixteen's theories of why women kill) suggests that violent people have either suffered strong physical abuse or seen other people close to them suffering from it. Myra fits into both these categories, as her father beat both her and her mother. Myra's mother also hit her, even striking the teenager across the face in the street one day after she'd missed the last bus home and been away all night.

One of the other stages of violentization is when someone coaches the initially normal person to be violent - and when she met Ian Brady he spent years encouraging her into violent ways. For many months he took her to see the films of violence and gave her books filled with violence. He spoke of bank robberies, Nazism and murder night and day. Then came the fantasized rehearsals, prowling the streets looking for potential victims and prowling the moors talking about what he'd do to them there. Only when he was sure that she was completely enthralled by his vision of superiority did he ask her to help him carry out his first murderous act.

Myra today

Even now she doesn't talk about certain aspects of what she did, writing about the other murders to a journalist - as broadcast in the BBC2 programme *Modern Times* - but in the case of Lesley Ann Downey saying 'I'm finding it very difficult... It just hurts so much to think that I could have been such a cruel bastard.' She was quoted in the programme saying that she 'chose to sacrifice Pauline so that my own family would be safe.' But if she'd wanted nothing to do with the abductions, Myra could have simply reported Ian's threats to the police.

If Myra was to admit that her own childhood rejection and her father's abuse had left her with suppressed rage, and that Ian Brady brought that rage into the open, she would sound more plausible. Certainly, the trial judge thought her redeemable if removed from Brady's influence - and even her harshest opponents don't actually believe that she'd kill again.

It's true that if Myra Hindley hadn't met Ian Brady her life would have been very different. She would probably have married and become a mother - she was distraught when her sister Maureen's first baby died and she has been kind to the children of friends and relatives who have visited her in prison. Under Ian's influence she became a very dangerous young woman but there's no evidence to suggest that she's a dangerous older woman now.

Searching for the truth

It's unlikely that Myra Hindley would have told the truth to psychiatrists during her first six years in prison when she still saw herself as the love of Ian Brady's life, when he was all she cared about. But after that, surely much could have been learned from her and put to good use to avoid others making the same mistakes?

This would have involved analysing Myra at length but the prison service seems disinclined to do this. One prison authority, who wished to remain nameless, told this author that 'prisoners don't receive any significant therapeutic help.'

You can argue that killers don't deserve help, in which case let's change the law so that it no longer gives the impression that prison is partly about rehabilitation, that people can change.

The Reverend Peter Timms is uneasy that he was prevented from fully counselling Myra, especially when she was starting to confide in him. He told me that he was 'willing to give ten thousand hours because it was important for her to know why.' (And surely for the public to know why.) He adds that he is 'seriously troubled about not being able to commit the time to counselling Myra to explore not when and how - which she was very honest and frank about - but why and what did it represent for her own inner life.'

He has tried to talk about this publicly but finds that the tabloids simply believe that men like him are seduced by the power of the female prisoner. Similar taunts have been thrown at some of Myra's legal representatives.

Aware that newspapers were still using pictures of the prisoner that were over thirty years old and that showed her looking deliberately emotionless, he gave them all one of her recent graduation photographs. But most papers prefer to use the old photographs, giving the impression that someone who commits evil acts as a very young woman in the thrall of a more sadistic man can never change.

Some newspapers also give the public an entirely erroneous impression of events. One reported that Myra Hindley had become a close friend of the child-abuser Rose West, profiled later. The report was completely untrue.

Update

On 31st March 2000 five Law Lords upheld the Home Secretary's decision that life should mean exactly that in Myra's case - in other words that she should die in prison. The reasoning given was her 'exceptionally wicked and uniquely evil crimes.' Ironically her former lover Ian Brady actually *wants* to die in prison as soon as possible - but earlier that same month he had lost his court battle to be allowed to starve to death in Ashworth Hospital where he has been treated for mental illness for many years.

Some criminologists view Myra Hindley as a political prisoner because successive Home Secretaries have refused to free her to avoid a public outcry. She apparently meets the usual criteria for parole yet has never been granted this.

4

IF I CAN'T HAVE YOU
The extreme reactions of Martha Ann Johnson

Martha Ann Johnson is one of a growing number of women (and men) who see their offspring as pawns to be used rather than as individuals to be nurtured. Between 1977 and 1982 she would kill all four of her children in order to hurt the man who cared for them.

She was born in Georgia, America, in 1955. Her IQ was a mere 78 - most people score at least a hundred. She was almost illiterate, spoke ungrammatically and often suffered from depression and a lack of self esteem.

Throughout her childhood Martha (who was sometimes called by her middle name of Ann) lived with her mother. She grew into an unhappy teenager with an increasing weight problem who had no confidence in herself and hated her small but heavy body, brown eyes and curly brown hair. Martha was desperate to find herself a boyfriend who would spend lots of time with her as she was afraid of being on her own.

She married for the first time when she was just fourteen. The marriage was to Bobby Wright and, like most teenage relationships, it was very difficult. The couple had a daughter, Jennyann, in 1971, who would remain with Martha when the marriage failed.

All of Martha's husbands would cheat on her, but she was always desperate to maintain the relationship or to remarry. Being a wife and mother was her entire existence as she had no educational or career prospects. She also had a very dependent personality and feared that she couldn't cope with running a household on her own.

After Bobby left her, Martha married Tommy Taylor and gave him a son, James, in 1975. This marriage was also argumentative and unhappy. Psychologists would later state that Martha had a personality disorder - presumably referring to her intense neediness - and that she found relationships with other adults difficult. She also moved around a lot from county to county, perhaps seeking a home or a relationship that would bring her happiness.

In 1976 Martha, by now an immature twenty-two, married for a third time. Her new spouse was called Earl Bowen. He was good to both of her children from her earlier marriages and loved them deeply and treated them as his own.

But his relationship with Martha was contentious from the start. She wanted him home all the time and he presumably felt trapped. She was also very threatened by his increasing bisexual activities and became intent on exacting her revenge.

He walked out after one of their fights, and stayed at a friend's house whilst he tried to decide how to resolve their many problems. Martha's entreaties failed to win him back so she decided to do something cataclysmic that he couldn't ignore...

The first death

On 25th September 1977 she went to two-year-old James's bed and sat on the sleeping child, suffocating him with her 250 pound weight. She then phoned her husband saying that she couldn't get the toddler to waken. Earl rushed round and found the little boy motionless in his crib. The body was cold and he could see immediately that he was dead.

Martha told the police that she'd gone to ask the toddler what he wanted for breakfast, only to find him rigid. The area around his mouth was a disturbing blue.

The doctors recorded the death as being Sudden Infant Death Syndrome, SIDS, and Martha was free to kill again. (Twelve years later the doctor would reverse this verdict in the light of the three subsequent deaths, saying that there was a ninety percent chance that this first death was homicide.) Martha was now reunited with her grieving spouse.

Another two births

She gave him a son, Earl, in 1979 and a daughter, Tibitha, the following year. She was still feeling afraid and inadequate and presumably hoped to cement her floundering relationship by giving her husband both a daughter and a son. Again, on the surface she was good to the children and they were always cleanly dressed and well fed.

The second death

But Martha and Earl fought again in November 1980 and Earl went to his lover, Stanley Hullen. Martha called Stanley in the hope of getting Earl back. She said that if something happened to the baby it would all be Earl's fault. Stanley was distressed by the conversation, though Martha would later deny to police that she made such a call.

When her husband still didn't return, Martha partially suffocated the three-month-old girl then left the room. Shortly afterwards - as she'd doubtless intended - a distraught Jennyann told her that the baby was gasping for breath.

Earl Bowen was called and told to go to the hospital. He found his wife and her mother there and asked his wife what she had done with their baby daughter. She denied harming Tibitha, asking why she would carry the children for nine months if she didn't want them? But her estranged husband still suspected the worst.

When Martha spoke to the police she said she'd been in the shower when her oldest daughter Jennyann appeared and said Tibitha was having difficulty breathing. Martha said she'd rushed to the baby's side to find sweets on the bed. She wondered if her toddler Earl had given the sweets to the baby, causing her to choke. But the autopsy wouldn't show any such sweets in the baby's windpipe and again the diagnosis was SIDS.

Earl Bowen told the medical examiner that this was the second time one of Martha's children had died after he'd argued with her, but this information wasn't acted on. One reason for this was that Martha's frequent house moves meant that she saw many different hospital staff, autopsy specialists and social workers and few of the personnel communicated with each other effectively about the case.

Inaction

All hospitals know that parents can injure or kill multiple times - but they hesitate to involve the law for fear that they can't prove it. Former prison officer Robert Adams told me that 'the best single predictor of future violence is previous violence.' But he admits that it's complex because many people have one violent episode and that most murderers don't go on to kill again.

Martha, though, wasn't in the category of having one violent moment. Two of her children were already dead and the circumstances were right for her to kill a third...

The third death

In early 1989 Martha was still missing her husband Earl. She spent part of January and the first days of February repeatedly taking his son, little Earl, to the local hospital saying that he'd swallowed rat poison or had a seizure. Unknown to her, at around this time Earl had applied for custody of the little boy because he feared for the toddler's life.

Incredibly, Martha now phoned Stanley again to say that if Earl didn't return home she'd do something to Earl junior. Stanley now strongly suspected that Martha had killed her first two children. He warned her that she'd burn in hell if she killed the third and he phoned the child protection services and told them of his fears.

But the enraged Martha was hellbent on creating another bereavement that Earl would have to comfort her over. She rolled her considerable weight on to the helpless child. She and her distraught daughter Jennyann then rushed Earl junior to hospital but he died on the way to the emergency ward. He was resuscitated and kept alive on a machine for three days after which he was declared brain dead and the machine was switched off.

This time the doctors thought the toddler had had a seizure and again failed to suspect foul play. It's possible that Martha, like many baby-killers, could act the part of a grieving mother. She also seemed an unlikely child killer, for those who knew her testified that she was always good to her kids and she and Jennyann were apparently close.

But Stanley Hullen's phone call to a child protection worker in Fulton County now started to produce results. The worker saw that Martha was indeed obsessed with the idea of getting Earl back and suspected she might go to any lengths to do so. Worried about the remaining child, Jennyann, she asked for the girl to be removed from the home, but a judge refused.

Earl Bowen was also concerned that Martha might harm Jennyann so he took her back to her natural father, Bobby Wright. The girl told her father that she was afraid of what her mother might do, and that she'd had a dream in which her mother suffocated her with a pillow. Both Bobby Wright and Earl Bowen got the impression she knew something about her siblings deaths but that she was too frightened to tell what she'd seen or heard. After a few days Mr Wright took his child to Martha's mother and she ended up back in Martha's care.

Sadly, such inactivity or lack of later vigilance on the part of the authorities isn't uncommon. Interviewed for this book, former prison officer Robert Adams explained that 'many researchers feel the true incidence of fatal abuse cases, including those against children, is vastly underestimated. For instance, some highly suspicious deaths in families where violence is previously known to have occurred aren't recorded as homicides because there is insufficient evidence to make a criminal conviction stick. Parents may admit some responsibility years later. This is not as rare as one might expect.'

He also cites research by Peter Scott in 1973 (*Parents Who Kill Their Children* Medicine, Science And The Law volume 13 issue 2) regarding parents who killed their children when they were under five years old. It showed that the parents who repeatedly killed weren't usually the aggressive psychopaths. Instead, Robert says, 'the really dangerous ones were the ones who were quiet and over-inhibited. When the otherwise passive person became unexpectedly violent the result was often fatal.' This was the final lesson that Martha Ann Johnson's three young children had now learnt. But Martha still hadn't achieved her goal of having Earl back full time so she prepared to kill again.

The fourth death

One year and one week after she'd killed her third child, Martha crushed eleven-year-old Jennyann into the mattress. Again, her motive was to regain contact with her former husband. This must have been a terrible death as a child of this age will fight for some time to draw breath. When her daughter went limp, Martha called her upstairs neighbour to say that the girl had stopped breathing and had wet the bed.

The neighbour found Jennyann face down on the bed clad in a t-shirt and dry briefs, apparently lifeless. She found Martha's demeanour odd, not that of a bereaved mother - especially a mother who had now lost all four of her children in a five year period. Instead, she was matter of fact and calm.

The police were also surprised at her lack of emotion and the paramedics were very suspicious of her child's death. Martha explained that Jennyann had fallen off a climbing frame a few days previously and had consequently had a brace fitted in hospital and that this had caused her to have breathing difficulties. The reality was that Martha had taken her daughter to the hospital complaining that she was having difficulty breathing. (She'd set up a similar alibi prior to killing one of her other children.) But when hospital workers examined and X-rayed the child they'd found nothing wrong.

Hours later, whilst conducting his investigation into Jennyann's death, Lieutenant Roberts realised that the woman was totally obsessed with getting back her estranged husband. When the subject of the deaths was brought up, she asked him, 'If I were two people and this other person did hurt the kids, would I go to jail?' He replied that she would.

Later, at the funeral, she was overheard to remark that though Jennyann was dead, Earl her husband was back home. This time the police feared homicide and ordered an autopsy. It showed that the girl had probably died of asphyxia. The crime lab strongly suspected homicide but just didn't have any proof. As a consequence, they didn't file charges against the now child-free Martha, who now went in search of husband number four.

Martha's fourth marriage

Soon she married Charles Eugene Johnson and went to live at Locust Grove, south of Atlanta. She was physically unable to have any more children but told relatives that she still thought of the four who had died, especially at their birthdays and at Christmas. She seems to have blocked out the truth of what she'd done to them. She added that she looked at photographs of them all the time.

She made friends with lots of the neighbourhood kids and took a job in the local convenience store. When asked to explain the deaths of all four of her children she said 'I think it was just bad luck.'

Reopening the case

But Martha's own luck was beginning to run out. At the end of 1988, seven whole years later, an investigative reporter in Atlanta found a medical report on Jennyann's death which admitted the death was suspicious. The newspaper, *The Atlanta Journal & Constitution*, made the findings public and as a result the autopsy details were looked at again.

The police now brought in FBI agent John Douglas and other specialists from Quantico to examine the case. The chances of a woman losing all four of her children to natural causes was deemed highly unlikely, and it was recognised that the deaths of the two-year-old and the eleven-year-old could hardly be attributed to Sudden Infant Death Syndrome as they were no longer infants. Various child protection workers, law enforcement personnel and Earl Bowen's lover, Stanley, also voiced their very strong concerns.

The arrest

In the summer of 1989 Martha Ann Johnson, now aged thirty-four, was arrested for murder. Sergeant Kenneth Stewart spent time sitting with her and helping her to dry her tears. Unknown to the accused, he had a video camera set up, hidden inside a box on a nearby shelf. Martha's confession was therefore taped without her knowledge, something that her defense would object to at her subsequent trial.

On the tape she confessed to suffocating Jennyann and James as a way of getting back at her husband after they'd argued. Her actual words to the police were `... I was just in a rage. I was mad. It hurt.' Of the suffocation, she explained 'I took Jennyann to bed with me and laid on her so she could not breathe. When she stopped moving I knew it was over with.' At another juncture she said 'I just hated him (Earl Bowen) so much for what he put me through.' But she denied killing the two children actually fathered by him.

Sergeant Stewart had had the children's graves bugged in case she apologised out loud for killing them, but she was always accompanied by relatives on her visits to the gravesides. Indeed, one of her aunts would speak in her defence at court. Though Johnson's defense would criticise the sergeant's tactics in going through Martha's garbage to ascertain more about her lifestyle, he would later receive a citation of merit for helping break the case.

The taped confession would remain a bone of contention throughout the trial for her defence would claim that it was meaningless. They said their vulnerable client was easily manipulated and would say almost anything under pressure. Martha herself would claim that she lied about causing the deaths in order to go home.

Her fourth husband clearly loved her and believed in her innocence. He promised that he'd look after her so she was let out on bail with the provision that she not be left alone with any child under the age of twelve.

The trial

In court she retracted her guilty statement, saying 'They had me convinced that I did it,' and later 'I didn't really understand. I was nervous and upset.'

But her original confession was played in court and the tape showed that she was aware of exactly what she'd done and she was heard saying that she was so sorry, that 'I knew over the years I did wrong.' She explained on the tape that suffocating the children with her weight was the only way she could think of to get her husband to come back.

Hearing the tape, she cried - possibly because her earlier statement helped prove that she was guilty. Towards the end of the tape she wept that she was afraid to go to jail.

On the last day of the five day trial she collapsed and had to see a doctor. She wept again that she hadn't harmed her kids. The jury - eight women and four men - didn't believe her and she was convicted of smothering eleven-year-old Jennyann. Though police, medical personnel and the fathers of the murdered children were in no doubt about her guilt, her fourth husband and some of her relatives continued to believe in her innocence.

Several sources suggest Martha was sentenced to the death penalty but in fact she was given a life sentence, which she immediately began serving at the Georgia Women's Correctional Institute in Hardwick. The District Attorney would later be criticised by a defense attorney in another case for not seeking the death penalty for both Martha and another woman due to gender bias.

Update

Martha Johnson largely disappears from the public record after her sentencing, only occasionally mentioned in articles about child killers. She cannot have any more offspring - and didn't ever harm a stranger's child - so presumably won't be a danger to anyone if she is ever released. The public still largely refuses to believe that some women kill their children though there have been many such high profile cases are the years, such as Alice Crimmins, Susan Smith, Waneta Hoyt, Marybeth Tinning, Diane Downs and Paula Simms.

5

SLAVE TO LOVE

The confused priorities of Charlene Gallego

Charlene Adelle Williams was born near Sacramento, California, in October 1956. Her father, Charles (known as Chuck) had started off as a butcher and worked his way up to being the vice president of a supermarket chain. He was a respected entrepreneur who had to wine and dine clients as part of his job. His wife, Mercedes, acted as his hostess and the pair of them regularly travelled as part of their business life.

Sometimes little Charlene would travel with them and at other times she'd stay with her maternal grandparents whom she loved dearly. She'd wear the beautiful floaty dresses with ribbons that her doting father bought her. She'd dance and sing and be his fairytale ideal of a little girl.

Her early school reports suggest that she was a shy, quiet child who had a good attendance record. Some classmates described her as mousy. She wore braces and had her hair braided in that least flattering of styles, pigtails, so didn't feel very good about herself. Like many only children who spend too much time exclusively in adult company, she probably found it hard to relax with people of her own age.

Charlene's father thought that young women shouldn't swear or be unladylike. He believed that good manners were important. Little Charlene more than lived up to his expectations - she was good at every one of her school subjects and was a regular attendee at her local church.

Mercedes was a small slim woman and Charlene was equally tiny. But despite her frail appearance her mother had a very brisk and no-nonsense approach to life.

Charlene remained shy until she reached fourth grade and found that she had a talent for playing the violin. It was a passion that would stay with her. She excelled in the school orchestra and also found the confidence to get involved behind the scenes in various drama club activities. Chuck was proud of Charlene's musical skills and bought her a very expensive violin.

Soon it rarely left her side. Later she'd talk of becoming a professional musician, but her mother didn't think this was a suitable career for her daughter so Charlene started to think about following her father into the supermarket business instead.

Then Mercedes was involved in a car accident and badly hurt her back. After that, she didn't want to travel very often. The schoolgirl Charlene, dressed like a princess as usual, took over the hostessing tasks. She'd travel in light planes and in boats with her father to meet his clients, most of whom would praise this intelligent and well spoken young girl. In return she was given lots of presents - especially dresses, which she adored. Charlene began to find that she could make friends with men and alienate women - but this suited her as she had always been a Daddy's girl. She was to remain her wealthy parents only child.

But there was clearly trouble in paradise for by puberty Charlene had started experimenting with drugs. By fourteen she was drinking heavily, getting by on a potent mix of Qualudes and gin. Her school kept wanting to expel her but her father intervened in her favour again and again. As her IQ was so exceptional, in the top one percent of the population, the school let her remain.

By now alternately quiet then boastful, she found it difficult to make or keep female friends. She also became very promiscuous but her parents were in denial that anything was wrong.

Two failed marriages

Charlene went to college but quickly tired of it. Still a teenager, she now decided to become a full time wife, perhaps emulating her mother. She promptly married a rich but equally lost young man and set up home with him. Unfortunately, he was a heroin addict who said that Charlene was obsessed by the idea of lesbian sex and wanted him to hire a whore that they could share in bed.

Charlene's first husband also found that she quickly let her appearance go to hell - hardly surprising given the amount of cocaine and marijuana that she was taking. He hated the fact that Chuck and Mercedes Williams intervened in their relationship a great deal.

The marriage soon failed and Charlene just as quickly remarried - this time choosing a soldier - in what she'd later call a desperate search for emotional security. But husband number two also quickly tired of his new wife, for if he refused her anything she'd call her parents over and ask them for whatever she desired. If they demurred she'd sometimes have an asthma attack and completely collapse until they gave in to her. The Williams believed she had asthma but her third husband, Gerald Gallego, would later suggest it was faked.

A suicide attempt

At just five feet tall, of a very slight built, and with blonde hair and blue eyes, Charlene looked younger than her years and very innocent - but by twenty-one she'd been divorced twice and had a string of unsatisfactory relationships. One of her more enjoyable affairs was with a married man and when he ended it she attempted to kill herself.

Her working life went equally awry. She worked in various meat companies but she was so overdressed and so flirtatious with the male staff that she quickly made enemies of the females. She had planned to follow her father up the corporate ladder but was increasingly sidetracked, taking long intimate lunches with the male employees. Charlene continued to drink heavily and could handle neat vodka and the inevitable depression that followed. She continued to date and discard various men.

Her father still doted on her, so when she moved into a nice apartment he bought lots of furniture for it. He also bought her a van.

Psychologists would later suggest that Charlene's father was too dominant a force in her life - and that she would spend her teenage years looking for a man who was equally forceful. She found him in Gerald Gallego who she met on a blind date. It was the autumn of 1977 and she was a thin and almost waiflike twenty-one. He was ten years older, a well built man with dark probing eyes and heavy dark hair. He'd been violent in most of his relationships and had done time for a string of offences, including car theft and armed robbery.

The lover's childhood

Gerald's own background had been a brutal one. His mother and her numerous boyfriends had beaten him during his formative years - and when his mother became a working girl Gerald was abused by some of her clients. He was often left hungry and dirty and was always pleading to be held and hugged. When he was nine his natural father, who had played no part in his life, was executed for killing two policemen - something Gerald wouldn't find out until he was fully grown.

Like Charlene, Gerald had failed as a lover and as a spouse - by the age of thirty-two he'd left numerous women when they ran out of money and possessions. He'd been married, albeit often bigamously, seven times. He had also started sexually abusing his daughter from one marriage when she was aged eight. (Some sources say she was aged six. Statistically, seven is the most common age for incest to begin.)

Gerald liked rough sex and Charlene responded to this. At first their sex life was so good that they simply couldn't get enough of each other. Some crime texts suggest that she was masochistic but it's more likely that she was sexually *submissive*. True masochism - in which pain is enjoyed for its own sake - is very rare. Indeed, she would later say in court that she hated the painful experience of being sodomised, an act which Gerald particularly enjoyed.

Sexual submission relies strongly on conversational powerplay. The submissive often indicates to the dominant party what he or she enjoys, so in a way it's the submissive that's in charge, the common term for this being 'topping from below.'

Sexually submissive people are often very strong characters in their day to day lives - as, in many ways, Charlene was. She was running rings around everyone at work but, like many women, wanted a man in her bed who could take charge. Gerald Gallego, who hated women deep down, originally rose to the challenge. He appeared streetwise and very masterful.

Within a week of meeting, the new couple had rented a house and moved in together. Gerald soon moved beyond the flowers and chocolates stage of the relationship and Charlene accepted that he was more interested in his own sexual satisfaction than he was in hers. Like most

serial killers who use sex to hurt and humiliate their partners, his preference was for anal sex then oral sex, with vaginal sex a very poor third. But
she was fascinated by his machismo and was soon sharing in his illicit fantasies.

When they had been cohabitating for a few months Gerald brought
home a sixteen-year-old dancer and they had a threesome together, but he
made sure that the two women only touched him and not each other. The
next day he returned early from work to find Charlene having sex with the
girl. Enraged, he threw the dancer out of the, thankfully, open window and
hit Charlene. He then withheld sex from her, saying that he had become
impotent. In reality, it seems, he no longer found her attractive because
she'd shown she wasn't fully dependent on him for sexual kicks. Inadequate
men like Gallego tend to choose very needy or very young girls who they
can overwhelmingly dominate and impress.

Gerald now sodomised his fourteen-year-old daughter and raped her
friend - prior to this he had only had vaginal sex with the confused teenager. He did so with Charlene's knowledge. It's unclear if Charlene was in the
room with them or just in the same apartment, but she evidently didn't find
anything immoral in Gerald's paedophiliac act. The fact that she condoned
the incest - and would later help him flee from the authorities when they
were ready to charge him with it - suggests she had the lack of conscience
found in the sociopath.

For the next few months Charlene worked at various jobs and
Gerald, who was uneducated, worked in a bar. He made many tips
because he was so attractive to women. Charlene suspected he was
sleeping with many of his customers, as by now he was sexually disinterested in her.

When the couple had been together for a year, he said that he needed a pair of love slaves to turn him on, and asked her to procure them.
Some sources suggest that she agreed because she saw the man's word
as law, that she wanted only to please him. But no one is completely
self-effacing so it's more likely that she wanted to satisfy her own
strong lesbian desires and totally control a helplessly tied-up girl.
Whatever her motivation, she agreed to lure teenage virgins to their
certain deaths.

The first two victims

On 11th September 1978 she approached two teenage girls in a Sacramento shopping mall, suggesting they come with her to her Oldsmobile van to smoke some marijuana. Gerald, of course, was crouching in the back.

Sixteen-year-old Kippi Vaught and seventeen-year-old Rhonda Scheffler happily accompanied Charlene to the vehicle where Gerald immediately locked them in and brandished his pistol. He told the girls that they were being kidnapped as he wanted to terrify them - their fear turned him and Charlene on. Charlene then taped their mouths, ankles and wrists, took the gun and kept it trained on the girls whilst he drove to a deserted area. They arrived late in the afternoon and Gerald and Charlene undressed and told the victims to do the same.

For the next six hours, the couple assaulted the helpless teenagers. Gerald sodomised them both and made them fellate him. He only had vaginal sex with one girl as the other was menstruating. The bite marks on one girl's breasts were very different to the bite marks on her friend's breasts, suggesting that Gerald bit one girl and Charlene bit the other. She would later tell a cellmate how ecstatic she felt during this cruel kidnap-rape. That's author Eric van Hoffmann's view of how the killings took place - but it has to be said that Ray Biondi's take on the subject is very different. He believes that Charlene had no sexual contact with the victims after she abducted them. This is very unlikely given what we know of Team Killers - the female half of every other killing couple in this book played an active part in at least one of the sexual assaults.

Gerald then told Charlene to drive around whilst he went off into the woods with his victims, carrying a sleeping bag. It's likely that he wanted to perform further abuses on the pair without having his girlfriend watching. The girls were clearly distressed when he eventually returned with them.

She now took the wheel and drove the girls on a fifteen mile journey to what would become their execution ground. She stayed in the van whilst her lover cracked their skulls with a jack handle then shot them, leaving them where they dropped. Kippi Vaught had only received a minor head wound but Gallego saw her moving and shot her again.

Charlene's third marriage

Charlene then drove Gerald home and for the next two weeks they relived the excitement. Soon they were looking for new kicks so decided to get married. The wedding took place on 30th September 1978 and was attended by Charlene's parents who took lots of photographs. Charlene seemed thrilled that she'd got her man. In truth, it's more likely that Gerald thought a wife *couldn't* testify against her murderous husband - when in reality it's merely that she can't be *made* to testify. It was a moot point as, despite the Reno marriage licence, she never legally became Mrs Gallego as the marriage was bigamous, Gerald not being divorced from a previous wife. Married or not, she'd later choose to testify against him and her evidence would put him on Death Row...

But for now, life settled back into its routine of drink and drugs and unfulfilling attempts at sex together. Both continued to give up jobs and find new ones, Charlene working in a bank at one stage and at a meat processing plant at another, whilst Gerald found a driving job. It wasn't enough to keep the adrenalin flowing so within nine months they were ready to kidnap and kill again.

The third and fourth victims

On 24th June 1979 Charlene lured the second pair of victims from a county fair in Reno, Nevada. Fourteen-year-old Sandra Kaye Colley and her fifteen-year-old friend Brenda Judd were approached by Charlene who asked if they'd like to make a few dollars by delivering leaflets. Like most teenagers they were eager to make some cash. They followed her to the van to collect the leaflets, only to find Gerald there pointing a gun at their heads.

This time Charlene drove the victims to a remote spot near Lovelock, Nevada. One of the girls was so frightened that she was sick and an angry Charlene slapped her hard. Gerald hurt himself when the van braked suddenly, after which he couldn't perform, but Charlene, according to author Eric van Hoffmann, went on to have sex with both girls.

Gerald then crushed their skulls with a spade and buried them in a shallow grave. They were considered missing for three years until Charlene admitted taking part in their deaths - but their skeletal remains weren't found for almost twenty years, dug up by a tractor driver in November 1999.

The fifth and sixth victims

In April 1980, ten months after the third and fourth deaths, Charlene lured her fifth and sixth victims from a Sacramento shopping mall. Seventeen-year-old Karen Chipman-Twiggs and Stacy Redican were driven to the Nevada woods, sexually assaulted by both Gallegos and shot by Gerald. He buried them near Lovelock, the battered bodies being found in July 1980 three months after they'd met their deaths. Until now the Gallegos had always kidnapped pairs of girls - presumably because they wanted one each, but now Charlene got pregnant so Gerald went on to choose a solo victim by himself.

The seventh victim

Charlene's pregnancy made her sick and she found it hard to sleep. Worse, she couldn't drink. Her condition made her miserable and the last thing she wanted was any kind of sex. Gerald, who had been so abused throughout his childhood that he had no empathy with other people, was totally unsympathetic to her condition and insisted they cruise about as usual in Charlene's van.

In early June 1980 the pair of them were driving through Oregon when he drew her attention to a lone female hitchhiker. Ironically, twenty-one-year old Linda Teresa Aguilar was also pregnant, four or five months gone with her second child. The Gallegos stopped the Oldsmobile and seeing the pretty Charlene in the van she was happy to accept a lift.

Gerald quickly ordered her into the back of the van, where she fainted from terror. Charlene became enraged and banged Linda's head against the van's floor. They undressed her and Charlene explored her pregnant body but apparently Gerald couldn't become aroused. Desperately Linda pleaded for her life, but he took her outside with her hands still tied behind her back. Then he beat her about the head, strangled her and buried her in a hastily dug grave.

The subsequent autopsy would reveal sand in her windpipe - proof that she was only knocked out by the rock that he'd hit her with. She had regained consciousness to find herself buried alive.

Around this time the pregnant Charlene moved back in with her parents as she liked her creature comforts. But she continued to date Gerald and sometimes sleepover at his house.

The eighth victim

Charlene and Gerald abducted their next victim, a Sacramento waitress, from outside the tavern she worked at. Virginia Mochel was thirty-four and had been talking to the Gallegos in the tavern. Witnesses would later say that Gerald was drunk and that Charlene was very quiet.

But Charlene was also clever. She left her jacket behind then knocked on the door after hours and asked Virginia to fetch it for her. Virginia did, but only opened the door a little so Charlene couldn't force her way inside. Undaunted, she and Gerald waited in the car park then forced the waitress into their vehicle at gunpoint. Gerald had touched Virginia's car, so Charlene hastily polished it free of prints.

They then took the terrified mother of two back to Gerald's home. There they stripped her and tied her hands behind her with fishing line before repeatedly sexually molesting her. Charlene forced the terrified woman to go down on her and whipped her and Gerald sodomised her several times. He then strangled her and the pair dumped her body early the next day. This murder took place on 17th July 1980, a mere month after the previous one. Afterwards Charlene drove back to her parents house for a nice long sleep.

The ninth and tenth victims

When Gerald phoned in August 1980 and asked her to spend the day with him she probably knew exactly what he had in mind - what she couldn't predict was how reckless he was becoming. They started to tour Sacramento, stopping off at various bars and restaurants in search of victims to abduct. Charlene couldn't drink much because of her pregnancy but Gerald got increasingly drunk.

That night they saw pretty Beth Sowers and her fiance Craig Miller leaving a dance at a restaurant. Gerald insisted that he had to have Beth, though Charlene thought it was too risky. But when he insisted, she pointed her gun at the young lovers, forcing them into the van. A friend of Craig's unwittingly intervened at which stage Charlene hit him across the face and told him to get lost.

The couple drove Craig to an execution spot - a lonely field - where Gerald shot him three times in the head. The Gallegos then took the terrified Beth back to Gerald's apartment. There she endured the same ordeal as their previous victims, an ordeal which lasted until the early hours. Charlene then drove to a remote area where Gerald shot Beth.

Meanwhile Beth and Craig had been reported missing. As they were intelligent young people from good families the police started to follow up on the registration number of the abduction vehicle. It led to Mercedes and Chuck Williams house and they explained that the vehicle belonged to their daughter, Charlene. She, in turn, spoke to the police briefly, claiming not to know anything about the missing Beth and Craig.

Fugitives

Knowing that the net was closing in, the Gallegos now went on the run, taking up residence in a Nebraska inn where they considered kidnapping the receptionist in order to steal her vehicle. They used assumed names but were caught when the Williams tried to wire them some money. Ironically Chuck Williams was afraid that his daughter might be harmed by Gerald - he had no idea that Charlene was actively luring victims into the Oldsmobile that he'd bought for her.

The FBI, using the charge of unlawful flight in an effort to avoid prosecution, took the by now scruffy pair into custody. The authorities strongly suspected they'd killed Craig and Beth - they just couldn't prove it yet.

Charlene's parents had already obtained an attorney for her and now got her a first class criminal lawyer. They filed motion after motion. She wrote to Gerald that they had a beautiful love together and that their relationship had been the most exciting of her life. He, in turn, reverted to being the romantic, sending her love letters with cute little drawings in the margins. Whilst in custody she gave birth to their child, a boy, who was immediately placed in a loving home. Seeing the baby as yet another bond between her and Gerald, Charlene felt very pleased with herself.

But after ten months in jail she became increasingly involved with another female prisoner and found less and less time to write to Gerald. Soon her prison lesbian lover was replaced by an informant who passed on Charlene's hints of what she'd done to young girls in the outside world...

Beginning to go stir crazy, Charlene contacted her legal representatives and said that she'd turn states evidence in return for a light sentence. As Gerald wasn't talking, they found this offer very attractive. She was promised immunity from the death penalty, and told that the prosecution would use those parts of her evidence which implicated Gerald, after which her statement would be sealed. A relieved Charlene went on to give details of all ten murders though she downplayed her part in them. It was agreed that if she testified against her husband she would receive a maximum sentence of sixteen years and eight months.

The trial

The first trial was held in California. Gerald had no money so was left with a public defendant. Instead he opted to become his own lawyer - which meant he was allowed to cross-examine Charlene when she testified against him in court. There she said that she'd procured the girls to fulfil his sexual fantasies and added that she herself didn't have any such fantasies. This was in direct contrast to what she'd told officials before: 'We had this fantasy, see...'

When further questioned by Gerald, Charlene would admit in court that she'd had a homosexual relationship in prison. And another prisoner was called who said that she'd rejected Charlene's advances and that

Charlene had then been very aggressive. It was clear that, despite her denials, Charlene could be dominant and that she liked sex with girls.

Charlene tried to give the impression that she too had been one of Gerald's sex slaves, that she'd been too afraid to deny him. But she had to admit that she'd sent Gerald letters whilst they were both in prison that said things like 'please don't ever leave me' - hardly the sentiments of a woman who was glad to be rid of a murderous man.

Gerald was found guilty at his first trial of murdering Beth Sowers and Craig Miller and given the death penalty, then extradited to Nevada and again given the death penalty for the murders of Stacy Redican and Karen Chipman-Twiggs. In 1984 he was put on Death Row where he still waits, lodging appeals against the sentence of lethal injection in one state and the gas chamber in another. A three judge panel met to discuss one of his appeals as recently as 1999.

District Attorney Wagner at first thought that Charlene was a timid and frightened girl. The police thought the same as she was almost pathetically eager to co-operate with them - albeit only once it suited her. Wagner spent weeks studying Charlene and eventually realised that she was manipulative, that she liked to pull the strings behind the scenes. He thought that she had been the number one girl in her father's life - and was determined to be the number one girl in Gerald Gallego's, even if that meant outdoing him in bravado and cruelty. She retained her religious streak and clearly thought of herself as special, saying that she had driven home drunk after kidnapping one of the victims but hadn't crashed, thanks to God.

Charlene said that she could do nothing to help these girls - a ridiculous statement given that it was she who lured most of them to the van in the first place. She also tried to give the impression that Gerald could have killed her at any moment - but one of her jobs meant that she was on the road alone for days at a time so she could easily have contacted police in a far away state. She'd also persuaded her parents to help Gerald evade the law and change his name by finding him the birth certificate of one of their relatives.

When it suited her she made coy comments to the court like 'I don't tell the man what to do.' Ironically her demeanour towards these court men was far from obsequious and the jury didn't like her at all.

The sentence

Charlene Williams served her full sixteen years and eight months in a Nevada prison. She spent her days reading and her evenings playing her beloved violin. She was freed on the 17th July 1997, age forty, and presumably reunited with her teenage son. She'd also said earlier in her sentence that she was looking forward to eventually going home to live with her mother. She is expected to inherit her parents wealth.

Update

By the year 2000 reports about Gerald Gallego's appeals were continuing to appear on American news bulletins, often posted on the internet. Most of those news items simply referred to 'serial killer Gerald Gallego' so that anyone not familiar with the case gleaned the impression that he acted alone. Already - as it so often does - society was choosing to forget the unpalatable truth that he had a female accomplice who lured the victims to the van, took part in their subsequent sexual assaults and knew of their cruel deaths.

6

LAND OF MAKE BELIEVE
The confused inner world of Genene Jones

Genene was born in 1950 in Texas and immediately given to her adoptive parents, Richard and Gladys Jones. Richard was an innovative man who ran a billboard business and owned a club. He would take Genene out in the truck with him when he drove around town putting up his billboards. She later said that these hours in the truck were the happiest times of her life. At six foot tall and weighing 240 pounds, her father had a powerful presence. She would remain close to him until his death from cancer when she was in her late teens.

One of Genene's brothers likewise died from cancer at a young age. She also had an adopted younger brother who she adored and who would die in his teens in horrible circumstances. And she had a sister, so the family was fairly large. Her adoptive parents were often busy - her mother taking care of the four children and helping her father to build a club which became the family business. He also built their home.

Genene would later report that she grew up lacking in attention and would pretend to be ill in order to obtain it: this started her childhood interest in medicine and in hospitals. At school she was loud and desperate to get noticed and loved to boss her peers about. Her high school graduation photo shows a teenager with a heavy face, thick bangs of hair and an unconvincing smile. No one knows exactly what happened to her during these formative years but she would later tell a friend that her childhood involved abuse.

The abused child grew into a slightly overweight adult of five foot four with a large nose and a small mouth. Her large grey eyes were her best and most expressive feature. She kept her brown hair cut short, something which emphasised her somewhat masculine face. Outwardly Genene seemed gregarious and fun loving but inside she nursed strong doubts about her self worth.

Her first marriage

She was dating in her late teens when her boyfriend announced that he was about to sign up for the navy. Genene panicked as she realised that she might lose him. So she immediately announced that she was pregnant, causing him to shelve his career plans and marry her instead. Genene was once more the centre of attention, the alleged future mother of his child.

But the months passed and she didn't get any bigger. When her husband confronted her about the situation she admitted that she'd lied to him. He was hurt and baffled as he would have been willing to marry her without a pregnancy. They stayed married but he now went into the navy as he'd originally planned whilst she stayed with her widowed mum.

Later the couple set up home in Tennessee together and had their first child, a son. When her husband was sent away on intensive training the twenty-something Genene went back to her mother without telling him - presumably an extreme way to show her displeasure at not having his full attention again. It's possible that she was also playing the games that many insecure women play, hoping that their partner will arrive in tears and beg them to come back.

It was whilst she was staying with the woman whom she called 'Mama' that her favourite younger brother assembled a home-made bomb in the garage and promptly blew himself up. Genene had been following her interest in medicine by helping out at the local private hospital and was there (leastways she told a friend she was) when they brought her dying sibling in.

When Genene's husband returned from his training course she told him that she wasn't coming back. It's possible that he didn't appear sufficiently upset at the news - after all, she was still desperate for very public shows of affection. Whatever her motivation, she went around telling everyone that he'd been hitting her - charges she seems to have made up. Like most embryonic serial killers, Genene told tall tales to make herself look interesting and was capable of lying about many things.

But after a couple of months she changed her mind and withdrew the charges of abuse then returned to her increasingly baffled husband. Investigators would later describe this first husband as gentle and sincere.

He appeared to genuinely love her and didn't want to speak badly of her even after her subsequent killing spree, but he did hint that there was something unusual about her sexuality. Given what we know of female serial killers it may be that she liked to experiment with other women or that she wanted to roleplay control games in the bedroom. Unfortunately she would later take this need for control into her workplace and push it to an ultimately fatal zenith.

The single nurse

Genene had never been particularly interested in her appearance but for some reason her mother paid for her to train as a beautician, after which she found work in a local beauty shop. Genene worked there for a few months but became bored with it and with her marriage and gave up on both, taking her son with her. She had complained of various aches and pains all her life and now told her mother that she wanted to follow her childhood dream of becoming a nurse.

Still only in her early twenties, she did just that, again funded by her mother. She studied for the Licensed Vocational Nurse (LVN) qualification, a course that took a year and resulted in basic nursing skills.

A second child

At this stage Genene became pregnant by a male nurse she'd been dating and gave birth to a daughter, but the relationship soon ended. She went on to have other relationships, all of which failed. Many people enjoyed her rancons sense of humour and saw her as a no-nonsense nurse and a good mother - but others found her overbearing and histrionic and noted that she caused disruption wherever she went.

Her hypochondria increased and she started to tell relatives that she had heart trouble, though medical reports didn't support this. One friend noted that as Genene moved into her twenties she looked increasingly withdrawn and tired. She was briefly admitted to hospital with a bleeding ulcer but was otherwise given a clean bill of health. Genene refused to believe the diagnosis. Moreover, she continued to smoke too much and eat too much and generally failed to look after herself.

Her very first child patient died, and the new nurse took the death very badly, drawing up a seat beside the tiny corpse and crying dramatically for half an hour. Nursing staff often feel sad when they lose a life, but Genene's behaviour always seemed to be more about people noticing *her* than about her latest dead patient. She would show this level of emotion throughout her nursing career.

Her strange behaviour continued apace. Her colleagues noted how she hated certain doctors (usually the ones who didn't carry out her many medical suggestions) and said that she set out to make her enemies look bad. On one occasion when a doctor wouldn't do as she demanded, she hyperventilated and had to be carried out of the room. Genene just had to get noticed, to be praised, on every occasion - without such external approval she felt so slighted that she wanted to hit back, to hurt her imagined enemies. She was starting to become dangerous.

Hypochondria

Genene's psychosomatic illnesses continued to affect her career. She visited the emergency room approximately twice a month complaining of various ailments. At other times she was briefly hospitalised for bronchitis, asthma, severe constipation and a bowel obstruction. Half-way through some of her shifts she'd announce that she had some mysterious ailment and would take herself off to Outpatients, much to the chagrin of her more stable workmates. She was increasingly self destructive, her smoking increasing the severity of her many asthma attacks.

The killing starts

Genene's first four years were spent at various hospitals in San Antonio, Texas, her home town, before she accepted a post at the local Bexar County Medical Center Hospital, working in the PICU, the Pediatrics Intensive Care Unit. This brought her into contact with numerous babies and children - and these same children soon began to die.

Between May and December 1981 an incredible twenty babies died in her care. Some died as a result of massive bleeding, others because their heartbeats stopped after suddenly becoming erratic. Yet others had seizures despite looking healthy only moments before. Children were going into the hospital in poor health, getting better under the direction of the medical staff - then suddenly dying when left for a short time in Genene's sole care. The other nurses on her shift were suspicious but they were inexperienced graduates who were often afraid of her loud manner and domineering ways.

She was on duty during May 1981 when a ten-month-old boy died unexpectedly of a cardiac arrest. Three days later she was tending a five-month-old child when he had a cardiopulmonary arrest. A fortnight later a two-month-old had two arrests within three days. These attacks were known as Code Blue emergencies, and the nearest doctors and other medics were expected to rush to the dying child with the crash cart and start resuscitation techniques.

Genene was invariably the first to arrive and the last to leave. She would insert an intravenous tube, tell the doctor about the baby's vital signs and hand over the required medications. Some saw her as the consummate professional - but others noted that she seemed to be enjoying the drama between life and death.

In early July one of her patients, a six-month-old boy, had a cardiac arrest. The next day Genene was his assigned nurse again when he had a second arrest that proved fatal. That same day a four-week-old infant suffered a massive bleeding episode and died. (Genene would later be found guilty of causing another baby to haemorrhage massively by injecting the child with the anti-coagulant heparin.)

The deaths of Genene's little patients continued throughout the year - but stopped for a month when she herself was admitted to hospital for minor abdominal surgery. During her absence, from the first week in November to the first week in December, the PICU didn't have a single Code Blue emergency or *unexpected* death. The two children who expired during this period were terminal cases who had been admitted to die.

Three days after Genene's return, the Unit heeded a Code Blue signal again. An eighteen-month-old boy was admitted with a severe viral infection, but seemed to be responding well to treatment until Genene came on duty. A doctor saw her in another part of the hospital and asked how the child was doing. Genene shrugged and said he seemed fine but the doctor went to check for himself.

He found the little boy blue and flatlining. The medic yelled for help and Genene quickly appeared with her crash cart and positioned an airbag over the infant's mouth. Three quarters of an hour later, despite heroic attempts to resuscitate him, the child was officially pronounced dead.

As the death toll mounted, another nurse heard Genene telling two parents that their son wasn't expected to survive. This was untrue, and anyway it wasn't Genene's remit to say such things to relatives. The nurse also noted that Genene had left the wrong bottles of solution lying at a bedside - if they'd been used they could have damaged the child.

The nurse plucked up her courage and complained to Jones' supervisors but was told to stop picking on Jones. Rumours about the number of Genene's patients who were dying continued to spread round the ward, but the hospital authorities put it down to personality clashes between the aggressive Jones and more easygoing newer members of staff.

Babies continued to die in Genene's care - at one stage there were seven deaths in fourteen days. Genene continued to exhibit strange behaviour. She wrote on her patients medical notes that she loved them and started to sing to their corpses. And she gave the doctors a possible diagnosis for one case, naming a medical syndrome about which little was known.

Some of the medics were impressed by a Licensed Vocational Nurse having such detailed knowledge and urged her to study for the superior Registered Nurse qualification, but Genene said that with two of her own children to care for this was impossible. In truth she spent so long at the hospital that her son sometimes called in to ask when she was coming home. It may be that she secretly questioned her ability to pass the more demanding course as she clearly had doubts about herself.

She may also have started to abuse alcohol by this stage. Leastways she turned up for work drunk on at least one occasion and had to be sent home. Like the Thrill Killer Carol Bundy, also a nurse and profiled later, she was failing in her romantic relationships and acting so oddly that she alienated her colleagues. And she was so obsessed with work that she was even failing her daughter and her son.

The killing continues

Babies continued to die on her 3pm - 11pm shift and it became known as The Death Shift. One nurse drew up a chart showing the number of mortalities on the late shift and took it to her superior, but the superior decided the death rate was not unreasonable. After all, it was an intensive care ward. Some of the nurses who directly or indirectly challenged Genene would later find threatening anonymous notes in their lockers at the hospital - Genene was known as a formidable enemy.

Then a three-week-old baby, Rolando, was admitted with possible pneumonia. Within six days of Genene's care he had two heart attacks, two seizures and episodes where he urinated uncontrollably. The doctors stabilised him and for three days he grew stronger. Then Genene took over his care again and within hours he was bleeding from various injection sites. This bleeding would start, then stop, then start again, to the other nurses dismay.

A doctor sent the child's blood for analysis and it came back saying that the blood contained heparin, an anti-coagulant. Shocked and bewildered, the man spoke to various nurses, trying to find out if this was an accident.

They again stabilised the baby but the next day, on Genene's shift, he started to bleed from his eyes, mouth, nose, ears, rectum and even his penis. Fearing that heparin was implicated again, the doctor injected its antidote. Genene left the room looking displeased. The doctor persevered with his hunch but found he had to inject even more antidote as the baby had been contaminated with a colossal amount of heparin, well over a hundred times the safe dose. The doctor then had Rolando removed to a different part of the hospital where he rallied within four days and was allowed to go home.

Another child died in Genene's care and she baptised it with water from a syringe. (She told her colleagues that she placed great value on running a good Christian household.) Other nurses noted that Genene insisted on carrying each dead baby in her arms to the mortuary, wailing the entire time.

By now the hospital authorities were conducting an internal investigation. When yet another of her patients died unexpectedly a new member of the medical team withdrew blood, intending to send it for toxicology reports. A nurse fitting Genene's description offered to take the blood to the lab for him. Needless to say, it never arrived.

As babies continued to die, the hospital admitted to themselves that they had a staffing problem but decided they didn't have enough evidence to implicate any one person. They therefore decided to get rid of *all* of their Licenced Vocational Nurses and instead employ only more qualified Registered Nurses in the PICU.

Genene was let go - but given a good reference. Some doctors had found her histrionic and said that both she and her family had problems of instability, but this information wasn't passed on to her new employer.

A new start

Genene's new boss was called Kathleen Holland. The two women had worked together very briefly in a hospital environment before and Kathleen had been impressed at how well the LVN responded to a Code Blue emergency, fighting to save each dying baby. Now Kathleen was setting up her own private pediatric clinic in Kerrville, Texas and asked Genene to be her nurse.

The move to Kerr County Clinic also involved Genene moving house and Kathleen offered to rent her house space. Genene and Kathleen were joined by Genene's two children, now aged nine and five, and by a pregnant friend of Genene's who babysat full time. The nurse spent her few leisure hours trying to make the place look homely and seemed full of admiration for Kathleen, a qualified pediatrician. Kathleen had the credentials and the authority that Genene herself pretended to have and clearly craved.

Genene was now given a badge that said Pediatric Clinician and revelled in this grandiose title. She would later act so self-assured during an emergency that the paramedics assisting her believed she was a Registered Nurse rather than the basic Licenced Nurse she actually was. Genene now had even fewer witnesses around her than she'd had on The Death Shift - and soon Kathleen's healthy young child patients began to collapse.

An eight-month-old girl, Chelsea, was brought in with a cold and Genene took her away to the play area whilst Kathleen talked with the mother. Moments later Genene reported that the child had stopped breathing and put an oxygen mask over the baby's face. She was rushed to hospital and soon recovered. Though baffled as to what had made their child collapse, the parents assumed that the fast-acting Genene had saved her. Nine months later they'd bring her back to the clinic - and this time she'd die at Genene's hands.

Meanwhile a severely disabled seven-year-old boy, Jimmy, was brought in suffering from seizures. Kathleen decided to send him to hospital in the air ambulance and instructed Genene to accompany the experienced paramedics in the helicopter. Genene immediately packed her medical bag.

She gave the impression that she was a trained and flight-practiced medic so the paramedics merely reminded her that it's impossible to listen to a patients heart or lungs through a stethoscope whilst a helicopter is in flight - but once the flight started Genene insisted on trying to do just that. She was then seen to inject something into the child's intravenous tube. She said it was to assist his breathing, but until now he had been stable. Within minutes he turned blue and went into cardiac arrest.

Genene then began to hyperventilate or to have an orgasm - she sweated, gasped and looked strangely high. The enraged army medics kept her to one side whilst they stabilised their child patient. Later she would lie to colleagues, saying that the paramedics didn't have a clue what they were doing and that she'd had to save the day. By now she'd also changed her story about what she'd injected and said it was Valium. She described the experience as one of the most exciting days of her life.

Strange things continued to happen at the clinic when Genene was around. A twenty-one-month-old girl was brought in with suspected meningitis and Genene set up the IV. Thirty seconds later the child went limp. Her mother would later report that the baby's eyes looked terrified, as if aware of what was going on. The mother pleaded with the LVN to do something but Genene said the child was just having a temper tantrum and holding her breath. Her boss, Kathleen Holland, revived the little girl and sent her to the largest local hospital. The baby survived.

Then Chelsea, who Genene had 'revived' before, was brought back in by her mother to have her inoculations. By now Chelsea was fifteen months old. Genene injected the child whilst she lay happily in her mothers arms. Chelsea soon started to whimper and her eyes became strange. Her mother asked Genene to do something but Genene said that Chelsea was just breath-holding and gave the baby a second shot. By now Chelsea was having difficulty breathing. Kathleen and a wide-eyed Genene did what they could then rushed the child to the emergency room, where she quickly died. She was the eighth baby to die in this way within a few months.

At this stage the local hospital started to investigate the new clinic, wondering why so many infants were dying after being treated there. Kathleen spoke with them then made sure that her drug consignment was in order. To her horror she found a bottle of the muscle relaxant succinylcholine - which could cause respiratory failure - was missing. She asked Genene about it and Genene admitted it had disappeared.

Later she said that the drug had turned up and was in the fridge. Kathleen investigated and found one full vial - and one with holes in the cap which had clearly been tampered with. Tests showed that most of the succinylcholine had gone, replaced with a saline solution. Further investigation showed that Genene had been ordering and signing for this drug. At this stage Genene asked Kathleen to pretend to the authorities that the vials had remained missing but the pediatrician explained that ethically and legally she could not do this.

A suicide attempt

Aware that the net was closing in, Genene now took an overdose and told Kathleen that she'd done so. The clinic's receptionist phoned the hospital and Genene promptly had her stomach pumped out.

A bewildered Kathleen sacked Genene and tried to keep her practice going, explaining to would-be patients about the recent fatalities. Suspicion inevitably fell on her as well as her LVN and she was subpoenaed by a Kerr County Grand Jury investigating the unexplained deaths.

Genene Jones was indicted for the deaths of two of her young charges by the Kerr County Grand Jury. (She was suspected of killing up to fifty.) That autumn she was also charged with endangering another baby's life, that of Rolando, by injecting him with the anti-coagulant heparin.

She failed a lie detector test and appeared at last to recognise that she was facing a jail sentence. But she continued to refer to herself as a 'good Christian woman' and seemed increasingly steeped in denial. She insisted on protesting her innocence to the outside world, holding frequent press conferences that told journalists how wronged she had been. Her legal advisers were horrified at these acts of exhibitionism but Genene seemed determined to keep getting herself noticed, no matter what the ultimate cost.

Genene's second marriage

But posing for local photographers wasn't going to pay the bills so Genene started working at a nursing home, training nursing aides in basic patient care (Her employers made sure she had no contact with the actual patients at all.) One of the other aides was a nineteen-year-old youth, Garron Turk, who was clearly mesmerised by her strong personality. She could also be very sweet and loving and caring - and if he knew about her history he probably believed she'd been wrongly accused. Genene married him a month after meeting him and neither party informed most of their relatives that they'd wed.

He and Genene then disappeared for a few weeks and her best friend refused to tell anyone where she'd gone, including the authorities. When law enforcement personnel tracked the newlyweds down they had their van packed and looked ready to set off for a new part of the country presumably using her new surname, Turk.

The new Mrs Turk was taken into custody and was soon telling the prison staff that the shock had made her miscarry - but the blood she'd shed was really due to her menstrual period.

In January of the following year she was tried in Georgetown, Texas, for the murder of Chelsea McClellan. She had written in the child's records that she would have given her life for her and had subsequently attended the baby's funeral. Chelsea's parents had initially only seen her charming side.

But details of her strange temperament had subsequently come to light. Chelsea's mother told of how she'd gone to her daughter's grave and was amazed to see Genene Jones there, crying and rocking back and forward and saying 'Chelsea.' When the mother spoke to the nurse, Genene got up and wandered dazedly away.

The trial

Genene was charged with little Chelsea McClellan's death and the trial began in January 1984. Acting on the advice of her counsel, Genene waived her right to testify. Her legal reps would later say that she was too easily upset, that she couldn't be trusted to act in her own best interests whilst in court. As it was, she sat there eating sweets and glaring at witnesses, and generally making herself unsympathetic.

The jury were told that the prosecution didn't have to prove why she'd killed the baby, only show that she had. They did, however, believe that the cause would be apparent. It was indeed clear that Genene had a massive inferiority complex and that reviving the children made her feel better about herself as it helped the rest of the hospital see her as a brilliant nurse. When she moved on to work with Kathleen Holland she wanted the area to set up a special unit for critically ill children which she, Genene, and her new boss, Kathleen, would be the ideal people to run. Some medics suspected that she had deliberately caused critical illness in her patients in the hope that it would ensure such a unit was formed.

The prosecution also showed that the Code Blue emergencies had all occurred when Genene was around and that such levels of seizure hadn't been seen before or since. They brought forth an expert who identified succinylcholine in the exhumed remains of Chelsea McClellan. They produced witnesses who testified that Genene would tell one person that she'd injected a young patient with one drug then contradict herself by immediately telling someone else that she'd used a different medicine.

Kathleen Holland testified that Genene had ordered succinylcholine then asked Kathleen to pretend she hadn't. At this stage in the trial Genene wept. She had an odd attitude to her former boss, in many ways admiring her and wanting to emulate her yet at the same time feeling envious of her superior qualifications and success.

The defence tried to suggest that succinylcholine was found naturally in human tissue. They suggested that Kathleen Holland could have made clinical errors and used Genene to cover her tracks. (This, of course, failed to explain the numerous babies that had had Code Blue emergencies under Genene's care when she worked for Bexar - but she wasn't on trial for the incidents at Bexar, only, at this stage, for the death of Chelsea at the Kerr

County Clinic.) The defence tried to paint Jones as an intelligent and devoted professional and said that the charges against her hadn't been proved.

The sentence

But the jury recognised her continued danger to the public and in May 1984 she was sentenced to ninety-nine years in prison. Five months later she was charged with the attempted murder of Rolando, the child she'd injected with anti-coagulant, a crime for which she received sixty years. At thirty-three she started her sentence in a women's correctional facility in her native Texas. Her second husband immediately filed for divorce.

Shortly after her incarceration, prison officials asked her former employers if she was a suitable candidate to work for the prison's hospital dispensary. Hopefully common sense made them say no.

The motive

Power seems to have been the strongest motive in this case, with witnesses to the babies deaths describing Genene Jones as being almost sexually excited during a Code Blue emergency. It's also clear that there was a Munchhausen's element for this woman had often faked illness as a child and as a young woman before going on to use Munchhausen's Syndrome By Proxy as her tool. With Munchhausen's the patient invents or exaggerates her own symptoms in order to win the attention of the medics. With Munchhausen's Syndrome By Proxy she causes or exaggerates the illnesses of her children and anyone else in her care.

This offender type has an overwhelming need for recognition. They also crave attention and have a strong desire to control others - nursing and half-killing little children satisfied Genene Jones' many needs. She could tell the other medics what to do and then make Herculean efforts to save the dying infant. If she succeeded she was seen as a heroine and if she failed she could revel in the histrionics of rocking the dead baby in her arms whilst wailing loudly before finally carrying the little corpse to the mortuary. People who knew her said that she perpetually lusted for control.

It's no accident, then, that Genene ended up working with an almost endless stream of helpless mute victims. Such offenders often take jobs in law enforcement and in nursing so that they can cause the frequent dramas they crave.

Such offenders are organised - Genene has asked for a lecture to be held on the uses of succinylcholine, the powerful muscle relaxant that she would later administer to some of her patients. She learned about the paralysis it would cause to the muscles, the diaphragm and eventually the heart. She also knew that, appallingly, the patient remains conscious and knows that they're becoming increasingly paralysed.

One of the themes that reverberates through this book is the fact that the murderesses invariably suffered as children before they went on to cause suffering as adults. Investigators didn't look into Genene's past too thoroughly as her widowed mother was ill by the time of her daughter's trial and Genene said that the trial had almost killed the older woman. But investigators believed that there had been something strange in her childhood and Genene had told a friend she'd been abused.

Admittedly, she told many lies to make herself look more important. But her overwhelming need for control, her inability to identify with others and her huge swings between low self esteem and grandiosity are all the symptoms of a child who hasn't been treated well. The authors of a book about the case, *Deadly Medicine*, say that she may have acted out as a nurse what had been done to her as a child - that is, she'd been physically hurt and then consoled so that physical damage and love became unhealthily fused.

Update

By the time she was forty-two Genene was eligible for parole but Chelsea's parents and their supporters campaigned to keep her behind bars where she continues to complain about the inexperienced doctors and nurses she used to work with. She will next be eligible for parole in 2009.

7

COLD AS ICE
The merciless acts of Judith Ann Neelley

Judith was born on 7th June 1964 in Murfreesboro, Tennessee, to a Mr and Mrs Adams who already had a son and a daughter. After Judith's birth, the couple would go on to have another two boys. Judith's mother, Barbara, was a housewife and her father was a construction worker. He also did carpentry. All seven of them lived in an increasingly cramped mobile home in an impoverished part of the United States. They weren't rich but they were reasonably fed and clothed and had access to a garden. There was also an adjoining wood filled with trees which the five children loved to climb.

Judith's father was often away from the trailer, working hard. Even when he was home he seemed remote, but she loved him and would later say that he never hit her. When she was nine he started his own construction company, so the family income increased markedly.

Judith was a bright child who did well at school, and was confident of her academic abilities. She had prominent front teeth and was big boned, but her large eyes and long dark hair helped compensate for this, though she thought of herself as ugly. She liked playing with dolls and when she grew up she hoped to become a nurse.

But when she was three months short of her tenth birthday, a tragedy happened that would change her life. Her father, who occasionally drank to excess, had a few drinks then went out on his motorbike and lost control of it. The bike veered to one side of the road and he was catapulted onto the pavement and killed instantly. Nine-year-old Judith was distraught to hear of his death, as was all her family. She had always been a quiet child but now seemed to retreat even further inside herself.

The Adams were now in financial trouble, for her father's pension wasn't enough to support six of them. For a while her mother, Barbara, found work in a factory, but then she had a car accident and had to give the job up.

Judith's mother didn't cope well with being alone. She started a relationship with a teenage boy and the courts charged her with contributing to the delinquency of a minor. She then bought a CB radio and began to make contact with many male strangers, calling herself the Indian Princess. (She was apparently half Cherokee.) Soon the men were turning up at the trailer at all hours of the day and night and they weren't there to talk...

There was only a blanket dividing Judith's sleeping quarters from that of her mum, so she could hear her having sex with various men. Soon Barbara became a full time prostitute. Young Judith was disgusted. She often left the trailer and climbed her favourite tree, spending the rest of the night there dreaming more grandiose dreams.

She was equally unimpressed by her siblings, who now began playing truant and watching mindless programmes on TV all day long. The older ones also took to beer drinking. Judith rightly saw education as her way of escaping a life as trailer trash. She had the IQ and energy to achieve this and the world would have been a safer place if she had remained on the scholastic path.

The next six years passed in this way, with Judith fighting off her mother's clients sexual advances. Rage understandably built in her. She'd come home from school and have to do most of the chores in the trailer then do her schoolwork, then listen to her mother having sex with yet another man. Determined to aim higher than this for herself, Judith rarely dated the boys in her class and defiantly remained a virgin. Still, she was desperately lonely and wished that her Prince would come.

Then, when she was fifteen she convinced herself that he'd appeared in the unlikely guise of Alvin Neelley, ten years her senior. He was a friend of one of her mother's client's, an overweight twenty-five year old and an obsessive user of prostitutes. He was married with three children and had a criminal record. He had also abused his wife, Jo Ann.

Alvin got by on jokes and compliments. His IQ was much lower than Judith's and he had no apparent ambition. But as history shows, if a person is desperate enough they will see almost anyone as their love object or their saviour, so Judith decided that Alvin had a nice smile, handsome blue eyes and that she was in love with him. She would say that they were so close that they were virtually telepathic. As Alvin wasn't the most articulate man in trailer park land, it presumably didn't take long to read his mind.

Judith's day to day life involved endless chores. Alvin, with time on his hands and ownership of a car, represented fun and freedom. She was also impressed at his cleanliness as many of her mother's clients were lorry drivers who hadn't always had access to a bath. At five foot ten and strongly built, Judith was a frightening prospect for some of her mother's male callers, but Alvin found her attractive and the sex was good.

He left his wife and fifteen-year-old Judith ran away to live with him. But life didn't get much better than it had been in the trailer as they were reduced to sleeping in his car. The increasingly unkempt Judith soon became pregnant but miscarried. In a bid to find some kind of happiness, they started driving around taking casual work for a few days or weeks at a time. The would-be nurse now worked in convenience stores alongside her lover and they made extra money by ringing up the wrong sale price and other illegal scams.

They married in the summer of 1980 as by then Judith was sixteen and their relationship was legal. By this time she was pregnant again, and money was getting short.

Armed and dangerous

Judith now committed armed robbery - at the end of October 1980 - by pointing a pistol at a student in a quiet corner of a shopping mall and demanding money. She called her victim a bitch and stared at her coldly. The terrified young woman handed her bag over and Judith fled.

If she'd been content with the money she might have gotten away with the crime, but she forged the victim's signature on her cheques, and was quickly arrested for trying to cash them. Judith was sent to a young offenders unit in Rome, Georgia, and later transferred to the Macon Youth Development Center. Whilst incarcerated there she gave birth to twins. Many months after being set free she would fire shots into the house of one of the Center's careworkers and firebomb the house of another worker, causing a fire to break out.

Alvin also went to prison at this time. He would be locked up for various theft and deceit crimes throughout the early months of their relationship. The couple wrote to each other throughout their enforced separation, the letters showing a mixture of love and control and emotional immaturity. None of the letters demonstrated the telepathic communication she'd earlier imagined and many bordered on the paranoid.

One missive he wrote her said 'No matter if you stick to me or walk out on me you'll get some things to answer to me about, and I do mean you.' In turn, she imagined that he was in touch with other women and wrote that 'None of them are woman enough to try to take you from me when I get out.' She also wrote of how brilliant their sex life was.

Judith was released in the summer of 1981 but was quickly rearrested on charges of shop theft. She was released again on 1st December. Alvin was still in prison so she stayed with his parents, though she complained in letters that his father could 'still raise hell' and was a 'son of a bitch.'

On his release she and Alvin - with the babies often strapped into the back seat of the car - continued to commit minor league criminal acts in and around their home area of Rome, Georgia. When they could, they stayed with relatives or shacked up in cheap motel rooms. Other times they slept in the car, Judith and the twins surviving mainly on peanut butter sandwiches, cookies and candy. Alvin favoured huge takeaway hamburgers and large amounts of Coca-cola. This overeating is symptomatic of unhappy people –food dulls the senses and essentially acts as a tranquilliser, an attempt to self-medicate.

Sometimes they managed to steal cheques from post office boxes and could afford to rent a room for a few days but at other times they were completely broke and found it hard to get even a change of clothes or a bath. Judith's previously glossy hair now hung in greasy tangles and her eyes were puffy. She was swiftly becoming the thing she most hated - an uneducated person with no clear goals, little cash and a series of dead end jobs.

Early revenge

When the going gets tough, the weak look around for a scapegoat. On 10th September 1982 Judith drove to the home of a Youth Development Center employee - who she would admit in court was kind to her - and fired shots into his home. He wasn't injured. The next night she threw a Molotov cocktail onto the drive of another YDC worker, a woman whom she would later praise publicly. She also phoned the woman and promised that both employees would die for abusing her.

Judith didn't leave her name but would later admit both crimes when taken into custody on a murder charge. She alleged that she'd been sexually abused at the home and forced to take part in a prostitution ring - but a subsequent investigation ruled this out and cleared the two people she'd tried to harm. As abuse is legion in children's homes it's very likely that *someone* abused her when she was in care. However it's also true that a man, presumed to be Alvin, made one of the threatening calls about his wife being abused to a careworker so Judith might have been trying to make her husband jealous during one of their many power games.

The first known murder

According to Judith, Alvin started to say that he wanted to have sex with a virgin and asked her to procure him one. But Alvin would say that Judith chose to pick up a girl to have power over her - and the police would later state that Judith clearly liked to control others and seemed stronger than her spouse.

Keen to make someone else feel worse than they did, the Neelleys went to the Riverbend Mall in Rome, Georgia on 25th September 1982. There they entered the video arcade and Alvin started playing the machines. When his back was turned, Judith approached Suzanne Clonts and asked her if she was alone, and if she wanted to drive around for a while. Suzanne looked at the dead eyed and dirty teenager and declined, a move that undoubtedly saved her life.

Lisa's abduction

Judith then approached thirteen-year-old Lisa Millican. The teenager was with a party from a children's home for neglected girls but had become separated from them. She was frightened as some youths had been eyeing her up and she'd had bad experiences with abusive men. She chatted eagerly to Judith as her care workers searched for her throughout the mall.

Lisa had already suffered greatly during her short life, as her family - who lived in a rundown trailer - had neglected her. She'd been sexually abused by her father from the age of eleven. Her mother had also taken her to bed with a man on various occasions saying that the man wouldn't rape her because he was too drunk.

Lisa and her three siblings had all been taken into care and she had been placed in several foster homes before being moved to the Harpst Children's Home. The attractive dark-haired teenager was actively bisexual - but clearly had no idea what the sadistic Judith Neelley had in mind.

Lisa now got into Judith's car, excited at the idea of an adventure. Judith may have had the twins in the backseat, yet another reason for Lisa not to feel alarmed. Alvin probably wasn't around at this stage, for by now the unlikely couple had a car each.

The reasons for this were myriad. Alvin liked a tidy vehicle whereas Judith kept hers littered with food wrappers and other junk. Plus they fought a lot and the separate vehicles allowed them to maintain a necessary distance. And it couldn't have escaped their notice that if a potential victim got into Judith's car and was driven someplace quiet, she would be especially taken by surprise when Alvin suddenly appeared.

At some stage on the journey Lisa was introduced to Alvin. It was easy for Judith to arrange this as the couple both had CB radios in their cars - ironic, given that Judith had so hated her mother's CB radio. Judith called herself Lady Sundown and Alvin called himself Nightrider. The hamburger diet hadn't been kind to Nightrider so he was a smiling, roly-poly kind of man. Lisa had no reason to fear the couple, and by now had no idea how to get back to the children's home even if she'd wanted to. So they all went to a cheap motel and booked a room.

One motel worker saw Judith walking through the building with Lisa following close behind her. She also saw Alvin going again and again to the vending machines which sold junk food. He clearly found it taxing to be active, his movements further hampered by a long-term injury that had resulted in a metal plate in his leg. Witnesses would describe Alvin as an overweight, breathless man who only ventured out of the room to obtain more sustenance. And Judith would admit that he liked to lie around for hours just watching TV. But his semen would be found inside thirteen-year-old Lisa's body so he clearly managed to have sex with the needy child.

When they were locked in their motel room, Judith produced her gun and told the terrified Lisa to do whatever she said. Then the couple gagged her and tied her to the bed. For the next four days Judith sexually assaulted her and Alvin raped her. Both Neelleys took turns in beating her whilst their own little children watched. At night they handcuffed the teenager to the bedframe and made her sleep on the floor. There was a spare bed in the room so leaving her cold and naked on the carpet was yet another instance of abuse.

Killing Lisa

After four days they decided to move on and Judith decided to kill Lisa - she would later claim this was so that the teenager couldn't identify her. Judith left the hotel very early whilst no one was around and handcuffed the girl to the inside of the car. She then drove her to a canyon in a remote part of Dekalb County, told her to get out of the vehicle and lie down. Lisa obeyed and Judith promptly handcuffed her young victim's arms around a tree.

Next, Judith produced a loaded syringe and injected Lisa in the neck with liquid drain cleaner. She would later claim that she did this to kill her quickly, but it's apparent from what followed that it was simply another form of torture, particularly when she had a gun available that could have instantly killed the raped and beaten child.

Lisa cried out and writhed on the ground but didn't die. After a time, Judith injected a different solution into the other side of Lisa's neck. Again, Lisa remained conscious. Judith ordered Lisa to walk about, ostensibly to make the solution work faster. Then she handcuffed her again, still at gunpoint. She went on to inject both of Lisa's arms and her buttocks using a total of three different syringes and waiting for a few minutes after each injection but the girl still didn't die.

Lisa pleaded to be allowed to go back to the children's home and said she was cold and could she have a blanket? The caustic agent was literally causing her flesh to bubble and liquefy and she must have been in terrible pain. Judith had taken care to drive to a remote region so there wasn't a rescuer for miles around.

Judith untied Lisa for the last time and ordered her to walk to the very edge of the canyon, which in some places is 600 feet deep. The pretty brunette teenager again pleaded for her life but Judith ignored her pleas and shot her from behind. The girl fell backwards onto the ground rather than toppling forwards over the edge so Judith pushed her over, watching her body plunge over eighty feet before it was caught by a jutting tree. Whilst rolling the girl over she'd gotten blood on her jeans so she now swapped them for a clean pair that she had in the car. She threw her blood-stained clothing and the syringes over the edge where they would be found near the body by Dekalb police.

Judith would say in court that she carried out the injections and the shooting on Alvin's orders because she was terrified of his violence - but there is no physical evidence linking him to the abuse at the canyon, only to having sex in the motel. She would also claim that he masturbated at the scene.

A taunting phone call

Shortly after Lisa's death, Judith Neelley phoned a radio station in Rome, Georgia and told them where to find the teenager's body. She repeated the detailed instructions in another phone call to the Rome police. The Rome police would search the area but fail to find the child's corpse. Judith now phoned the Dekalb County Sheriffs Office and told them where to find 'a young girl's body' adding 'where I left her.' They searched and finally found Lisa with a bullet through her head. They also found Judith's blood-smeared jeans and the three syringes that had been used to torture Lisa immediately before her death.

Criminologists always state that female serial killers never make taunting phone calls to the police - but Judith Neelley is a rare exception. Her motive for doing so is still unclear. What's certain is that the taped calls helped show that she was confident, calm and completely without remorse for her vicious crime.

Other potential victims are approached

On the afternoon of 3rd October 1982, Diane Bobo was approached by Judith Neelley, who tried to get her to go for a ride with her. She refused immediately. The next day thirteen-year-old Debbie Smith was walking home from school when Judith did the exact same thing. She too declined. Both felt uneasy after their encounter with the staring teenager in the brown Dodge - and Debbie's mother would report the incident to the authorities. Both witnesses were later able to identify Neelley from photographs.

Judith shoots John

The approaches to Diane Bobo and Debbie Smith having failed, that evening Judith drew up alongside a couple who were out walking, John Hancock and Janice Chatman. She said that she was lonely and repeatedly asked them to ride around with her. John Hancock, a gravedigger, had a bad feeling about the offer, but foolishly ignored his intuition. He had recently become a Christian so thought he should satisfy Judith's request for companionship. Janice, his common law wife, had learning difficulties so was quite happy to get into the car.

Judith started to drive along country roads with her two new passengers and her two small children in the car. Soon she switched on her CB radio. When someone calling himself Nightrider started to speak she responded immediately. She called herself Lady Sundown as she arranged to meet up with him. She sounded calm and assured, not the battered and brainwashed wife she would later try to make herself out to be.

After a while she drew up on a dirt road north of Rome and Alvin Neelley drew up in a red car beside them. Alvin suggested that John Hancock ride with him and Janice Chatman stay with Judith. John's uneasiness increased but Janice seemed quite happy with this arrangement. The two cars then drove north looking for a cheap source of drink that Alvin had apparently heard of, but finally stopped because John Hancock needed to urinate.

Both cars stopped and John Hancock walked a little distance away and relieved himself. He was aware that Judith and Alvin had left their vehicles and were standing watching him. He could hear them whispering. Then he heard Alvin say 'If we're going to do it, let's get it over with,' and Judith approached him pointing her gun.

She ordered him to walk with his back to her. He did, his heart beating heavily in his chest. She told him which directions to take, marching him backwards and forwards until Alvin, by now out of sight, shouted to hurry up and get it over with. (John, who miraculously survived the shooting, would later say that Alvin sounded scared.) He asked if he could talk to her but she said 'Hell, no' and remained disinterested and cold. She added, ambiguously, that they were going to take care of his girlfriend - at which stage Alvin shouted again for her to hurry up.

Seconds later John felt a bullet enter his shoulder. The force of the shot threw him forward onto his stomach. He played dead, feeling his blood run down his back and into the ground as he heard his assailant, Lady Sundown, rush away through the woods.

John Hancock lay there for some time, hearing both cars drive away and knowing that twenty-three-year old Janice Chatman was in one of them. At last he dragged his bloodstained body to the road and tried to flag down a car.

Janice's murder

Now it was Janice's turn to be driven to a cheap motel for the couple's sexual pleasure. Judith would later say that Janice was quite happy on the journey and this is possible as she hadn't seen John Hancock being shot. He himself would later explain that Janice was almost childlike and had often been sexually used by men. But Alvin Neelley would state that when the two cars stopped - moments before Judith shot John Hancock - he saw that she'd handcuffed Janice to the inside of the car.

Once at the motel, Judith Neelley sexually assaulted Janice and Alvin allegedly raped her. Alvin would say that Judith also mocked the mentally retarded woman for talking so strangely. This murder, like that of Lisa, seems to have been about power, although that power was sometimes expressed in sexual terms.

The next day Judith decided to get rid of her victim, so drove the woman to a rural part of Chattooga County. There she marched Janice out of the car and shot her. Janice continued to scream and Judith angrily shot her twice more in the chest. She would later say that Alvin had ordered her to do so, but in his version he only heard about the death from Judith as he'd driven on ahead (A jury didn't believe that he'd only helped to abduct and rape her and he was charged with causing her death.)

The listeners

A kindly stranger picked up the bleeding John Hancock and rushed him to the hospital. There he received emergency treatment and soon recovered from his gunshot wound. He was able to give an excellent description of Judith and Alvin Neelley, though obviously he only knew their CB names.

A Georgia detective invited him to come down to the station and take a lie detector test, to make sure that he'd played no part in the disappearance of his partner Janice. (Though feared dead she was still officially listed as missing.) Incredibly, whilst he was there, he heard Judith Neelley's voice emanating from another room. A policeman was playing tape recordings of Mrs Neelley's phone calls to one of her almost-victims, Debbie Smith, the schoolgirl who'd declined a ride. John Hancock exclaimed that he was listening to the voice of the woman who'd shot him - and he proved to be right.

Debbie, John and other witnesses now picked out Judith Neelley's face - and, in some instances, Alvin's - from crime photographs that the police showed them and a warrant was issued for their arrest.

The arrest

By now the couple were back in Judith's home town of Murfreesboro, Tennessee, staying with her mother, Barbara. On 9th October Judith went to a hotel there and tried to pass a bad cheque. She was arrested - and word soon got back to Sergeant Kenneth Kines, who knew Neelley was responsible for John Hancock's shooting and Lisa's torture and death. After all, her taunting phone calls had told them where to find Lisa's body, information no one but the killer could know.

The police searched Judith's mother's house and found some of the Neelley's killing kit, including handcuffs, guns, knives and masks.

Alvin was also arrested the same week and when Janice Chatman wasn't found with either Neelley the police strongly suspected she was dead. Alvin would later tell police where to find her body - in a rural backwater in Chattooga County. He'd claim that Judith told him where she'd shot the girl, that he wasn't directly involved in her death. He even drew them a map of the killing fields and they did indeed locate the young woman's body in the vicinity. Unfortunately she was too badly decomposed to undergo forensic tests.

He said, she said

Alvin now claimed that Judith was the powerful one - and certainly the police found her hard and cold, whilst several people said she had the most chilling stare they'd ever seen. A police photo at the time of her arrest showed her expression as one of repressed rage. It wasn't the first time she'd looked frightening - she'd certainly terrorised the female student she mugged and unsettled Debbie Smith and Diane Bobo with her compassionless gaze.

Police thought that Alvin, in contrast, was a wimp, a weak man who seemed permanently close to tears and who admitted he liked to ride in a separate car to his wife because she had terrible mood swings and would pick arguments. (Possibly the peanut butter diet played havoc with her blood sugar.) He talked about the firebombing, shooting and killings that she'd instigated, and said that he'd begun to fear that she'd shoot him too.

When first brought into custody Judith denied everything. She was pregnant again and looked unkempt and impoverished. Her eyes were blank as she stared at the police and her voice was flat. Living in a car with two children whilst expecting a third would take its toll on anyone's health - but it still didn't give her an excuse to inflict misery on others.

The police let her hear tapes of the various calls that she'd made. Thereafter, she admitted firebombing one careworker and shooting into the house of another. When they played the tapes she'd made after Lisa's death, she started to talk matter of factly about the girl's sexual abuse, the drain cleaner torture and eventual death. She also admitted shooting Janice Chatman three times.

Asked if she was afraid of her husband Alvin, she shook her head and said that he was the only person she'd ever trusted. She would later change this story to suggest that he'd abused her almost every day of her life - though the endless beatings mysteriously left not a single bruise. She was driven to Fort Payne, Alabama, and charged with the murder of Lisa Ann Millican. (Janice had been killed in a different jurisdiction so charges relating to her death would have to be brought separately.)

Keeping up appearances

Judith Neelley gave birth to her third child, a boy, whilst waiting to go to trial. Bob French, who intially didn't like her, reluctantly agreed to act as her defense. He arranged for her to have dental work so that her buckteeth looked better. He also arranged for her hair to be styled and got her upmarket clothes. At the end of this grooming period she looked healthy and attractive. She was also intellectually fit - tests showed her IQ was still well above average. It appears that Bob French also had her coached so that she lost her aggressive air.

Whilst putting together Judith's defense, he found out about Alvin's first wife and mother of his three children, Jo Ann Browning (she had married Mr Browning long before obtaining a divorce from Alvin Neelley, making the marriage bigamous) and managed to track her down.

The trial

Judith Neelley went to trial on the 7th March 1983. The venue was the Dekalb County Courthouse in Alabama. Seven women and five men made up the jurors. It had been clear from Bob French's original questions during the jury selection process that he was going to take the woman-as-victim approach.

The prosecution stated that when Judith had started talking to Lisa in the mall, her plan had been to abuse her. They said that Judith was not Alvin's victim - after all, she had acted alone during several of her crimes. She had approached complete strangers and engaged them in persistent conversations, and she had sounded confident during her calls to the police. The people who had declined to go with her also said that she was not bruised or cowed and that in some instances Alvin hadn't even been around.

Bob French called Jo Ann Browning, Alvin's first wife, to the stand. The couple had been married for three years in the seventies and had produced three children. Jo Ann had helped Alvin rob the stores where he worked - she would state that he made her do so. The couple had either inhabited trailers, where she said he hit her daily, or moved purposelessly around. When the stormy marriage faltered, he had insisted on keeping the children, so Jo Ann had good reason to hate him even more. A clearly immature man, he had used his offspring as pawns to hurt his ex-wife - for after insisting on custody he'd eventually given the children to relatives.

Alvin had left Jo Ann after he met the younger Judith, so she had another reason to make him look bad in court. (Alvin Neelley was tried separately from Judith for the murder of Janice Chatman. He was found guilty and given two life sentences.) Jo Ann would claim in court that he'd beaten her over eight hundred times, often using heavy implements. The prosecution queried this as she had never had a broken bone. Whatever the reality of the relationship, it was clear that she detested her former spouse. The prosecution suggested that Jo Ann's story was a lie or at least hugely exaggerated, the words of a woman scorned.

Prior to her trial, Judith had never alleged that Alvin had abused her - but now she followed Jo Ann to the stand and gave a defence that amounted to Battered Wife Syndrome, even though she didn't fit the true definition of a battered wife.

The syndrome was coined to describe women who kill their abusive *partners* - not women whose abusive partners allegedly tell them to kill *someone else* who they've abducted for sexual kicks. Moreover, studies of battered women who have killed their violent men show that the women had tried to escape on numerous occasions but been tracked down and re-abused. And they'd been beaten more severely than the battered wives who didn't go on to kill. In other words, these women had tried hard to escape their particularly violent abusers and had only killed them as a last resort.

Judith Neelley didn't fit this pattern at all. She had been free at times when Alvin was locked up. She could have gone anywhere she wanted - indeed, in one letter she had told him so, stating that she only waited for him to leave jail because she wanted to be with him. She wasn't dependent on him for her livelihood - she had taken a cashier's course whilst in the youth correctional centre so could have taken legitimate shop work anywhere in the states.

Judith produced just one photograph where she was bruised and claimed that Alvin had hit her, bit her, kicked her and raped her, but a mental health expert said that she could have gotten these injuries in many ways. He said that she retained her free will, that she hadn't been brainwashed by Alvin. Other photographs showed the couple smiling happily as they posed with various guns. Judith had been *au fait* with guns for years and owned several weapons of her own. She now said that Alvin had made her smile for each of the photographs but neither the prosecution or the jury were convinced.

Judith explained Lisa's abduction by saying that Alvin had decided he wanted a virgin. She was allegedly afraid not to comply with this request, so duly got thirteen-year-old Lisa for him. She would at first give the impression that Lisa was happy to stay with the Neelleys - but later slipped up and mentioned handcuffing her to the car. She said that Alvin had made her help him beat Lisa at the motel whilst their babies watched.

She gave a similar story when it came to Janice Chatman's sexual assault and death, saying that Alvin had made her do it. But John Hancock was able to assert that *Judith* had shot him. At the time Alvin was out of sight so if Alvin was truly the instigator she could just have pretended to fire at John and let him go. Under questioning, John admitted that she'd fired the shot when Alvin told her to hurry up - and that it was Alvin who had determined where the two cars would meet up. But Judith Neelley had done the actual shooting - she'd taken a malicious pleasure in taunting him in the previous moments and hadn't appeared at all intimidated by her spouse.

Her defense suggested that if one of the women she'd approached had given her 'Christian witness' (talked to her about religion) then Judith -

already an armed robber, persistent thief and mugger - wouldn't have gone on to kill. In reality, more serial killers come from deeply religious areas of the world than from more secular ones. And Alvin Neelley's possessions included tracts from a TV evangelist - but that hadn't stopped Alvin having sex with underage girls.

The jury now recommended that Judith be sent to prison for life without possibility of parole - but in Alabama the final decision is the judge's and he sentenced her to die in the electric chair. It was the only time she cried throughout the trial, and the tears were clearly for herself.

The death penalty

At eighteen, Judith Neelley was the youngest woman ever to be sentenced to death in the states. But then she wasn't like most young woman - she'd tortured a thirteen-year-old child and ultimately murdered her. And she'd sexually assaulted and killed a twenty-three-year old woman of limited mental ability and shot her companion, leaving him for dead.

She'd also fired bullets into one house, probably knowing it contained children as well as an adult careworker. She'd firebombed the home of another careworker, again having no control over who was potentially maimed or killed. She'd mugged a student and had scammed money from many of the convenience stores that gave her work. She'd often stolen cheques from people's mailboxes and she'd tried to entice other teenagers and women into her car.

By the time she was eighteen she'd had three children, all born whilst she was incarcerated. She'd driven the first two - the twins - around the country, never giving them a stable home.

Death row

Judith was sent to a prison for women in Alabama to await execution, and spent much of her time there reading and lodging various appeals. She had a cell to herself, an improvement on the car-based living she was used to. She took her exercise periods and her meals alone, presumably because child killers are often assaulted by other prisoners. She might also have been seen as a risk to other young women given her aggressive tendencies.

She continued to be visited by her defense attorney Bob French, by now an expert on Battered Wife Syndrome. Local feeling against her was high, and people understandably turned against Bob too and stopped being his clients. Eventually he had to file for bankruptcy.

Meanwhile Judith's appeals - including one which alleged that Bob French had failed to represent her properly and that he'd already decided to write a book on the subject at the time of her trial - were turned down. Her final appeal was heard in 1998, after which she was left with no further legal redress.

A convenient conversion

Suddenly Judith decided she'd seen the light and became a Christian Fundamentalist. Alabama's governor was also a Christian Fundamentalist. He only had a few days left in office, so had nothing to lose in voting terms when he commuted her sentence to life imprisonment. He added the term 'without possibility of parole' - and the local newspapers then reported that she would spend the rest of her life behind bars. In reality, a governor cannot prevent the parole-consideration process, so she will eventually be eligible for parole.

Other victims

Occasionally crime encyclopaedias state that Judith Neelley tortured fifteen young female victims to death in Alabama, Georgia and Tennessee, but fail to give names beyond those known; Lisa Ann Millican, Janice Chatman and the wounded John Hancock. One sociology book started that Neelley claimed six victims. Again, no concrete details were given.

It's certainly true that serial killers are often tried for far fewer killings than they are believed to have actually committed, but I contacted various true crime writers in the states and they were unable to find names or any other details of these deaths.

This author read what is considered the definitive book on the subject, *Early Graves* by Thomas H. Cook, which only names the victims profiled here.

Why she did it

Although the crimes were of a sexual nature, it's apparent that Judith Neelley's motivation was power. She clearly took pleasure in hearing her victim's plead for their lives and in watching them writhe on the ground. Alvin, police and other witnesses would say that 'Judy liked to be in charge.'

It's also possible that she was trying to kill an earlier version of herself. She'd written to Alvin when she was in the youth correctional facility, describing his other women as 'a little bunch of nothings.' She doubtless saw the abused, impoverished Lisa and the low IQ Janice as being akin to the trailer trash background she so despised.

Judith had dreamt of a nice home and a career, a life a million miles away from the crowded trailer with its endless fornication and drinking. Yet here she was, driving from state to state, staying in cheap motels and conning stores out of cash. The girl with the high IQ had fallen low - but through a mixture of cruel words and even crueller actions she could make her victims seem even lower than herself. To the women who passed her in the shopping malls, Judith Neelley was an unwashed drifter with an equally shiftless husband - but to Lisa, Janice and John she became omnipotent, holding the key to their immediate wellbeing and having power over whether they lived or died.

It's a well known fact that the person who has the most menial day job is often the person who is a despot and a sadist to his family - and indigent Judith Neelley was sadistic enough to inject drain cleaner into a thirteen-year-old child and watch the child's flesh bubble and liquefy.

Update

The fact that Lisa was tortured and killed in the Grand Canyon of the South upset the local people and made the canyon seem more sinister than it had before. In the early 1990's various volunteer groups banded together and worked hard to clear it of trash and restore it to its natural beauty. Locals also started an energised campaign called *Save Our Land*.

Judith's sister and three brothers launched a 'save Judith' statement in January 1999, claiming that she too was a victim of Alvin's alleged violence. 'Domestic violence goes more deeper than just a beating,' (sic) one of her relatives said. They added that her family loved her very much.

And of Judith's own much-travelled offspring, all born in custody? Her twins have been adopted by Alvin's mother, whilst her third son - whose middle name, at her request, is Alvin - is being cared for elsewhere in the states. She has been appealing to have the children returned to her. Her own mother is now dead.

Coming to a shopping mall near you?

Judith Neelley will be eligible for parole in Alabama in 2014, assuming she doesn't manage to file a successful appeal before that. She will be fifty years old. However, she may remain behind bars because she was also sentenced to life in Georgia for kidnapping when she abducted Janice Chatman there.

8

GIVING IT UP FOR YOUR LOVE
The dependent world of Catherine Margaret Birnie

Catherine was born in Australia on 31st May 1951. She was only ten months old when her mother died, at which stage she went to live with her father in South Africa. This arrangement lasted for two years, after which she was sent back to Perth, Australia to live with her controlling grandparents who wouldn't allow other children into the house.

Given few treats and little fun, Catherine had such a loveless and lonely childhood that people who knew her would report that she rarely smiled. She also endured the trauma of watching her grandmother die in front of her during an epileptic fit. She would remain in poverty throughout her life.

By the time she was eighteen, Catherine was burgling factories and shops with her friend and next door neighbour David, who was the same age as her. Both were convicted, though Catherine received probation for the early breaking and entering charges. The third time she was imprisoned for six months and the previously-jailed David Birnie got two and a half years.

The pair of them were at one stage caught with wigs, coshes, gelignite and guns, everything needed to cause serious damage to property. Their criminal kit was chillingly similar to that owned by female serial killer Judith Neelley, profiled previously.

Catherine gave birth in prison and the baby was taken from her until her release. The child wasn't David's and indeed it isn't known who the father was. It's likely that, like most unloved young women, Catherine was desperate to be held and cared for and tried to achieve this by being promiscuous. When she and David drifted apart he married someone else.

The thin, pale Catherine now got herself a job as a couple's domestic help in Freemantle, Western Australia - but found herself more interested in their adult son, Donald. When she was twenty-one she married him and soon had a child by him. She was outside with the boy when he was seven months old and saw him crushed by a car. He died immediately.

Catherine went on to have another five children by her husband, but he refused to get a job and she had to work hard to support him plus their offspring. She also helped to support two of her adult relatives.

Catherine hadn't been parented well so she had few parenting skills of her own. She also hated housework and had very little energy left for it by the time she finished work for the day. It was an impoverished and unrewarding life - but the only type of life that she had ever known.

This exhausting marriage lasted for sixteen years, after which she again met up with David Birnie. His own childhood had partly been spent in care as both his parents were out of control alcoholics. He'd been brutalised all his young life. Catherine resumed her love affair with David and he wooed her with chocolates and flowers and made her feel that she mattered to someone. Within two years she had left her husband and moved in with him.

David was no knight in shining armour - but then embryonic female serial killers rarely manage to attract knights in shining armour. He already had a failed marriage and numerous failed relationships and career starts and had been fired from a previous job because of sexual assault. He sometimes saw sex as a weapon and would inject numbing chemicals into the head of his penis so that he could thrust into a female for hours. He was so highly sexed that if a woman wasn't available he would make do with a male.

Catherine now convinced herself that she loved him more than anything else and that she would do anything for him. This 'perfect' love gave meaning to her otherwise unfocused life, a life without her children and without educational or career prospects. She changed her surname to Birnie by deed poll so that he became her common law husband, but they were never officially wed. The couple set up home in Willagee in a modest old house that they rented from the local authorities. As with her previous household, Catherine let the place get very untidy and the garden hopelessly overgrown.

In fairness, she had other things to think about. David wanted sex all the time - and when he wasn't having it he was watching videos that depicted it. He was insatiable with a preference for very young women, and he had enjoyed many before settling down with the thin, clingy Catherine.

She was a low dominance female and he was a high dominance male, so before long she wasn't enough for him. He began to dream of kidnapping a girl who could become his sexual slave.

The first victim

David worked as a labourer in a car-wrecking yard. When a twenty-two-year old psychology student, Mary Neilson, called at the yard to buy tires, he suggested she come to his house where he could sell her them cheaper. When she did so, he dragged her inside and held her at gunpoint. It's not known whether this was all his own idea or whether he and Catherine had discussed it first.

Whatever the original sequence of events, thirty-five-year old Catherine now watched approvingly as her common law husband chained the younger girl to the bed, stripped her, gagged her and repeatedly raped her. Catherine had no time for her own gender - after all, her mother had deserted her by dying and her grandmother had abused her horribly. All that she cared about was that her beloved David was enjoying himself. She noted exactly which acts with the girl were giving him most pleasure and she would later emulate these acts, possibly as a way of retaining his love.

Mary, the psychology student, did what she could to please the man who was raping her and the woman who was watching, doubtless drawing on all her knowledge of human behaviour to try to save herself. But the couple discussed the situation and decided she had to die.

Late that night they drove her to the Glen Eagle National Park where David raped her again before he strangled her with a nylon cord. The killing too, was sadistic, as he used a tree branch to slowly tighten the noose. He and Catherine then took turns in stabbing the lifeless body so that the air would escape and it wouldn't bloat excessively and burst out of its shallow grave. Catherine helped him dig such a grave and cover up the mutilated corpse. The date was 6th October 1986 and within four weeks they'd kill another three times.

The second killing

A fortnight later Catherine and her common law husband cruised around for hours in search of a second victim. Finally they espied Susannah Candy, a fifteen-year-old hitchhiker who was pleased to accept a lift. When she entered the car she was held at knifepoint and her wrists were tied. She, too, was driven to the couple's squalid home. There, Catherine forced Susannah to write to her parents assuring them of her wellbeing. She would make the teenager write a second such letter later in her ordeal.

In a chilling reconstruction of what had happened to Mary Neilson, the fifteen-year-old was now chained to the bed and repeatedly raped. This time Catherine actively participated in the teenager's ordeal. She got into bed with David and sexually molested the girl. She also took photographs of David raping the teenager, something that he did again and again over several days.

Finally, David Birnie forced a sleeping draught down Susannah's throat and told Catherine to strangle her. Catherine did so, seemingly jealous of the length of time her common law husband had kept the pretty girl alive.

She now helped him bury the fifteen-year-old's body near to the previous girl they'd killed. So far no one had suspected them and they were on a high.

Victim three

Ten days later Catherine and David went out looking for sex slaves again. This time they saw Noelene Patterson standing beside her vehicle, which had run out of petrol. She knew the couple slightly so had no reason to suspect that their offer of assistance wasn't genuine. They helped her to push her vehicle to a service station then they forced her at knifepoint into their car.

Like the others, the thirty-one-year old was chained to the bed, gagged and raped. She was beautiful and classy so an infatuated David Birnie delayed killing her. By the third day Catherine was insanely jealous and insisted he kill the woman now. He drugged Noelene, strangled her and buried her in the forest near to the others. Catherine picked up a handful of earth and threw it over Noelene's face as her corpse lay in the hollow they'd dug for her in the woods.

Catherine would photograph some of the corpses for her own and David's pleasure. And the police said that when she led them to the thirty-one-year old's body, she spat on the grave.

The fourth victim

Early the following month, on Guy Fawkes Day, Catherine spotted twenty one year old Denise Brown at a bus stop. Denise loved dancing and night-clubs and tended to see the best in everyone so she was happy to accept a lift from the slim, unassuming-looking couple who seemed so much in love.

She too, was treated like the Birnie's previous victims, though her terror lasted a shorter time, for that day and most of the next. On the second day the Birnies made her phone a female friend to say that she was well. Thereafter they drugged her and drove her towards a pine plantation where they planned to bury her.

On the way, they drew up alongside a nineteen-year-old university student who was walking home. David sat staring straight ahead in the driving seat whilst Catherine did all the talking. She asked the teenager if she wanted a lift. Between sentences she sipped from a can of rum. The girl felt uneasy that someone should be drinking in the afternoon - and felt more uneasy when she saw a small dark haired figure asleep on the back seat of the vehicle. She explained that she enjoyed walking and hurried away.

Now the Birnies took the sleeping Denise to a pine plantation. David raped her in the car and they held her there until darkness fell. Then Catherine helped David drag the distressed victim outside where he raped her once more, stabbing her twice in the neck at the same time. Catherine stood over them, helpfully shining a torch so that he could see the best way of carrying out his bloody task. Denise was still alive so Catherine fetched a larger knife and told David to stab his victim again. This time she lay still - and they erroneously thought she was dead.

The Birnies then dug a grave and put Denise into it, but as they were shovelling in the dirt she sat up. David grabbed an axe and hit her with it. Again she sat up, and he used the axe to club her to death. Her corpse would be found five days later by police with the skull brutally cracked open. Catherine Birnie, the unloved child who rarely smiled, had become a young woman who enjoyed watching other women being killed.

Fifth teenage victim escapes

She and David went out cruising for new sex slaves almost immediately. This time they spotted a sixteen-year-old girl walking home and they dragged her into their vehicle at knifepoint. Their need was clearly escalating as they had invited rather than forced their earlier victims to enter the car. Back at their house, they stripped the teenager and chained her to the bed by her hands and feet. David Birnie then raped her again and again whilst Catherine licked around his testes. At other times she licked his anus as he thrust into the suffering girl.

Catherine told her to phone her family to reassure them that she was with friends and hadn't come to any harm. She did so. Throughout her ordeal she tried to remember everything about the house so that if she was freed she could identify it to the police. The Birnies, of course, planned to murder her like the others so made no attempt to conceal their identities.

They unchained her the following day and were then distracted by their drug dealer ringing the doorbell. The Birnies went into the living room to buy cocaine and the victim managed to clamber out of the bedroom window and run for help.

The half-naked girl staggered into a Freemantle supermarket screaming hysterically. She was taken to the police station and told them the whole terrible story. Crucially, she was able to identify the address in Willagee where she'd been held. She'd even memorised the telephone number on the Birnies' phone when they'd forced her to call her relatives and lie about being safe and well.

The arrest

The police went to the house and apprehended the couple within moments of each other. Both were calm but hellbent on denial. Catherine was interviewed separately from her common law husband but refused to admit anything. She said that the girl had gone willingly with them, that they'd had consensual sex. She denied that they had anything to do with the other missing women who the police now strongly suspected were dead. For five days she denied everything, determined not to incriminate David. She only cracked when police told her that he'd admitted to killing four women and given details of where the bodies were.

They were now driven to the grave area by police, where David pointed out the last resting places of Denise, Mary and Susannah. Both Birnies seemed to revel in being the centre of attention and were totally without emotion when the decomposing corpses were unveiled. Catherine said that she'd like to be the one who showed them where Noelene - who she'd hated - was buried. She gave police lots of details about why she'd loathed the elegant woman and she spat on her grave.

Their hatred for these young women had been extreme. Police personnel who saw the Birnies' photographs of the victims said 'pack animals do not debase their prey to such an extent.'

The trial

At the trial, held in Perth's Supreme Court in February 1987, the couple held hands and Catherine was seen to pat David's arm and constantly smile at him. He was the only one charged at this stage, as psychiatrists were still determining Catherine's sanity. He was given life imprisonment.

The following month Catherine - who had been found sane - was also sentenced to life imprisonment and was sent to the maximum security Bandyup Prison. Her psychiatric report said it was rare to find someone with such strong emotional dependency on another person. That dependency remained, with the couple exchanging thousands of letters and petitioning to be married. The request was refused.

When word of David Birnie's crimes reached his fellow prisoners, they began to beat him up. He was attacked so often that he attempted suicide a year after being imprisoned and was transferred to another establishment where he'd be safe.

But the couple's life sentence doesn't actually mean life; under Australian law it signifies a maximum of twenty years.

Update

Another macabre event took place a year after the Birnies' imprisonment, when one of their friends, Barrie Watts from Queensland, was sentenced for killing a twelve-year-old girl, Sian King.

In 1999 Catherine's ex-husband Donald died and she applied for compassionate leave to attend his funeral. Prison rules for lifers deny attendance at the funeral of anyone but an immediate relative, so her request was turned down. Catherine stated this was unfair, and in doing so understandably aroused press and public rage.

Because the term ex-husband was used in various reports, most internet sites wrongly reported that it was David Birnie who had died. But I was able to check the facts with the Australian police who confirmed that it was the man she'd had six children with who had expired - and that her team killing partner David Birnie is still very much alive in prison.

9

TRYING TO GET THE FEELING AGAIN
The murderous aphrodisiacs of Gwen Graham &
Catherine Wood

Catherine May Carpenter was born in 1962 in Michigan, USA. Her father was a warehouse truck driver who had served in Vietnam. Her mother was a book keeper who went on to have two more children, a boy and a girl. Catherine would later admit that her father drank heavily and beat her and that they had a very poor relationship. Cathy's father was a distant and angry man - like his father before him - who publicly called little Cathy names and mocked her chubbyness. And the overweight child felt equally unloved by her mother who was always giving her offspring tasks to perform and who seemed preoccupied and cold.

Cathy spent her childhood either looking after the younger members of the family or hiding away from the world in her bedroom. From an early age she showed one of the traits that unloved or abused females often suffer from, an obsession with eating vast amounts of food.

She grew into a six foot tall, broad shouldered teenager who loved reading. When she was sixteen she met Kenneth Wood and almost immediately began to test his love for her, getting her friends to phone him up and ask him out. She demanded that he choose between her and his hobbies, making it clear that she needed unconditional love.

Cathy moved in with Ken after a family fight. Shortly afterwards she announced that she was pregnant and they decided to get married, Ken taking out a loan to pay for the reception. Her parents gave them a cake and a few dollars for alcohol then asked for change. The wedding took place in August 1979 when Catherine was just seventeen and Ken twenty. He worked in a car plant and she went to school until nearing the birth.

From the start it was clear that Cathy had few maternal feelings towards their only daughter. Her husband would later state that she was always criticising the little girl and ignored her childhood illnesses. Indeed, Cathy would later tell the authorities that when she was around children she wanted to hit them, including her own desperate-to-please child.

She also hated housework and Ken would usually come home to a house filled with dirty crockery and fast food wrappers, Cathy having spent the day eating junk food and reading everything from the classics to crime novels. As she refused to go shopping, he often brought in more takeaway for their evening meals. For years after her daughter's birth she lived like this, rarely venturing out in the daylight, and her weight soared to almost four hundred and fifty pounds.

In her favour, she was bright and well read and was able to work out other people's strengths and weaknesses, perhaps using the hypervigilance that many abused children develop. She had an impressive general knowledge, kept up with current affairs and was good at games like chess.

By 1986 even Cathy had had enough of her workless existence. Deciding that she could cope with helping the elderly, she applied for and got a job as a nursing aide at Alpine Manor, a local nursing home in Grand Rapids, Michigan. The home had over two hundred bedrooms, each containing two patients, many of whom were suffering from Alzheimer's or other organic brain diseases. Others had multiple sclerosis or severe arthritis. All required extensive nursing care.

At first Cathy seemed hesitant and shy as she spoke to her supervisors. Other aides found her almost excessively polite and so self conscious that she ate alone in the dining room. They were seeing the nice side of what many people would later note was a Jekyll and Hyde personality. Within a few months she would gain in confidence and the dark brutalised side would reveal itself. She would drink heavily, become physically violent with some of her colleagues and ultimately help kill the helpless patients in her care.

Thanks to her hard physical work as a nursing aide, Cathy soon lost one hundred and fifty pounds and started to take more interest in her appearance. She dyed her hair platinum, bought new clothes and had a brief lesbian affair with a co-worker. This was her second Sapphic relationship for as a young teenager she'd had sex with another girl.

Her new lover's obvious devotion seemed to boost Cathy's ego to the extent that she thought she was irresistible to the other lesbian women who worked alongside her and she would flirt with and then spurn them. In short, she was showing some classic serial killer traits, a dangerous mix of omnipotent periods, violent outbursts, emotional distress and very low self esteem.

Cathy started to play mind games with those staff members she didn't like, pouring water onto their patient's sheets, then claiming that the beds were urine-soaked because the nursing aides had failed to change them. She also started being rough with some of the patients, reporting injuries from them that in hindsight were clearly defense marks from lashing hands and feet. Some of the patients were visibly afraid of her and at least one family complained about Cathy's roughness to another member of staff.

A few months before, this twenty-four-year old had felt too worthless to do anything but eat, read and find fault with her bewildered daughter. But now Catherine was in a position of power, with emotionally fragile co-workers claiming their desire and their love. More potently, she had an almost endless supply of patients who were completely dependent on her for hours at a time.

Some of the senior citizens were tied to their beds with soft restraints at night to stop them sleepwalking, which rendered them completely help-less. Others had lost their voices as the result of strokes or brain disease so couldn't shout for help. At this stage Gwen Graham joined Alpine Manor and was soon to join Cathy's bed.

As her attraction to Gwen deepened, Cathy asked her husband to leave the marital home. Angry and upset he did so, taking their daughter with him. Gwen moved in and the two began an affair. Both seemed immature and would write each other bad poetry and leave adolescent messages for each other on the answering machine.

Gwendolyn Gail Graham

Gwen Graham's childhood had been even more loveless than Cathy's. She was born to Linda and Mack in 1963 in Santa Monica. She was their first child - though her mother would go on to have another two children in quick succession. By the time she was twenty-two Gwen's impoverished mother had three offspring under the age of five and a husband who was often away due to work. She would later admit to journalists that at the time she couldn't cope.

Linda would hit the children with her belt and later admitted hitting

Gwen with an electrical cord when the little girl was just eighteen months old.

Gwen's father kept switching employment, working in everything from law enforcement to welding and each job change caused him to move the family around California with all the change of schools and childhood friends that entailed for the younger Grahams. The five of them rarely had enough money - and Gwen's dad believed that you shouldn't pick up a crying baby because this made it spoilt - so family tensions grew. Gwen would later recall incidents where someone forced her head down the toilet and flushed it, leaving her with a phobia about water faucets. She had nightmares and became increasingly accident prone.

By her teens Gwen's arms were badly scarred by cigarette burns. When asked about this she explained that her father had sexually assaulted her for several years and that she'd self harmed in order to ease the emotional anguish. A woman on Gwen's paper round would later say that Gwen looked like an abused child.

By seventeen she'd had several lesbian relationships and had moved in with a woman in her mid-twenties who loved her. Despite the good times, the pair drank heavily and sometimes got into physical fights.

Gwen grew into a woman of five foot two with reddish hair and a smile that many people would later describe as cute and innocent. When her lover took up a job in Grand Rapids, the needy Gwen followed her out there and got the job at Alpine Manor. But the relationship deteriorated and so she began an affair with her co-worker Catherine May Wood.

Gwen's work performance had originally been first class but after she began her relationship with Cathy her patient's care deteriorated. The two started whispering and giggling together and leaving doors shut whilst they cleaned and turned the patients, something that was against the Manor's open door policy. A supervisor tried to get them assigned to different shifts but no one acted on her suggestion - and even when the pair were working separately they often swapped duties with other aides so that they could be in the building at the same time. Soon some of the patients were telling the other aides that someone had threatened to kill them. As many had Alzheimer's they simply weren't believed. Patients started dying, but no one initially suspected murder as they were old and ill...

The deaths

The deaths took place between January and April of 1987 when the lovers were on the same shifts at Alpine Manor, though they weren't usually assigned to the same patients. Cathy would later claim that Gwen held a washcloth over each patients nose and mouth, kneeling on them if necessary to restrict their struggles. She herself, Cathy said, would keep anxious watch at the door. The pair would then hurry to a nearby anteroom and make love, enjoying intense orgasms as they relived their murderous acts. They also took souvenirs such as socks and part of a table decoration from the victims and kept them on display at Cathy's home.

During this period five patients died. The first was sixty-year old Marguerite Chambers who had been diagnosed with Alzheimer's five years previously. Her family was surprised to hear of her sudden death in January 1987.

The following month Myrtle Luce died. Earlier a nurse had noticed Myrtle's nose was bleeding, but put it down to high blood pressure or to the heat in the nursing home. Later Cathy would admit to pinching patient's noses closed with her fingers to see how much they struggled. It helped her and Gwen decide which of their charges would be the simplest to kill. Whatever the reason for Myrtle's nosebleed she couldn't tell anyone as a series of strokes had left her brain malfunctioning. As she was ninety-five and had been losing weight, the nurses weren't alarmed to find her dead in bed.

Mae Mason was the third woman to die. Cathy would later say that she kept other people talking in a nearby part of the building while Gwen carried out the killing. Mae was seventy-nine.

Seventy-four-year old Belle Burkhard was murdered in late February. A nursing aide who Cathy detested went in to turn her patient, and found the woman dead with her arm bent beneath her. The arm was bruised, but as Belle often had fits nothing more was thought of this.

The final victim, octogenarian Edith Cook, was very ill and kept sedated. Cathy would later say in court that this amounted to a mercy killing. An alternative explanation is that Edith was debilitating to care for as she had advanced gangrene.

In more than one instance, doctors had told the patient's relatives that the patient had a strong heart - yet the sudden death was put down to heart disease. In another, the patient's teeth had been removed, possibly to stop her biting her own tongue as she was suffocated with a washcloth over her mouth and nose. Cathy would later say that Belle's bruised arm was caused by Gwen Graham kneeling on the old lady to hold her down as she suffocated her to death.

What really happened at Alpine Manor may never be known - for the bodies of the supposed victims didn't show conclusive trauma to constitute physical evidence. All that is certain is that Cathy and Gwen had promised never to leave each other - but the relationship deteriorated over those four months into suspicion and mutual violence and Gwen began to have another lesbian affair. In April 1987 she moved with her new lover to Tyler in Texas and began work as a nurse's aide, this time with babies. She worked there for several months but none of her young charges were harmed.

Cathy's confession

Cathy brooded over Gwen's departure for the next four months then in August 1987 she told her husband what she had done, saying that she and Gwen had killed several elderly patients. Believing that the killing spree was over, and that the patients had been near to death anyway, Ken Wood didn't immediately go to the police.

For the next fourteen months he went over the information in his mind and watched his wife closely, finally deciding she was still emotionally unbalanced, cold and full of hate. In the autumn of 1988 he told the full story to police officers, but at first found it hard to be believed. After all, his separation from Cathy had been bitter and they had gotten into disputes in which they fought so loudly that they caused breaches of the peace. Officials had to be sure that this wasn't a rejected suitor trying to set up his innocent ex-wife.

But when Cathy was brought in for questioning she admitted the deaths within minutes, stating that Gwen had suffocated the women whilst she, Cathy, kept watch at the door. She couldn't remember all of the names of the victims but narrowed the time period down to a few weeks. She gave details of which shifts she and Gwen had been working on and who else was working elsewhere in the building, information later validated by the nursing home's records. She further told the amazed police personnel that she and Gwen had enjoyed spectacular orgasms as they relived the deaths.

Later Cathy agreed to take several lie detector tests, but she was seen to press her legs down hard on the floor as she answered certain questions, a tactic that is known to distort the detector's readings. She admitted to officials that she had lied constantly for as long as she could remember, something that her ex-husband wearily verified. She told officials that if she appeared anxious it was because she'd pressed washcloths against some old people's faces to see how they'd react and as a rehearsal for the suffocations she'd promised Gwen she'd carry out.

Gwen Graham was also arrested and charged. She had told her new female lover, Robin, that she'd killed six women but Robin hadn't believed her. Both Gwen and Cathy had had a macabre sense of humour when they worked together, pretending that they got turned on when bathing the elderly patients. Robin saw the confession as Gwen's warped way of getting attention or as a mind game that had gone beyond a joke. Other nursing aides had also heard Gwen and Cathy talk about killing the invalids, but chose not to believe it - perhaps because society doesn't think of young females in murderous terms.

The trial

In September 1989 Cathy Wood pleaded guilty to second degree murder and agreed to testify against Gwen Graham. She said that the pair of them had agreed to take turns in killing, so that each had imprisonable evidence against the other. That way neither could ever leave the relationship. She also said that she had been unable to keep her part of the murderous bargain, and had simply watched Gwen start to suffocate the first victim, Marguerite Chambers, but had looked away before the killing was complete.

She gave the impression that she had only been able to hear - rather than see - Gwen suffocating Myrtle Luce, Mae Mason, Edith Cook and Belle Burkhard. She added that Gwen had later told her she'd had to kneel hard on the struggling Belle, which is why Belle had discolouration on one of her arms.

Cathy said that she hadn't wanted to lose Gwen, so she went along with the deaths. She also gave the impression that she was physically frightened of her lover. Yet Cathy weighed three hundred pounds and was six foot tall, whilst Gwen was an elfin five foot two. And at least one witness had seen Cathy pick Gwen up and throw her violently across the room during a fight. Other witnesses had seen Gwen fighting with another woman, and both Gwen and Cathy had attacked Cathy's ex-husband, Ken, when he came to the house to collect his clothes. Children who'd been violently punished had once again turned into violent adults.

Within hours Gwen Graham was found guilty of all counts and given multiple life sentences. The girlfriend she had followed to Grand Rapids said later to the papers that she was incensed that Gwen had been convicted on hearsay and mainly on Cathy Wood's confession. This woman was the only person who knew Gwen to attend her trial. In contrast, Cathy's mother and ex-husband spoke publicly in Cathy's defense.

The following month Cathy appeared before a Kent County judge and was sentenced to between twenty and forty years in prison. She asked that she not be sent to the same facility as Gwen Graham - and when she briefly found herself in the same holding area she refused to make eye contact with her former lover and became visibly upset.

Psychological profiles

It's hard to build up a true picture of Cathy Wood. The media's first impressions of her came from her former husband, Ken, who presumably felt some guilt at contacting them and had some loyalty towards his ex-wife. He therefore told journalists that Cathy had been led astray by the more dominant Gwen Graham. Some true crime authors then echoed this trend in their articles on the subject, describing Wood as passive, depressed, afraid and less culpable than Gwen. Others noted that she was miserable because her marriage had broken up.

But as Lowell Cauffiel points out in her impressively detailed book on the case, *Forever And Five Days*, Cathy chose to end the marriage because

she'd taken a lover. Her unassertiveness also dissipated when she had elderly patients in her care and she was often the one chosen to subdue the
more exuberant patients because of her no-nonsense manner and large
size. She also frightened other patients into passivity by swearing at and
generally threatening them. Cathy admitted holding the noses of some
restrained patients - hardly the actions of a timid woman. And she admitted throwing ice cold water in her baby daughter's face to stop her infant
tears.

Yet Cathy had her supporters, including many of the staff at Alpine
Manor and she was promoted shortly before the killings came to light.

Other psychologists have suggested that Cathy fits into the narcissistic
category of people who tap into and exploit the needs of others. This certainly squares with the way she behaved towards her ex-husband and
towards the women at the nursing home who fell in love with her.
Narcissistic personalities see themselves as special and don't believe they
have to follow the same rules as the rest of society. They are deeply envious of other people's accomplishments - Cathy hated the more beautiful
and talented nursing aides. They also lack empathy.

This lack of empathy is understandable in that she appears to have been
exploited throughout her childhood and given so many chores to do that
her youth had little fun in it. Clearly the adults she grew up with didn't
empathise with *her* and she had to replace the lack of love with food. When
she was arrested and offered a meal, police were surprised at the size of
takeaway she ordered. A relative described her as 'emotionally starved.'

Gwen, the more physically scarred of the couple, fits into the borderline category of people who don't bond in infancy with their mothers.
Gwen's mother was young and unsupported and always ignored her crying babies, believing that this would toughen their characters. She and her
husband also physically chastised Gwen harshly from her formative years
until she was eighteen. Gwen had once confided in a friend that her mother once almost choked her to death in a fight. She went on to play choking games with Cathy as part of their erotic activities.

Because borderline personalities miss out on that crucial early parent-
child bond, they spend their adult lifes trying to create it. They therefore
fall quickly in love with other people and have intense relationships that are
more based on fantasy than reality. That's why Gwen could claim she'd love

Cathy forever, yet would move on within a few months to another woman's bed.

Gwen had a lower IQ than the well-read Cathy and could have been easily manipulated by her so it's unclear which woman was the dominant party. Indeed, some sources have suggested that the patient's deaths may have been natural, and that Cathy made up the killings to get back at Gwen for leaving her. Cathy had said at one stage that she found paying her bills hard work - and indeed her mother later evicted her for non-payment of rent. Cathy also said to a friend that she'd probably find life easier in jail.

Yet Gwen did tell Robin that she'd committed the murders and that she feared Cathy would go to the authorities. Later she retracted this statement and has never publicly acknowledged her part in the deaths.

Gwen Graham's sentence excludes the possibility of parole so she will never be released unless new evidence leads to a new hearing. Cathy Wood is eligible for parole after serving sixteen years in prison which makes her first possible parole date due in 2005.

10

LOVE DON'T LIVE HERE ANY MORE
The brutalised household of Rose West

Rosemary Pauline Letts was born on 29th November 1953 in Northam, Devon, a quiet village in England. Her father, Bill, had been a radio operator in the navy for many years but was now an electrical engineer. His own childhood had been marked by loneliness and excessive discipline and he was a violent schizophrenic who battered Daisy, his unassertive wife and the seven children she would have with him.

Daisy, increasingly unable to cope with his brutality, was a depressive who had suffered a series of nervous breakdowns. (Her own father had beat her throughout her childhood.) Horrifyingly, she even had Electro Convulsive Therapy, colloquially known as electric shock treatment, whilst pregnant with Rose.

Rose came into the world to find that she already had an elder brother, Andrew, and three elder sisters, Patricia, Joyce and Glenys. Later she would also acquire two younger brothers, Gordon and Graham. The children would be kicked, beaten, thrown against the wall and locked out by their sadistic father. It was a life of fear. Playing was forbidden as was speaking at mealtimes, and their sole entertainment consisted of long walks with their mother who was determined to keep up appearances.

Clearly picking up on the tension in the household, the toddler Rosie would rock herself back and forward for hours at a time. Howard Sounes says in his excellent book on the subject *Fred And Rose* that this is one of the signs of learning difficulties. But it's also something that babies do to comfort themselves when frightened or to self-stimulate when they are neglected and bored. Rose also had nightmares and sucked her thumb well beyond the age where other children stop.

Outwardly she was a pretty child with big dark eyes and long dark hair - but inside she increasingly lived in a world of her own. She would stare into space and often not hear other people when they called to her and some writers have mistakenly assumed that this automatically points to subnormal intelligence. It may indeed signal that - but it's also the behaviour of abused children of all IQ levels, who go into constant daydreams in order to tune out from the horror they're experiencing at home.

And it was a terrible home. Rose and the others would be woken first thing by their father - who never played with them - and given an extensive list of chores to do. If these weren't completed to his excessively high standards all hell would break loose. He used bleach in all the rooms and even on the carpets, something he had learnt to do whilst in the navy. If the children were late going to bed he would come into the bedroom and throw a bucket of cold water over them. He hit them so viciously that the neighbours often heard them scream.

The older girls would leave home as soon as they could and one of her brothers would ask to go into care for his own safety. But poor Rose and her remaining siblings stayed on in a house where their father would frequently throw out all the food in the kitchen and smash up the furniture in a blind rage.

Rose's mother would tell him to hit the children where it didn't show. She alleges that he rarely hit Rose as she was his favourite. Her brothers have confirmed this, saying that she was so quiet that she never gave him a reason to pick on her. Rose was also the most attractive of the family and rumour had it that Bill was attracted to young girls.

School days

Rose was bullied throughout primary school and given the name Dozy Rosie. In truth she was seen as 'sensible' which is often the description given to abused children who don't run about and have fun in a normal childhood way. She found it hard to talk to children her own age so settled for mothering much younger ones. She adored her two younger brothers - babies always brought out her maternal side.

But by age twelve she had realised that only the strong survive and had become the schoolyard aggressor. By now she was of a fairly big build so no one wanted to get on the wrong side of her. As she moved into puberty she became understandably interested in sex, but her strict religious mother and outwardly puritanical father refused to tell her or her siblings the facts of life.

By thirteen she was becoming sexually precocious and was masturbating her ten-year-old brother. Because the household was so poor and overcrowded they shared a bed. But it was more important for Rose to get *older* men on her side - after all, the older man in her life, her father, could kill her or her siblings at any moment. Older men had to be turned into allies at whatever price. She consequently began to display exhibitionist tendencies when middle aged men were around, an exhibitionism that would stay with her. And she would walk round the house naked in front of her brothers when her parents were at work.

In 1969, when Rose was fifteen, Daisy at last left Bill and took Rose and the younger kids to stay with relatives. It was a plan born out of desperation and one beating too many. Rose now helped out in the relative's cafe - but spent more time sleeping with the truck drivers who came in for their meals. The few compliments they paid her were probably the kindest words she'd ever known and the casual sex was the closest she'd gotten to love.

But her relatives house was now crowded and the atmosphere wasn't good. At this stage Rose did what she'd always done to make things temporarily better - she made sexual advances to a man, in this case to the married male relative that they were staying with. Some of their other relatives think that her mother caught them in bed together. Whatever happened, she was thrown out and went back to live with her increasingly strange dad. She would never forgive her mother for abandoning her and still talked about the emotional pain many years later. Her father's moods sometimes drove the fifteen-year-old from the house and she was picked up on the streets by the police, suspected of soliciting.

Rose now briefly had two unsatisfactory low paid jobs, then went on to a third at a bread shop. Whilst waiting for the bus home from work one teatime she was chatted up by a man called Fred West. She was still fifteen and he was twelve years her senior. He was married but separated.

Rose didn't like him at first as he was covered in grease - he drove a van and did building work on the side - but she was flattered by his attention. Eventually she agreed to a drink in a nearby pub. Prior to the date he sent a go-between into the bread shop to give her two presents from him, a lace dress and a fur coat.

Rose explained that she couldn't take the gifts home - her puritanical father, Bill, would kill her if he knew she'd been on a date as she'd never even had a proper boyfriend. (She kept denying to her relatives that she'd been having sex with truck drivers and other men she met casually.) Bill was still falling into rages or day long silences at home.

Fred then suggested that he could keep the coat and dress for her in his caravan. He took the impressionable teenager there and she met his daughters, Anne Marie aged five and Charmaine aged six. Both children had the same mother, Catherine Costello, known as Rena, but only Anne Marie had been fathered by Fred. Charmaine had been fathered by a Pakistani student and Rena had already been expecting her when she met the equally promiscuous Fred West.

Fred had taken both children from Rena as a way of hurting her, but wasn't at all paternal. He often shouted at the children or rubbed them inappropriately on his lap. At other times he would take off for pastures new and put them both into foster care.

But for now both little girls were living with him in the caravan, looked after by whoever was available, often other caravan dwellers who pitied the neglected children. Some of their carers were girls Rose had been to school with. Fred used the children to lure young women into his life as untrained nannies and most of them ended up having sex with him.

Fred would weave tall tales about his numerous jobs in various parts of Scotland and England, his hotel chain and his career at sea. It was the kind of talk that intelligent adults quickly see through as his anecdotes were all about his successes yet he was a grubby little man living in a tiny and dirty caravan. But young love-starved girls like Rose were intrigued and impressed.

Rose immediately made a fuss of the children and they responded as they'd had little attention in their lives. Fred, who had probably been planning this since setting eyes on the lonely, big-busted teenager, turned to her and suggested she'd make an ideal daytime babysitter. He'd pay her the same money that she was getting at the bread shop and she could tell her father that she was still working there.

So fifteen-year-old Rose now made her covert way to the caravan every morning; a child looking after children. At first it was fun playing at house, and she got to escape from the little girls in the evenings. Then her controlling father found out...

Determined to keep her from Fred (some criminologists believe that

Bill had been having sex with his daughter since she turned thirteen) he put her in care. Whilst she was there she didn't have a single visitor. During her three months in this home for troubled teenagers she sneaked out a few times to see Fred. She would write him a letter that said 'we are two people, not two soft chairs to be sat on.' And relatives would indeed watch her softness, her vulnerability, leach out of her over the years.

A defiant pregnancy

As soon as Rose left care at sixteen she went to Fred and got pregnant by him. It was her only means of ensuing that he'd have to stay in her life. After all, he'd been having sex with almost every young woman he encountered at work or who babysat for his children. She possibly thought it would also make her father accept him and accept that she was no longer a child. By now her parents were reconciled and the verbal and physical violence in the household had started up again.

But Bill Letts didn't accept the news of his impending first grandchild - instead he said that Rose could only stay if she had an abortion, and booked her into an abortion clinic without her permission. Rose would tell her children many years later that at this stage her father also gave her the beating of her life. The teenager turned to her mother for support but Daisy was too angry to even talk to her. Rose was, as usual, emotionally alone.

Despite this ultimate cruel rejection, Rose felt happy as she left her parents house - freedom was hers at last, as was sudden adulthood. The crying child and abandoned teenager was about to become a stepmother of two and a birth mother of one. She would also start on the journey that would make her one of the most prolific and cruel female serial killers in British history...

Rose moves in with Fred

Without a friend in the world, Rose now went to Fred and he rented them a single room in Cheltenham. The place was dirty as he kept all his oily tools there. There were also clothes and food scraps littering the floor. They were two semi-literate people living with two neglected children, so it was hardly *Romeo and Juliet* but romance-craving Rose convinced herself that it was perfect.

Her contentment increased when he found them a flat in Gloucester, at 25 Midland Road. That October she gave birth to their first daughter, Heather. The couple would tell each other that she was a child of love and Rose would promise to love Fred for as long as she lived.

Their physical love - at the start - was very good as Fred was into heavy sadomasochism and Rose was more than willing to flog him for his sexual pleasure. She also enjoyed being beaten - and would later ask her female lovers to treat her equally aggressively. Meanwhile, Fred imbued the relationship with a special quality that went beyond the sexual, saying that they could virtually read each others minds. (Something that Judith Neelley and her husband, profiled earlier, also beleived.)

But he apparently didn't read the signals that she hated being left alone with two school age children and a tiny baby. He worked long hours, leaving her trapped with the children in the barely furnished and uncarpeted flat. Keen to get something for nothing (a trait he would show throughout his life) he soon stole some tyres and was traced and sent to prison for ten months, the sentence to run from October 1970 until the summer of 1971. Heather was just a few weeks old.

The teenage Rose was left with three kids, little money and no support. When her parents eventually visited, they could see she had recently been crying. Every time they called thereafter her eyes were red-rimmed and she lost an unhealthy amount of weight.

She started to beat Anne Marie and Charmaine for being slow to eat their cereal or for laughing and talking together, the very things her father had beaten her siblings for. She pulled their hair and hit them on their heads with whatever crockery was available. She even beat them for wetting the bed.

One of Charmaine's friends rushed in to the house one day to find the little girl standing on a chair with her hands tied, whilst Rose stood behind her brandishing a wooden spoon. On other occasions Rose tied the children to the bed and went out for hours leaving them hungry and helpless. The children looked increasingly unloved and afraid. But, like all toxic parents, she was in denial about the damage that she was doing and wrote to Fred in prison that Charmaine liked 'being treated rough.'

Rose kills Charmaine

During one of her attacks on Charmaine - in May or June of 1971 - she went too far and murdered the child. Many people think that she strangled her, as, during a rage, she would choke one of her later children, Stephen, into semi-consciousness. When neighbours asked where Charmaine had gone, Rose told them that she'd gone back to her mother, Rena. The school accepted this explanation too. In truth, Rose had dumped the little body in the coal cellar and turned her full rage onto seven-year-old Anne Marie. It was still a few weeks until Fred was to be released from prison but Rose wrote him increasingly romantic notes and he responded in his poorly spelt and ungrammatical hand.

Bill Letts had at first visited the house with his wife Daisy but afterwards he would often visit on his own. It's likely that at this juncture he began to have sex with Rose again.

Fred came out of prison and buried Charmaine's body in the backyard after taking the corpse apart and inspecting the way the bones fit together. Knowing that Rose, too, was now a killer he may have told her about a murder he'd committed on his own in 1967 - namely that of Anne McFall, his nanny turned lover who was eight months pregnant with his child. He would tell other people that he loved Anne, so it's possible he killed her by accident during extreme bondage sex. Many couples indulge in exciting tying up games, but Fred also liked to restrict his partner's breathing by using masks or tubes and bind and gag them so hard that they couldn't move or verbally communicate. Suffocation could take place if their nostrils clogged.

Whatever he did to kill Anne McFall, her body would eventually be found almost three decades later, in 1994 in a field near Fred's childhood home, with the wrists bound and the fingers and toes cut off, presumably post mortem. The near-term foetus had been cut from her body and was buried a few feet away.

Fred and Anne had been living in a caravan which doesn't make an ideal dismemberment site - but Fred also had access to a lockable garage that his friends said had a horrible atmosphere. It's likely that he carried her corpse there and cut it into pieces, something he'd done with animal carcasses when he worked in an abattoir. He would enjoy the comparatively unusual sexual thrill of dismembering female corpses throughout his life.

The police and many locals would also later suspect Fred of murdering Mary Bastholm, a waitress at a cafe he frequented. She disappeared from a bus stop in 1969 - and Fred (sometimes accompanied by Rose) would later abduct other women from bus stops. Her body has never been found.

After hearing his confession of killing Anne McFall and possibly Mary Bastholm, Rose might have told Fred that she was sleeping with Bill Letts, her father. Leastways Fred would later tell the police that he'd seen Rose and her dad having enthusiastic sex. Rose would have figured Fred wouldn't mind - after all, he had allegedly slept with his own mother and sister. And *his* father had allegedly slept with his own daughters, Fred's sisters. Fred's father would also tell him how to disable farm animals in order to have sex with them. Moreover, Fred loved the idea - and the actuality - of Rose sleeping with someone else as long as he could watch or could hear all the details afterwards.

Rose and Fred now had a special but terrible bond between them as they were both killers - and killers who had gotten away with it.

A far from ideal husband

Fred's sex life with Rose was based on consensual sadomasochism - but his earlier sexual experiences had been coercive and abusive. Many people believe that his mother took his virginity at age twelve. She was a huge woman who wore a belt around her waist with which she beat her other children - but Fred was her favourite so he escaped the worst of her wrath. He would later tell his own sons as they reached twelve years old that they were now old enough to have sex with their mum.

The twenty-year old Fred came home after working away and was soon having sex with his thirteen-year old sister. It's rumoured that he was the cause of her underage pregnancy, but in court she refused to say. He also had sex with animals in the fields around his simple village home. A tethered sheep makes few demands for satisfaction so he got used to being an impatient and selfish lover - Fred always came within about a minute of having sex with a woman and seemed to prefer the tying up or voyeuristic side of things. He also liked to keep mementoes such as his lover's lingerie.

When Fred wasn't fashioning implements to use on Rose or making home improvements he was usually out of the house. He was an incredibly hard worker and was always doing overtime or doing up neighbours houses. He also walked the streets looking for dropped coins and went through rubbish dumps looking for clothes and toys that he could bring home. Rose was frequently left on her own with the crying baby Heather and equally tearful Anne Marie.

The great escape

After a few months of this Rose had had enough. She left, taking Heather, and went back to her parent's house but her father said that she couldn't stay permanently, that she had to remain in the marriage. After a few hours Fred turned up and said 'Come on Rosie, you know what we've got between us' - presumably a veiled reference to Charmaine's murder and illegal burial. He also said that if she wasn't back in a few minutes her place in the marital bed would be taken by someone else.

Rose turned to her parents and said 'You don't know what he's capable of - even murder,' but they thought that she was just being melodramatic. Fred said that he'd wait for her in the van and after a few moments she walked towards it with the baby and climbed inside. It's not clear what motivated her return the most - the fear that he would tell the authorities that she'd killed Charmaine or the fear that he would replace her, Rose, with another woman and that she'd never be loved by anyone else. Earlier she'd professed her amazement that he thought so much of her. After all, she'd been brought up to see herself as worthless, stupid and bad.

Rosie does Gloucester

Within months of Rose and Fred getting back together, he started to say that he wanted her to have sex with coloured men because they were genitally bigger than white men and could last longer. She could have as many coloured lovers as she wished in their Gloucester home and enjoy the resultant orgasms as long as he was allowed to watch.

Fred wanted to know how far Rose could widen vaginally using different vibrators. He wanted to know how much semen another man produced. The wrongly-raised builder wanted to measure everything as if it was a building work project. He wanted to watch and hear rather than to directly participate.

Till death us do part

Despite his flaws, the teenage Rose continued to cohabit with him and asked him to become her husband, to give her increased stability. Fred might have wanted a wife that couldn't testify against him. So they booked their wedding for 29th January 1972 at the local Registrars.

Fred worked all morning then turned up at home just before the ceremony in his dirty working clothes. Rose was mortified that he wasn't prepared to make the slightest effort. She had to beg him to get changed.

It is telling that he conveniently forgot he was still married to Rena and put his marital status down as bachelor. Many writers made the assumption that he'd killed Rena by this stage, but it seems that he killed her later after she started trying to track down Charmaine. Pretending to be a bachelor meant nothing to Fred as - like most serial killers - he lied constantly.

One of Fred's brothers and a friend acted as witnesses and they all had a swift drink then went back to work. Rose asked for an alcoholic drink but Fred, who was virtually teetotal, snapped at her and bought her a soft drink. He was already intent on controlling her and would later get her to sign a slave contract saying that she would do whatever he desired.

The move to Cromwell Street

In the spring of that year Fred found the family a bigger house at 25 Cromwell Street, a few minutes walk from their existing flat in Gloucester. He worked all hours of the day and night to turn part of the house into cheap bedsits for students and other young people who wanted to tune in and drop out.

Fred himself didn't take drugs but he let it be known that he was liberal minded, that his lodgers could have a wild time. Rose also showed her liberal side, having sex with several of the male lodgers and, later, making passes at the female ones. Again, Fred made it abundantly clear that he didn't mind. Whenever possible he would turn conversations with the lodgers round to sex or home-based abortions or to what bodies mutilated in car crashes looked like.

Rose began to prefer females because they were softer and warmer, more giving. As long as Fred could watch or hear about it he was rapt.

Life went on in a semblance of domesticity for a few months then Fred heard that Rena, his first wife, was back in the area, having formerly been living in Scotland. Worse, she was at Fred's parents house and was asking to see her daughter, Charmaine.

Fred was horrified. Rena probably wouldn't care about his bigamous marital status - but if she found out that her child was dead she'd go to the police and he and Rose would go to jail.

In August or September 1972 he consequently arranged to meet Rena at a quiet pub and got her very drunk. He probably walked or carried her to his car, pretending that Charmaine was waiting for her at his home.

What happened next can never fully be known - most writers have speculated that he strangled her and dismembered her in the field where her body was ultimately found. But a length of piping was found in the grave, something that he could have used to let her breathe whilst the rest of her face was tightly masked to prevent her screams being heard. So he probably took her, semiconscious, to an abandoned outhouse and abused her before driving her body to its lonely burial plot.

Anne Marie wouldn't find out for many years that her mother, Rena, had died. Anne Marie hadn't been quite as unhappy as Charmaine, because Fred was her natural father and he occasionally made a fuss of her. But all that was about to change...

Anne Marie is raped

During their first year at Cromwell Street, Fred spent a great deal of time doing building work in the cellar. One day, he and Rose started grinning strangely at eight-year old Anne Marie. Then they marched her down the stairs, saying that they were going to break her in, something that all good parents did.

Anne Marie was uneasy, but, as always, she did what she was told. When they got to the cellar, Rose stripped her. The child started to cry, but Rose was impervious to her tears. She forced her down onto a mattress then sat on her face. Rose also scratched her stepchild's chest until it bled.

At a later date such scratches would be found on Anne Marie when her school took her swimming - and Heather would refuse to go swimming because the teachers would see her many bruises - but the authorities didn't intervene.

Fred now tied his daughter up and raped her, whilst a smiling Rose looked on. Rose then followed her usual tactic after any kind of abuse, by threatening the victim. She also kept Anne Marie off school for the rest of the week as she was bleeding internally and found it hard to walk.

Some time after the rape, Rose tied the child to a metal frame that Fred had made and beat her then assaulted her sexually with a vibrator. (Later she would make her son Stephen strip, then tie him up in the bathroom and beat him in an equally sexually-sadistic way.) Rose was by now placing photographs of herself in contact magazines, so had as many willing partners as she wanted. She was also having consensual sadomasochistic sex with a female neighbour, but she clearly found it more exciting to have an unwilling victim - and found an easy target in her helpless stepchild Anne Marie.

The brood mare

Over the years there would be more and more helpless children in Rose's care because she gave birth almost annually. Fred would father Heather, Mae, Stephen and Barry by her. She would also have a miscarriage and possibly an early abortion. Later Rose would go on to have four children by her Jamaican lovers, children who Fred was proud of, though their dark skin made it absolutely clear that they weren't genetically his.

Sadly, despite his pride at their births, he would treat these children as badly as he treated the ones he had sired. Rose's relationship with her own mother had been strained for many years but after she gave birth to half-caste children Daisy told her not to visit again and ignored the letters that Rose sent.

Rose would later say that she had so many children because her husband refused to wear condoms and because the pill made her sick - but it's more likely that she was repeating history and having as many children as her own mother had had. She would also recreate the hellish fear and tension of the household that she'd grown up in - only this time she'd be the one in charge.

The cruel mother

Like her father before her, Rose was only kind to children whilst they were babies that had no strong personalities of their own. As soon as they began to walk and talk she would fly into her frequent rages, hitting the children because they dropped a fork or trampled a little mud into the carpet. She made them finish every meal even if they strongly disliked that particular foodstuff and clearly saw children as having absolutely no right to respect, choice or love.

Once when they were talking to each other from their beds, she threw them outside in their nightwear and locked the door, leaving them frightened and frozen. Her children would frequently be seen at hospital Accident & Emergency departments, but, again, the authorities failed to intervene.

The babysitter

However, for a few weeks there was some happiness in Anne Marie's life when Rose took on a live-in babysitter, Caroline Owens. Seventeen-year-old Caroline got on very well with Anne Marie and little Heather. Rose also had a new baby, born that May, who she called Mae. But Rose made it clear that she wanted to have a much more intimate relationship with the pretty babysitter. She kept coming into the bathroom when Caroline was having a bath and would talk to her whilst suggestively stroking her hair. Caroline's own childhood had been unhappy so she welcomed Rose's friendship, but she didn't want to indulge in lesbian sex.

Fred told the babysitter that Anne Marie wasn't a virgin but when Caroline looked horrified he added that she'd broken her hymen in an accident on her bicycle. Meanwhile Rose's advances intensified so Caroline left.

But Rose wasn't prepared to let this object of desire get away. She had power over her children and over the men who she met through contact ads - by now Fred had installed secret peepholes and recording equipment in the master bedroom and Rose would position her lovers so that Fred got the best possible view of her having sex with them. Most of these men were so impressed at her sexual skills that they became regular visitors. Now she wanted to exercise the same power over Caroline.

She and Fred decided to kidnap the girl. They recalled the route she travelled to visit her boyfriend - and knew that she had no reason to fear violence from them.

On 4th or 6th December 1972 the Wests drove along until they saw the unsuspecting teenager. They picked her up, but as soon as she got into their car she detected a strange atmosphere. Rose said that they should chat and quickly got into the back seat with her. Fred started driving and Rose began to touch Caroline's breasts. She protested but Rose continued to assault her, stroking her legs and trying to kiss her on the lips. Caroline tried to fend the older teenager off - despite her life experience, Rose was still only nineteen - at which stage Fred turned around and punched Caroline, knocking her out. They then parked, taped her limbs together and drove her to Cromwell Street.

She regained consciousness as they neared the Wests house, and found that Rose was still grinning strangely. They marched her into the house and up to their bedroom, where Fred beat her vaginally with a belt buckle, causing her intense pain. Both Wests extensively caressed her and Rose went down on her - until then, the teenage Caroline hadn't even known about oral sex. Though they blindfolded her, she could feel Rose's long nails entering her intimately.

A long night of such abuses followed, during which she had sticky tape wrapped around her face - this would become one of the Wests' trademarks in their later sexual murders. She could hear Rose laughing after she was gagged and bound. At one stage Rose went away for a few minutes and Fred raped her and then cried. He said that Rose had devised the plan to kidnap Caroline because she had especially strong lesbian desires when she was pregnant. (Rose must have been a month or so pregnant with Stephen at this time as he was born in August 1973.) As the sexual assaults continued, Caroline fully expected to die.

Early the next morning she heard visitors arriving at the house and tried to make a noise to let them know that she was there. Enraged, Rose put a pillow over Caroline's head and began to suffocate her. Fred was also very angry when he re-entered the room. By breakfast time, however, the couple seemed to have worn themselves into a post-orgasmic lull, and they began to speak to her normally, asking if she would become their live-in babysitter again.

Acting for her life, Caroline said yes and they freed her from her bonds. She was allowed to clean herself up, then she helped Rose tidy the house and care for the children. When all of them left the house to go shopping, she said that she'd go back to her mother's house and pack a bag.

Instead, Caroline went to her mum's house and bathed repeatedly. When her mother saw the injuries caused by Fred punching her and by the actions of ripping the brown tape off, she asked her daughter what had happened. Caroline told her and her mother contacted the police.

Rose in court

The police went round to Cromwell Street and were met with verbal abuse from Rose. She denied everything, but the police found one of

Caroline's buttons in the Wests' car. They also found the sticky tape used to bind the terrified teenager. Fred should really have been charged with rape - but Caroline was too afraid to testify in court against him. Instead all parties settled for the more minor charge of assault.

Rose and Fred answered this charge in January 1973. Their solicitor managed to play down the abduction till it sounded as if a consensual threesome had just gotten slightly out of hand. As a result, the couple were merely fined a total of one hundred pounds. Letting one of their victims go had clearly backfired against them. The sensible solution would have been to stop creating victims - but instead, Fred and Rose decided that their next sexual plaything would have to die.

Rose would ultimately be found guilty of all of the murders that are listed below - but a very few writers and at least one of Rose's children believe that she played no part in the deaths, that they were all committed by Fred West acting on his own.

Linda's murder

Three months after Caroline's abduction, in the spring of 1973, Linda Gough came to the Wests for support having had an argument with her parents. The nineteen-year-old seamstress had visited the house often in the past as she had had relationships with two of their lodgers. She had also babysat for the Wests.

Now someone took Rose's former babysitter to the cellar and bound her face with surgical and brown tape. What happened next will probably never fully be known, but it's believed that all of the cases involved sexual torture. The Wests vaginally penetrated and sodomised many of their consensual sexual partners with large vibrators, so it's likely they did the same thing to the young woman they eventually killed. Fred had also told one of his earlier potential sexual partners that she could burn or flog him or let him do the same to her...

It's likely that Linda was suspended from the ceiling whilst these abuses were taking place, as Fred had fashioned holes in the beams. When finally imprisoned, he told one of his sons that he hung his victims there.

After Linda died, Fred completely dismembered her body and buried it below the house. It would remain there for the next twenty-one years and when it was finally unearthed by the authorities, some small bones would be missing. The tape that had been used to silence her was found still wrapped around the skull.

Meanwhile, Linda's parents began to search for her. Her mother went to Cromwell Street and Rose answered but said that she didn't know a Linda Gough. But Mrs Gough pointed out that Rose was wearing Linda's slippers - and that some of her daughter's clothes were drying on Rose's washing line. At this stage Rose admitted she'd remembered who Linda was, but said that she'd gone. Linda's recent relationship with her parents had been awkward, so though they searched for her they didn't assume the worst when she didn't get in touch.

Carol's murder

The Wests had gotten away with murder again - and for a few months their memories of abusing Linda presumably sustained them. Rose may also have been tired throughout the summer as she was increasingly pregnant with the son she'd ultimately name Stephen. He was born in August 1973, and by November the couple were ready to kill again.

In November a fifteen-year-old girl called Carol Anne Cooper was seen waiting for a bus that would take her to her grandmother's house. Thereafter she vanished. She had been in care so was desperate for affection and probably accepted a lift from the smiling Wests.

She, too, was bound and gagged and suspended from the cellar's rafters. When her body was eventually found it had a deep mark in the skull, suggesting that she'd been stabbed through the head. This particular injury may have been post mortem as Fred liked to decapitate the dead women. He also enjoyed sawing off the thighs and would later hint to his son that he had sex with the corpses, the ultimate controlling sexual act.

It seems that Fred liked to take care of the bodies after death - though he also enjoyed brutalising them whilst they were bound and gagged in the cellar. It's not clear whether Rose took part in the dismemberments, but the way she acted after abducting Caroline Owens, and with even younger girls whom she lured to the house for juice and biscuits, makes it clear that she enjoyed forcing large objects into her victims to make them cry out. She also liked to scare her consensual female sexual partners, tying them tighter than they liked and partially restricting their breathing then gloating about her intensifying power.

Lucy's murder

Carol's murder didn't seem to satisfy them for long. Leastways only a month elapsed before they abducted their next victim, Lucy Partington. She was a religious university student, the twenty-one-year old niece of the late writer Kingsley Amis. Lucy had visited a disabled friend on 27th December and was waiting at a dark bus stop to catch the bus home when Fred and Rose presumably drove past.

It's likely that they forced her into the car - she was an intelligent, cautious girl who wouldn't have accepted a lift from strangers. Fred would later lie that she and he had earlier been lovers, but in truth she would have had nothing in common with this semi-literate man who was rarely clean.

Lucy was taken to the Cromwell Street cellar, bound, and treated as badly as her predecessors. She may have been kept alive for up to a week as Fred attended casualty seven days later with a bad hand wound, probably received whilst cutting her body up. He also decapitated her corpse and buried it in the basement. Another young life had been cruelly stolen in exchange for a few days of depraved lust.

But not every hunting trip was a success - so Rose and Fred decided that they would now only advertise for single female lodgers. If a girl was beholden to them for the roof over her head then it was harder for her to resist their requests for sex.

The couple also took to loitering about outside orphanages, where Rose would engage the most needy girls in a motherly chat. Later she'd invite them round to play with the babies. Word soon got around that Cromwell Street was a good place to go for a nice afternoon out.

But after a while Rose would start stroking the young girl's hair and telling her that it was alright to touch. Many of these girls just froze, but some felt too scared to protest and allowed the paedophiliac acts to continue. On other occasions she'd answer the door wearing very little then make it clear that she had no panties on under her skirt.

On one occasion Rose tied up two girls and buggered them both with a candle or a vibrator then Fred had intercourse with them. One of the girls might have been Fred's daughter Anne Marie as both parents had been abusing her for several years. Rose regularly beat Anne Marie and locked her in the cellar. Rose also took pornographic photos of the child and let her be sexually abused by Rose's own father, Bill Letts.

Rose even made Anne Marie dress up and go out to pubs with her in the hope of attracting men to make up a foursome. By the time Anne Marie was thirteen she would be forced to have sex with several of Rose's clients.

After these abuses, the girls from the orphanage were in great pain and they often bled. (Anne Marie would have an ectopic pregnancy by her father when she was fifteen.) But they would also feel confused. After all, Rose had been so nice to them up till now. Had they sent her the wrong signals? These girls had been abandoned by their families and had sometimes been criticised or punished within the care system. They had little sense of self worth and tended to blame themselves for everything.

Thankfully, some of the girls would find the courage to tell of their abuse at Rose's hands when Rose finally ended up in court, though the fact that they had taken money from the tabloid press somewhat tarnished their testimony. For now, though, Fred and Rose weren't finding these assaults on orphaned teenagers exciting enough, so another young female stranger had to die...

Theresa's murder

In April 1974 Rose and/or Fred picked up a twenty one year old Swiss girl, Therese Siegenthaler. It's possible that Fred had someone other than his wife already in the car with him as the police suspected at least one other man was involved in the murders. Theresa was studying in London, but they gave her a lift when she was hitchhiking between London and Wales. She had taken self defence classes in the past but was clearly no match for whoever overpowered her. Theresa was driven to Cromwell Street where someone wrapped a brown scarf tightly around her mouth and bound her limbs with rope. The inevitable abuses followed until finally Fred dismembered and decapitated her corpse and buried it in the cellar.

Another death?

Four months later Rose presented herself at the hospital with a very badly cut finger that required a hospital stay. She made up various stories about what had happened, which later made the authorities wonder if she was trying to conceal another murder. Then again, she'd lied often since childhood and may even have been covering up the fact that she'd attacked one of her children with a blade. Later the children would testify that she'd sometimes lunged at them with kitchen knives during a rage.

It's also possible that Fred cut her during an argument. The children would say that the atmosphere worsened when Fred came home at night, and then he would get angry if Rose didn't want to prostitute herself for him. But apparently Rose also lunged at Fred with a knife on one occasion, and when he slammed the door the blade went into her hand.

Shirley Hubbard's murder

Three months after this hospital stay, in November 1974, they encountered fifteen-year-old Shirley Hubbard. A witness had seen her getting on a bus, so presumably the Wests offered her a lift when she got off at her journey's end.

This teenager was more heavily bondaged than the other victims buried under the floorboards. It's been said that the female serial killer often tries to kill an earlier representation of herself, as if trying to snuff out a painful memory. At fifteen, Rose had been rejected by both parents and soon made pregnant by Fred - so she possibly hated everything about this girl aged fifteen. And Shirley - who had been in care since her childhood - was beautiful and interested in clothes and makeup, whereas twenty-one-year old Rose wore old clothes and schoolgirl-like white socks and had heavy unstyled hair.

The killer or killers bound the teenager's face very heavily, leaving only a slender tube protruding from one nostril to allow her to breathe. They left her eyes uncovered so that she could see what was about to happen - and so that they could see her terror. They stripped her and assaulted her, then Fred dismembered her corpse. When her makeshift grave was finally discovered, many of the bones and part of the torso had gone.

Juanita's murder

Five months later, in April 1975, one or both of the Wests picked up eighteen year old Juanita Mott as she hitchhiked to a friend's house. Earlier Juanita had rented a bedsit from them and had babysat for their children so she had no reason to assume that they meant her harm.

Her abductors now gagged her with a pair of long white socks and tights then bound her using several feet of plastic rope. When the body was eventually found it would be clear that the eighteen-year-old had been trussed up like a mummy. She too was suspended before the sexual torment took place. Juanita may have ultimately been killed by a hammer as her skull was indented when it was unearthed in the basement of Cromwell Street.

A period of domesticity

After this April 1975 death, life seemed to return to normal - or as near to normal as was possible for the Wests - for a couple of years. Fred decided to make extensive renovations to the house and this included turning the torture chamber into bedrooms for the children. Rose still entertained clients in the master bedroom upstairs. He also built an extension into the garden and made the lodger's flats in the upper part of the house completely self contained.

Rose continued to go out to pick up men, and during one of her trips she met and began talking to an eighteen-year-old girl called Shirley Robinson. Other accounts say that it was Fred who met Shirley first, chatting her up in a cafeteria. Shirley had had a very hard life and was working as a prostitute. Either Rose or Fred invited Shirley to come and stay with them and their children. She would ultimately become the second victim called Shirley that they would kill.

Shirley moved into Cromwell Street in the late spring of 1977. At first they all got on well. Rose was newly pregnant, this time with one of her coloured lover's babies, so appreciated the help that Shirley could give around the house. Shirley had had other lesbian relationships so it's likely that at the start they made a sexual threesome, but over time Shirley started to have feelings for Fred. She assumed that Rose wouldn't mind - after all, she was still having sex with Jamaican men.

By the early autumn of that year, Shirley was expecting Fred West's child. She was happy about the pregnancy - but Rose became jealous of the closeness between them. Her jealousy was compounded by the fact that Fred kept joking that Shirley would be his next wife.

Eighteen-year-old Shirley had by now seen Rose lose her temper with the kids - and realised that she would make a fearsome enemy. She tried to keep out of Rose's way yet still attempted to stay close to Fred. As 1978 progressed, she started to sleep on the floor of one of the other lodger's rooms, not wanting to be left by herself when Rose was at home.

Fred told various people that Rose was really enraged at the situation. He added that Shirley would have to go. Everyone thought he meant that she'd have to leave the West household - but he and Rose had really decided that Shirley would have to die.

Shirley Robinson's murder

In May 1978 one of the other lodgers came home to find Rose in Shirley's room, packing away her stuff. Rose said that Shirley had left to visit relatives abroad and that she wouldn't be coming back.

In truth they had killed her, most likely by strangulation. Either Rose or Fred also cut the eight month baby from her womb and buried it near to her. One of them scalped the body then Fred dismembered it as he always did.

By now Rose was in charge of all the money - from rent, her prostitution and husband's wages. This suggests that she played an increasingly dominant role in the relationship. But Fred was equally capable of dominating, insisting that she still sleep with his coloured friends. Sometimes when they argued he hit her - at times she looked frightened of him and one client remembers seeing her with a badly blackened eye. In late 1978 she gave birth to her first mixed race daughter and the following year she gave birth to a second mixed race girl.

Alison Chambers death

After the 1978 birth, the Wests started enjoying their sex life again, this time with Alison Chambers, a seventeen-year-old girl who was clearly vulnerable. Alison had been in care until the Wests invited her to stay. She had few friends and was a dreamer who was desperate to be liked.

Fred and Rose always had to have their own way, and it's likely that at some stage Alison protested that the sex was becoming too violent. Thereafter (in September 1979) they apparently stripped her and gagged her with a belt, fastening it around her skull and under her jaw. They also tied her up and abused her then killed her and buried her in the garden. They had promised her that they'd take her to live on their fictitious farm in the country, but instead put her in a premature grave.

In the same year Rose's sadistic father Bill Letts died - and the murder of girls being buried under the Cromwell Street house stopped abruptly. The only body to be buried after this date would be that of Heather, their daughter, eight years later. Fred and Bill had become friends and had at one stage run a cafe together. Some crime writers have wondered if they also went out driving together looking for girls.

An increasingly vicious mother

After her father's funeral, Rose continued to treat her children intolerably. She had always been cruel to Anne Marie - Fred had raped the child for years in his van and in derelict farms - so the terrified teenager left home when she was just fifteen years old. Fred then turned his incestuous attentions on his fourteen-year-old daughter Heather and increasingly molested her.

Rose just laughed at Heather's attempts to ward him off or erroneously called her firstborn a lesbian. And the abuse wasn't just verbal and emotional - Heather was frequently beaten by Rose and was so badly bruised that she refused to participate in school gym lessons, a fact that earned her school detentions again and again.

Other than that she was seen as a bright child, but an increasingly withdrawn one who had few friends. (The Wests wouldn't allow their children to bring schoolfriends home, and timed their journeys back from school to make sure that they didn't speak to anyone at length or go to the authorities.)

At home, Heather would rock herself back and forth for hours - just as Rose had done as an abused child - and she had terrible nightmares. She bit her nails so badly that her fingers bled.

Yet despite Rose's poor relationships with Heather, Stephen and to a lesser extent, Mae, she continued to produce yet more children. In the summer of 1982 she had another daughter, and yet another in the summer of 1983, both by Jamaican men.

Heather is murdered

Desperate to escape from the brooding atmosphere of Cromwell Street, Heather left school in May 1987 and applied for a job at a holiday camp. She thought the job was hers but later got a phone call telling her that she hadn't been successful. Heather was disconsolate, crying for most of the night.

In June she was strangled by either Fred or Rose - Rose had previously almost strangled Stephen into unconsciousness during an argument so may have done the same thing to Heather, this time going further. Her remains were naked when found, suggesting sexual abuse, but she hadn't been gagged.

The other children came home that night to be told that Heather had left. Rose had been crying. A few days later she went to see her brother and sister in law and said that Heather had left because she was a lesbian. She added that they must not mention Heather's name ever again.

At other times she told neighbours that Heather had been hitting the younger children so she'd got rid of her. On yet another occasion she pretended that Heather had phoned to say that she was well. Later the other children contacted a Missing Persons programme in the hope that their beloved sister could be traced but they got no response so suggested calling the police. At this stage Fred said that Heather was involved in illegal activities and that they'd get her arrested if they set the police on to her.

The reality was very different. Fred had dug a hole in the back garden and buried his daughter, paving over her makeshift grave with a patio at a later date.

It's possible that Rose didn't know that Fred had killed Heather - she would sound genuinely shocked when eventually told of her death by the police and refused to eat for the next three days whilst in custody. And she would cry whenever her name was mentioned in court.

Another threesome

After Heather's death, Rose continued to work as a prostitute but by now she restricted her business hours to one day a week. However she was still keen on ongoing sexual satisfaction. Fred did some work for a new neighbour called Kathryn and when he heard that she was bisexual he invited her home to meet Rose.

Kathryn found that Rose was sexually aggressive from the start, sitting close to her and making it clear that she wasn't wearing any panties. After a few drinks, the three of them went to bed.

The threesomes - or more often twosomes when Fred was at work - became a regular occurrence, but soon the sex became more violent. The couple allegedly showed her bondage masks and restrictive suits that were too small for them but which had clearly been worn. And she claimed Rose put a pillow over her face and whispered 'What's it like not being able to see?' She also asked how Kathryn would feel if she was left tied up all day and just tormented occasionally - a chilling account of what they actually did to victims who wouldn't be missed.

After one of those sessions, Kathryn decided not to go back to the Wests and soon she moved away from the area. If she had protested *dur-*

ing a bondage session they may well have increased their abuse and then snuffed out her life.

That said, she had contacted the press and accepted their offer of eight thousand pounds before going to the police, so, as was pointed out in court, she had good reason to make the sex sound frightening even if it hadn't been.

A break for freedom

By the late nineteen eighties even Rose seemed to have had enough of Fred and their home-based life. She wanted him to take her out more. After all, she was in her mid thirties yet had never had a social life. Fred was now fifty and had no time for anything other than work and voyeuristic sex. So she started going alone to a country and western bar and became friendly with the bar staff. She and Fred would argue about this and he would hit her. She hit him back.

In the same period she rented a flat of her own to take her lovers to. Observers say that Fred went to pieces at this time. Unable to control his wife totally any more he tried to control other aspects of his universe, cleaning compulsively and talking endlessly of seeing bodies in car crashes, crashes that were never mentioned on the news and that no one else knew anything about.

It's likely that these car crash fantasies gave him an excuse to talk about what a dismembered body looks like, as he was still obsessed with thoughts of corpses. He was also very curious about the insides of living women and would keep a diary of his daughters' menstrual cycles and take many videos of Rose's vulva up close.

Rose, for her part, always seemed willing to pose pornographically for the camera. Either she enjoyed being the voyeuristic centre of attention or it was an easy way to please Fred. Sometimes she'd be tired after shopping, cooking and cleaning all day and wouldn't want to have sex with his Jamaican friends, but he would nag her until she gave in, saying, in a throwback to the Dark Ages, that a good wife always did what her husband said.

Kathryn had been thirty when she got involved with the Wests - but Fred hadn't lost his desire for much younger girls. One day he abused a child, both raping and sodomising her in the house and videoing the entire abusive episode whilst Rose was out at the shops. The girl was screaming and other people in the house tried to intervene but he'd locked the door. The child remained traumatised by the rape and in the summer of 1992 she told a friend who told the police.

A visit from the police

The police visited Cromwell Street to search for the video of Fred raping the girl. He was at work but Rose answered the door and lashed out at one of the constables. She had always seen her home as her castle and resented any intrusion from the outside world.

She was arrested for assaulting the officer and charged with that and with the neglect of two of her children. She warned the bewildered youngsters not to say anything (about being sexually, physically and emotionally abused by her and by various relatives) then she was taken away.

The five youngest children were immediately taken into care. Stephen was asked if he'd been abused, but he denied it as he'd been brought up to see the police as the enemy. Anne Marie told the truth but later tried to retract her statement as she was afraid.

With all of the young children out of the house and Fred on remand, Rose found Cromwell Street a lonely place. She went to the local pound and got two terrier-like dogs for company. But she beat them viciously for the least imagined misdemeanour, just as she'd done with her kids.

Whilst Fred was in jail pending his court case for rape, the Wests became very romantic towards each other on the phone. They also wrote loving letters. In one of those letters Rose apparently said that if Fred was found guilty she'd do time with him. Meanwhile she got a part-time job as a cleaning lady to bring some more money into the house.

When Stephen visited his father, Fred wept and said he'd done some terrible things whilst Stephen was in bed at night. He obviously thought that the murders would be discovered any day.

But soon he was released to a halfway house that he only had to return to at night. It looked as if once again the Wests might get away with it. Rose - sometimes accompanied by her grown up children - would travel there to meet him outdoors during the day. Fred and Rose would fondle each other quite openly during these visits to the amusement of passers-by and the embarrassment of their children. In the end the couple bought a small tent and had sex there.

But even sex couldn't take their minds off the fear of imprisonment. Rose must have realised that the net was closing in - leastways, when the police offered to return her pornographic videos she told them to burn them. She explained to Fred that they'd cost her her children - like most toxic parents she was unable to see that it was her cruelty that had led them to be taken away.

The case against her and Fred collapsed when the terrified young girl refused to testify. But all five of the younger children opted to stay in care - and Rose seemed surprised by this. People who have seen pictures of the youngsters whilst they were with her say they looked lost and very subdued. Chillingly, she decided to have another child and had her sterilisation reversed, but miscarried at age 39.

Settled in their foster homes, the little Wests began to say that Heather was buried under the patio. Fred had often joked about this but the older children had been worried that it was true when they could find no trace of their sister. The children had been close, united as fellow victims of abuse.

Fred was let out by the end of the year and immediately returned to Cromwell Street and went back to work. But he was clearly frightened of something. Rose was also nervous, and they would sit on the settee holding hands and doubtless wondering what life would be like if the corpses under their feet were ever found.

Meanwhile, a social worker contacted the authorities about the allegations that Heather was buried under the Cromwell Street patio. The police made extensive inquiries and realised that Heather West, Charmaine West and Rena West had all disappeared. Fred had allegedly raped a young girl, so had he raped Heather and then murdered her? They decided to investigate...

The search of Cromwell Street

On 24th February 1994, Rose's twenty-one-year old daughter Mae opened the door to find a police team there with a search warrant. It said they were there to search for Heather's body. Rose dismissed the search as stupid - but when they started to dig up the garden looking for Heather she went into shock.

She told her son to phone Fred, to get him home no matter what - but his mobile phone was out of range and eventually his employer had to telephone direct to the house he was working on. When the family did get hold of him and told him what was happening he said he'd be home in a few minutes. Instead he disappeared for several hours.

It's likely that he went somewhere to destroy vital evidence - later he'd tell Stephen that he'd previously dismembered some of the bodies at a disused farmhouse so perhaps he returned there to hide certain clues. Most of the bodies found at the Cromwell Street address had many bones missing so he may have kept them as grisly trophies at a derelict place.

Rose cried and cried and refused to go to the station to make a statement. She was so upset at the view of the police digging up the garden that the children drew the curtains on the increasingly eerie scene.

Fred protects Rose

When Fred at last arrived home he told police they were looking in the wrong place, presumably hoping they'd find Heather and not the other bodies. He wanted to keep Rose out of the picture and clearly saw himself receiving a light sentence as he just told his children he might be going away for a time.

The day after the digging started, the searchers found Heather West's body. They also found an extra femur, which showed that a second body was buried nearby. Police arrested the Wests and Fred was charged with his daughter's murder and sent to jail.

Fred told police again and again that Rose had nothing to do with Heather's death or the disposal of her body. He said that Heather had been rude to him when Rose was out shopping and that he'd strangled her with his hands or with a pair of tights or with an electric flex. An impulsive strangling, however, doesn't explain the body's nakedness.

Fred had already told friends that he'd gotten Rose so young that he'd been able to train her to do whatever he wanted. Did that include covering up violent deaths?

Rose is questioned

The police asked Rose why Heather, Charmaine and Charmaine's mother, Rena, had all disappeared. Rose told the story about Rena coming back to fetch the child. She was then asked about Heather and said that she was glad that Heather had left as she was a lesbian. At another juncture she said that they'd fallen out because Heather was hitting the younger kids.

When told that Heather was dead and asked how she felt, Rose appeared to be deeply shocked. For the first time it occurred to the police that she genuinely might not have known Fred had killed their daughter. She told the police that she 'didn't know nothing' and said that if Fred had killed Heather then he wasn't right in the head. It's clear that from this point onwards she decided to disassociate herself from Fred.

She was questioned for two days then released pending further inquiries. The next day she left Cromwell Street forever and moved with Stephen and Mae to a safe house. Meanwhile the police were still digging up corpses from the grounds.

The suicide attempt

Rose must have known that imprisonment was near - and she either decided to end it all or to make herself look emotionally vulnerable in the hope of obtaining a lighter sentence. Whatever her motivation, she swallowed the contents of a bottle of painkilling tablets then staggered through to her grown-up children in the other room. They phoned an ambulance and she had her stomach pumped out.

Later she was treated for depression. It's quite common for female serial killers to be treated for depression after their arrest or imprisonment - though they are usually depressed about their own fate rather than retrospectively feeling guilty about the incredible suffering that they've caused.

Throughout February and March the police discovered partial female skeletons in the Wests' garden - namely those of Heather West, Shirley Robinson and her foetus, Shirley Hubbard, Alison Chambers, Lucy Partington, Theresa Siegenthaler, Juanita Mott, Carol Anne Cooper and Linda Gough.

In April they turned their attention to the Wests' previous flat at Midland Street and found little Charmaine's skeleton there. Later that month they unearthed Rena's remains from a field near Fred's childhood home. In June of that year they found the skeleton of his former lover Anne McFall and that of her unborn child.

Rose was now charged with sadistically assaulting an eleven-year-old girl in Rose's home in the seventies and of attacking a little boy. (The identities of child victims cannot be disclosed for legal reasons.) She was jointly charged with a man in his late sixties but the charges against him were dropped.

She was soon charged with Linda Gough's murder - Linda's mother had gone looking for the girl and found Rose wearing her slippers. Linda's other clothes had been hanging on the washing line.

Later that year she was charged with a total of ten counts of murder; the girls buried in the garden and Charmaine. She wasn't charged with Rena and Anne McFall's deaths as their bodies were found far away from Cromwell Street so their murders were solely attributed to Fred.

Whilst awaiting trial Rose took to lying around watching children's TV and eating confectionery so that by the time of the conviction she'd put on three stone in weight and looked expressionless and plain.

The charges

On 30th June 1994 Rose and Fred were charged together. He touched her shoulder as they stood in the dock but she shrank away from him. She continued to ignore him during the months when he was in prison, though he kept writing to his children asking after their mum.

On New Years day he wrote Rose a short love letter that said 'All I have is my life. I will give it to you, my darling.' Then he hanged himself in his cell.

When Rose was given the news she was put on suicide watch, but she didn't shed a tear. Some people thought that she would now be freed as the case against her was circumstantial. There was no fingerprint or other forensic proof that she'd been involved in the victim's deaths. Rose entered a not guilty plea to all ten charges - and Mae delayed having Heather buried as she was sure her mother would want to attend the funeral when she was found not guilty and set free. But the legal system decided that Rose's living victims should be allowed to tell of their ordeal in court, and that gave the trial enough substance to go ahead.

The trial

Rose's trial opened on the 3rd October 1995 at Winchester Crown Court. It soon became clear that Rose could be a sadistic and callous woman. Caroline Owens relived her ordeal of being fondled, stripped, intimately probed and assaulted at Rose's hands.

Rose's horrific cruelty as a parent was also brought to light. One witness was her stepdaughter Anne Marie, who recalled the numerous times that Rose had hit her, beat her and mocked her. Rose had also helped various men assault Anne Marie when she was still a child.

Rose was now trying to present herself as a timid quietly spoken woman - but the court was allowed to hear her taped interviews with police in which she swore constantly, was loud and obstructive. She told police 'what Fred says goes' and tried to make out that she was totally under his thumb. The defence also tried to present Rose as a victim as indeed she had been - until she became the aggressor who beat her children and possibly took young girls' lives.

Rose insisted on taking the stand, though her legal advisers warned against it. She alternately laughed and made bad jokes, got angry and showed her true rage. She even criticised some of the deceased and came over as a generally objectionable human being - though, as crimewriter Brian Marriner says, we shouldn't find people guilty of murder just because we find them unlikeable.

A voluntary prison worker took the stand and said that Fred had told her that Rose was involved in some of the murders and that Rose had killed Shirley Robinson, her pregnant rival. Other women who'd had sado-masochistic relationships with Rose testified that she'd become increasingly violent during the sex sessions, taking them beyond their limits and clearly getting off on their fear. Unfortunately these witnesses had all taken money from tabloid newspapers so may have had a vested interest in making their accounts sound more sinister than they might actually have been.

Rose's mother, Daisy, said that Rose had been afraid of Fred. She said that Rose had been childlike for her age when she met up with him. Daisy didn't even look at her daughter whilst giving evidence and admitted that she hadn't seen her for seven years.

After a six week trial, the jury retired to consider its verdict. Over the next two days they returned several times to announce they'd found Rose guilty of more of the killings until she was eventually found guilty on all ten counts of murder. The judge recommended that she should never be released.

Rose betrayed little emotion when the verdict was read out but wept afterwards downstairs.

The legacy of abuse

Rose wasn't the only family member whose life would be ruined by her brutal childhood. Her brother Graham became an alcoholic by his early teens, whilst another brother Gordon spent his adult life in mental hospitals and in prisons. And her older brother Andrew never forgot the terror that he'd suffered at his father's hands.

Less is known about Joyce and Glenys who moved away from the home as early as possible. Patricia developed Alzheimer's disease and was dying by the time of Rose's trial.

The other victims - Rose's children

Rose's children also continue to suffer the legacy of abuse, just as she and her siblings did. Stephen's marriage quickly broke up amidst rumours of domestic violence. And Anne Marie - who lost her mother, Rena, and her sisters Charmaine and Heather to Rose and Fred's violence - has tried to commit suicide, taking an overdose in 1995 when she heard of her father's death and another one during Rose's trial. In November 1999 she jumped into a freezing river to drown herself and was finally pulled from it unconscious and treated for hypothermia.

Life after life

In prison Rose started to read voraciously, something she hadn't often found time for before. She also applied to become a prison listener, a kind of jail Samaritan. But no one wanted to confide in this woman who had abused her own children so viciously, so the authorities turned down her request. She also 'got' religion, as most long term prisoners conveniently do, and became friends with an elderly nun.

Further crimes come to light

In 1999 pornographic videos were found at the house of a known paedophile which apparently implicated Rose West. It's doubtful that further charges will be brought against her because of all the extra costs that this incurs. There's little point, as the judge at her trial has already said that she should never be released.

11

MIDNIGHT AT THE LOST AND FOUND
The chaotic life of Carol Mary Bundy

Carol was born on the 26th August 1942 to Charles and Gladys Peters. They already had a seven-year-old son, Gene, a child actor. Unfortunately he resented her arrival and they would never be close. Sadly, her parents weren't close either. They had a negative mindset that saw the worst in everything and everyone.

Home was a succession of American states, everywhere from Louisiana to Los Angeles, as their father pursued his career in cinema management. Poor Gene was constantly being taken to new film production companies and to different schools. When Carol was three her mother gave birth to a third child, a daughter, Vicky. Ultimately both girls would be abused by their violent dad...

Carol was beautiful at birth, but, like most children of unhappy and disapproving households, she soon became clumsy and awkward. Her father was an alcoholic and a control freak. Her mother had been a starlet with tap dancing talent - but she now settled for a career in hairdressing and lived life secondhand by putting little Gene onto the stage. He would star in over a dozen movies and the toddler Carol would have a bit part in one of those films.

But there was little stardust back home. Gladys proved to be so violent a mother that her husband wouldn't allow her to physically punish the children for fear of what she'd do to them. Gladys was afraid of her husband so she outwardly agreed to this command. Nevertheless, Carol's younger sister Vicky would watch on one occasion when Gladys lashed Carol across the face again and again with a belt. Other beatings left them all with welts on their skin and she would occasionally draw blood. Charles also beat his children with implements and both parents were emotionally abusive to them. Young Carol gained weight, lost confidence and became a heavy, bumbling child.

Perhaps she could not bear to see the horror of her everyday life for by the age of nine she had a wandering eye and had to have special glasses with extra thick lenses. Her schoolmates laughed at her and she retreated into the world of books, reading science fiction tomes for hours in her room. There, she concentrated on the good times she'd had with her family and convinced herself that all was well in her harsh and ungiving world. It was a level of self deception that would dangerously continue throughout her adult life - for in the end her murderous fantasies would prove more vital to her than reality.

The maladroit child grew into an overweight and self conscious teenager. Carol had the type of thin brown hair that flops easily and her parents had it cut in an unflattering short style. She also had thick glasses and difficulty in maintaining eye contact. Her slim and pretty mother continued to mock her. Carol was so distraught that she drank iodine at age twelve or thirteen in an attempt to kill herself.

Then one day when Carol was fourteen, her mother suddenly said she felt ill and took to her bed. Her husband took her to the doctor but she went into cardiac arrest and died. That same night Carol's father said that he didn't want to sleep alone. He then sexually abused her eleven-year-old sister, Vicky. (As an adult, Carol would go on to sexually abuse an eleven-year-old child.) Later he sexually abused Carol, introducing the crying bereaved teenager to oral sex.

The emotional damage continued, with him calling them names, pointing out Carol's weight problem and her general physical awkwardness. Their brother Gene, by now twenty-one, had left home so escaped this escalation of abuse.

Within months of his wife's death, Charles remarried, presenting Carol and Vicky with an instant stepmother. This wife, too, was soon at the mercy of his anger and depression - during a rage he even tried to kill her with his gun. They struggled and he only succeeded in shooting dead Carol's cat.

At this stage Carol and Vicky were fostered for a few months and then delivered to their controlling grandmother in Michigan. Soon their father, in the throes of a divorce, took them back to California and the insults started up again.

Fifteen year old Carol was by now exhibiting extremely disturbed behaviour, running naked through the streets in order to get attention or peering into other people's bedrooms. She also became promiscuous, sleeping with any schoolboy who would have her because she was so desperate to be held and loved. Again, this pattern would continue into adult-hood as she believed she had nothing to offer except casual sex.

She dropped out of school and her father suggested she get herself a beauty qualification that he would fund. Carol did, but soon got tired of the course. She had a creative mind and was good at writing fiction so would have been suited to more intellectual pursuits - but she had no sense of self worth and had been desperate to appease her controlling dad.

Carol's first marriage

Despite her attempts to placate him, her father was never pleased with her and her misery continued. She dropped out of college and took up with a man in his mid fifties who had a drink problem. In a bid to escape her hate-filled home, seventeen-year-old Carol married him. Unfortunately he too wanted to exploit her and planned to become her pimp. Carol left him and moved in with a writer, Richard, who was fifteen years her senior. At last she had met an intelligent and creative man who saw that she, too, had many talents. But she was too damaged to fully grasp this new chance.

She started various creative projects - including a book - but saw none of them through to the end. Two years passed in this way and then she was told that her father had killed himself. Carol was only nineteen but already completely brainwashed into the role of the doormat. She thought that his death was her fault, that she should have done more for him.

Female love

After her father's death, Carol went to bed with a female for the first time, hoping to find genuine love in another woman's arms. She was ultimately rejected by the woman and returned to having casual sex with men. At twenty-one she was diagnosed as suffering from diabetes, a condition which exacerbated her ever changing emotional moods.

She was still living with the long suffering Richard who could see how talented she was but feared that her terrible childhood had ruined her for-ever. When she asked if he would support her through nursing school, he said that he would providing she kept up her grades. Carol did - and qual-ified in 1968 as top of her class.

But she still saw sex as the way to make friends, to keep people on her side, so continued to sleep with both men and women. Her promiscuity strained her long term relationship with Richard past breaking point, though they kept in touch.

Carol's second marriage

Carol now dated and married a fellow nurse called Grant Bundy and had a son by him. But the marriage deteriorated after the birth and Grant sometimes threatened her and slapped her. Foolishly they went on to com-pound matters four years later by having a second child, another boy. Carol worked hard during these years, though her martyred conversations made it difficult for the other nurses to like her. Still, she was a reasonable moth-er to her boys, taking them out for hamburgers and giving them rides on her motorbike.

But in an effort to buy their love, she ran up huge credit card debts and this led to many rows. To add to the misery, her ongoing eyesight problems had now worsened to the extent that she was going blind and could no longer work as a nurse or ride her bike or do the sewing that she'd always been so good at. During an argument Grant blurted out that he didn't want her moping around all day and that he couldn't afford to support the fam-ily alone, then he allegedly ran at her with his fists raised. Frightened, she sought refuge in a shelter for abused women, taking her sons, now five and nine.

The affair

Within a fortnight she'd moved into an apartment house and was flirting with the married housing manager, a womanising country and western fan called Jack Murray. Her feelings for this cowboy-hatted man quickly became obsessive and he was flattered by her attentions, going to bed with her in various empty apartments and in his van. She'd go down on him until he orgasmed but he rarely gave her an orgasm in return. Carol, who had known so little love in her life, didn't seem to expect sexual gratification - having a new lover to dream about was more than enough.

Jack was physically attractive in a Tom Jones lookalike kind of a way, whilst Carol was an older looking mid thirties, still overweight, with large heavy-lensed glasses. To compensate, she spent her savings on new clothes and makeup. She also gave Jack cash and gifts whenever he asked and would wait at home for hours in the hope that he would come round.

Carol was desperately lonely whilst he was at work or with his attractive blonde wife and kids. She'd lost her husband, her house and was facing the possibility of losing her eyesight. Jack, obviously flattered by the way she looked up to him, found out about an operation she could have to save her sight and even drove her to the hospital for her appointments, albeit getting oral or anal sex from her as a reward each time. Carol convinced herself that this was love and that they'd eventually marry. She overlooked his lies and his numerous faults.

Clearly playing on this unconditional love, he insulted her and broke their rare dates to coffee houses or to the cinema - most of those 'dates' simply involved her giving him sexual satisfaction. When she got money from selling her marital home he persuaded her to put it into a joint account. Jack was also treating his wife badly, beating the distraught woman and hitting their children. Carol was sure that he'd leave the marriage and live with her. She even had an affair with his brother-in-law in the hope of making him envious.

Eventually she confronted his wife, and Jack then told Carol to leave them both alone - at which stage Carol's complete lack of pride became even more apparent. She wrote to Jack begging him to give her a pet name and make her a loving tape recording of his voice. She said that she was tired of belonging to everyone, of sleeping around, that she only wanted to belong to him.

Jack didn't want to know - he had access to the joint account, which was all that he cared about. He'd found younger girlfriends to replace the thirty-something Carol. He was tired of her always hanging around.

Devastated, Carol moved to a different housing block - but masochistically went to a country and western bar and watched Jack and his wife dancing together. Her mood only lifted when she was approached by a good looking man with a smooth, soft voice called Doug Clark. She wasn't to know that Doug made a habit of targeting fat, lonely woman and encouraging them to fall in love with him before asking for free accommodation, gifts and cash.

Doug moves in

Carol was immediately won over by Doug's soft voice and firm hands as he manoeuvred her around the dance floor. He phoned her to arrange a second date - and at the end of the evening, which consisted of a meal in her home, he went to bed with her. There he told her that she was intelligent and fun and spent the night concentrating solely on her pleasure. She was in heaven.

Doug obviously realised that he had an especially easy touch on his hands, for the next day he asked if he could move in. Carol was probably ready to tie him to her bedposts by now but she contented herself with just saying yes. He also asked if he could have a pair of her knickers to wear so that he'd spend the day feeling close to her - he had been wearing women's clothes since he was four years old.

When Carol bashfully handed over her large colourless panties, he handed them back saying that they were too big for him. It must have been obvious to Doug just by looking at Carol that her panties would be capacious so this was clearly a move to make her feel uncertain about herself, to humiliate her.

Doug Clark would prove to be another Ian Brady or Gerald Gallego, men who pick up insecure women and confuse them with a mixture of insults and pretend love until the woman feels she is nothing on her own.

Carol's eyesight had now improved enough for her to go back to work as a vocational nurse. Doug was an engineer in a factory but he made it clear that he was an educated man who could do better. He seemed to like Carol's sons and they initially liked him, so life was looking up. Carol had always enjoyed bondage and humiliation and Doug was eager to try it so they had fun in the bedroom. Doug took her to her sadomasochistic limits and Carol was eager to find out how far she was willing to go.

She got in all Doug's favourite foods and fixed him all his favourite meals.

Soon she was even bringing his lunch to him each day at the factory. She bought a station wagon for herself because he admired it, but when she found it hard to drive she gave it to him. Carol bought Doug clothes and gifts and praised him lavishly in an attempt to keep him by her side.

Deep down Doug hated almost everyone, perhaps because his parents had sent him abroad to boarding school and hardly ever visited. His mother had migraines and his father worked long hours and was rigid in his behaviour, but psychiatrists were later convinced that something much darker than this must have happened in Doug's early home life.

Now he no longer had to hide his contempt of Carol - after all, she loved him no matter what he did. She left him notes saying that their minds were exactly similar, that no one had made her feel the way he made her feel.

He started to stay away for days at a time, clearly sleeping with other overweight and unloved women. Carol was so distraught that she drank, which played havoc with her diabetes and her always volatile disposition. She also answered an advert in a singles magazine and started seeing another man through it. Her new partner, who was very rich and very overweight, wanted marriage but soon saw that Carol was emotionally lost. She would sleep with Jack Murray one week if his other girlfriends weren't available, and sleep with Doug Clark the next.

Carol told this new man all about the sadness in her life and he urged her to start protecting herself from these exploitative men and to close the joint account with Jack Murray. But Carol didn't want to hurt Jack's feelings so kept the joint account open, sure that he wouldn't abuse the privilege. She simply couldn't believe that she was a worthwhile companion to be with for her own sake and in the end the new lover walked out of her life.

Folie à deux

Reassured that he had her unconditional love, Doug now said that he'd always wondered what it would be like to abduct a girl for sex and commit a murder. Pleased that he was sharing his fantasies with her, Carol asked him for further details. Doug said that he'd like to have a woman fellate him as she died. They started to talk more and more of murder and of keeping love slaves, and Carol convinced herself that this gave them a special bond. Incredibly, she let Doug bring his other girlfriends home and sometimes sleep with them in her bed. Carol felt sad and hurt and worthless as she sat alone in the adjoining room. Doug had said that she was completely unattractive to him and that he preferred other women. But at least he was sharing his murderous daydreams with her...

In April 1980 he asked her to buy two guns - and Carol did so. He asked her to come out with him to find a prostitute. The desperate Carol did this too. She even paid the prostitute to go down on Doug in the front seat whilst she, Carol, watched quietly from the back. The session was not a success as Doug, whose sexuality had always been fantasy and masturbation-based, was becoming impotent during ordinary sex.

Doug now knew that he could do anything he wanted and Carol wouldn't object. He hit her sons - and persuaded her to hit them too. She even used a belt on them as her father had done to her. He also took her car and brought it back damaged - he'd later admit that a death struggle with a sex partner had caused the gearshift to break.

Doug allegedly injures a prostitute

He came home with scratches on his face and blood on his clothes and Carol tried to persuade her sons that he'd been in an accident. Later he came back to Carol with blood all over him and told her he'd been in a fight. In truth, he may have stabbed a prostitute who was giving him oral sex in his car, but she had managed to kick the door open and throw herself onto the street. Carol knew that Doug was lying, that he'd started to act out his fantasies, but she pretended to believe his tales.

She now - early June 1980 - sent her sons away to live permanently with their father, who immediately sent them on to his parents. For years she had seen her role as that of wife and mother, had cooked and cleaned the house and did the laundry, so that her children were well fed and beautifully dressed. Now she had turned her back on that role and found herself a new role as the unshockable accomplice of a potential murderer, a man with whom she was totally obsessed. Carol sold the children's bunkbeds and planned to move to a house closer to Doug's work. Her own nursing career had to take second place.

This plain overweight woman with the increasingly damaged psyche had failed to please her father or her many lovers. But she had another chance, could become the most special person in Doug Clark's big talking but under-achieving life. In the next few weeks he would kill several times and she would either assist him or be shown the dump sites where the corpses lay.

Doug kills two victims

A few days after her sons left home, in mid June 1980, Carol found bloody clothes and blood soaked tissues in Doug's car. Most of us would have run a mile, but Carol apparently threw away the most scarlet-stained garments and laundered the rest, then asked him what had happened. Doug said he'd met two teenage siblings aged fifteen and sixteen and offered them a lift. The girls, Gena and Cynthia, were later described by one witness as look-ing totally out of place in their surroundings. They had been regularly whipped by their mother so had run away from home.

One of the girls had gotten into the front with Doug and he'd shot her in the head, after which he shot her half sister. Then he drove both girls to his garage and had oral sex with one and sodomised the other. One girl was dying as he abused her and the other was already dead so he cut off part of her clothing and indulged in necrophiliac sex.

His semen would be found in one girl's throat and vagina and in the other girl's rectum - and he would make a phone call to a girl in their address book saying how much he'd enjoyed raping them. This necrophili-ac orgy took place in the second week of June 1980, and was apparently Doug's finest hour.

Thereafter he went to a girlfriend's house and borrowed her camera to photograph his blood smeared dead victims, spending several more hours with them. Then he wrapped up the bodies and dumped them far away from his rented garage.

Doug told Carol all of this - and she felt flattered that he trusted her with this special knowledge. (Prosecutors would later suspect that Carol witnessed this double murder or at least saw the corpses, but they couldn't prove it.) Carol would later say that Doug took her out for a drive and showed her approximately where the bodies lay.

Doug's previous killing

He then went on to tell how he'd previously killed another girl at the end of May, in Carol's car. The victim was a beautiful blonde prostitute called Marnett Comer. That was why the gearstick was broken, as the seventeen-year-old had struggled before he managed to shoot her dead. Doug had then stripped Marnett and sexually abused her corpse.

He would later tell a friend that if you drove to a secluded area and put a dead girl on your car bonnet with the engine running then you could feel the vibrations going through her corpse as had sex with it. Doug then slit the dead Marnett's stomach open so that the insects would invade it faster and help it to decompose.

Doug had given some of Marnett's clothes to Theresa, an eleven-year-old neighbour of Carol's who he was intent on seducing. He kept Marnett's panties for himself as he still enjoyed wearing woman's clothes.

Carol would later tell police that at this stage she thought she'd better co-operate with Doug in case he killed her and her kids. In truth, the children were away at their grandparents and Doug was often at other girlfriend houses. She could have phoned the authorities when he was out of the house and he'd have been arrested at his work the next day. The reality is that she wanted to please him no matter what he did - and she saw no especial worthiness in preserving other young female lives.

Police don't believe a woman is involved

She did phone the police at one stage, giving a false name and saying that the murders had been committed by her boyfriend, but they refused to believe that a woman was involved in the deaths and thought she was a crank. They were so dismissive of her on the phone that they alienated her completely. After all, Carol was desperate for attention, a few words of praise.

They'd later find that bullets had been fired from guns like the ones she'd bought - and would find that a woman exactly matching her description had bought the box that one of the dead girl's heads was later found in. But they didn't attempt to track her down, convinced that they were looking for a man.

In fairness to the police, Carol sounded confusingly edgy, hurt and arrogant on the phone. After all, Doug, the love of her life, was still having sex with other women. She'd given up her children and her colleagues didn't like her. Plus Jack Murray was alternately ignoring her or just using her to give him head. The desperately needy Carol had always tried to romanticise her relationships, but even she had to admit that her Prince hadn't arrived.

As a result she was only sleeping for five hours a night and was sometimes drinking to elevate her mindset. She was also taking tranquillisers in an ever increasing dose.

Child molestation

She had good reason to be depressed and guilty and afraid, for she was now joining Doug in molesting her eleven-year-old neighbour Theresa. Carol had originally refused to have sexual relations with the child but Doug had accused her of being jealous of the well built and outwardly mature looking eleven-year-old. He and Carol took the girl into the shower with them and to bed where Doug would ultimately take her virginity.

Carol would rationalise that the child didn't seem to mind, conveniently blocking out the fact that lonely children are desperate to please outwardly friendly adults. Carol took photographs of her lover and little Theresa engaged in various sexual acts.

The couple took the girl to the cinema and to burger restaurants and on shopping expeditions where they paid for everything. On other occasions Doug took Theresa out in the car and asked her to pick him out the wildest prostitutes. He sometimes had sex with them in the front seat whilst Theresa watched from the back.

Carol often had oral sex with Doug and Theresa, just as her father had had oral sex with her and her eleven-year-old sister. Theresa's mother saw

Carol as a homely woman, a matronly type, and had no idea that her child was being abused.

Carol kills

On the 20th June 1980 Carol and Doug were out cruising late when they saw a cute teenager hanging around. They offered her a lift and she hesitated but then accepted. The seventeen-year-old said she was called Cathy and accepted forty dollars, her price for giving Doug oral sex.

She went down on him with Carol sitting in the back of the car. Carol had her gun ready. Doug had suggested that Carol might like to kill the next victim so that she would be as involved in the murders as he. What happened next is open to dispute - Carol would later claim that Doug changed his mind and shot the girl himself. Doug would say that Carol did it. She would be found guilty of this teenager's death.

One of the killers shot Cathy through the head but she continued to struggle. Doug snapped at Carol that she mustn't freak out, but Carol calmly reminded him that she was a nurse who saw blood and death all the time. She was now as caught up in her role as a killer as she'd been in her role as the all-American mom.

She got into the front seat of the car and undressed the badly injured teenager. The girl was bleeding and writhing and soon making the death rattle, but the two sociopaths were impervious. Carol simply put Doug's jacket over Cathy so that no one would see what was going on. They drove to a quiet area and dumped her naked body. Presumably, given that they'd stripped her, they abused her corpse.

Doug kills another two girls

That same month - on 23rd June 1980 - Doug went out driving on his own and paid a twenty-year-old prostitute called Exxie Wilson to get into the car with him. He drove to a car park where she started to give him oral sex. At the point of orgasm he shot the mildly retarded young woman through the back of the head. She bit him in her death throes and he was so angry that he threw her out of the car, ripped off her clothes and used a knife to hack off her head. He left the torso where it was and bagged the still warm head.

He then drove back to the area where he'd picked her up and found her friend Karen Jones who he feared could identify him. He shot her in the head then dumped the body, before taking Exxie's head back to Carol's apartment. He had sex with it then put it in her freezer for future fun.

Carol would later say that she found the head gross - but if that's true she didn't say so to her lover. Instead she got out her makeup kit and prettified the thawing head so that Doug could have sex with it again. She then bought a chest for them to hide the head in, wearing gloves when she went to buy the piece of furniture. They dumped the chest and its grisly contents in an alley where it would be found by a horrified passer-by.

A celibate life

Carol had hoped that these shared acts would make Doug love her more - but instead he seemed to like her less and would only sleep with her as part of a threesome with eleven-year-old Theresa. He spent more time at other women's houses leaving Carol to drink alone or phone her sons at their grandparents house. The grandparents kept wanting to send the children home and Carol said this wasn't a safe place for them just now.

In desperation, she called her former lover Richard, the writer, and told him all about Doug and his killing spree. Then she had second thoughts and called back saying that the murders were fictitious, that she was writing a short story with that plot and wanted to know if it sounded tenable. Given her drinking, her mood swings and her tranquilliser dependence, Richard was not surprised by the content of this call.

Another suicide attempt

More lonely and friendless than she'd ever been, Carol went to her garage and injected and ingested insulin and tranquillisers. It was more of a cry for help than a genuine attempt to end it all for she called her work saying that she planned to take her own life. She also left a 'goodbye-cruel-world' note for Doug. She was found semi-conscious and taken to hospital by the paramedics where she had her stomach pumped out. Jack Murray reluctantly drove her home the next morning, bringing a female friend with him to keep Carol at bay.

Carol's morality slipped even lower now and she brought eleven-year-old Theresa to Jack and let him fondle her. But she wouldn't let him have sex with her, saying that this privilege belonged only to Doug.

Carol kills Jack

Doug continued to treat Carol like shit and Carol began to go to bits. She also found out that Jack had taken a great deal of money from their joint account and that he had lied about what he spent it on. Her work performance became so poor that no one wanted to share a shift with her. She had always talked nervously nineteen to the dozen and now - on 3rd August 1980 - she went to the country and western club and began to tell Jack that Doug had killed several girls and that she had been involved.

Jack, in turn, told the group he was with. They urged him to contact the police, but he seemed to have a change of heart and said he was sure that Carol was only joking. In truth, he'd probably realised that if she went to the police she'd tell them that he'd fondled an eleven-year-old girl and asked if he could have intercourse with her.

Later Carol said she wanted to talk to Jack in his van. He agreed and got inside with her where she allegedly offered to perform his favourite sexual act, that of licking his anus. He took off his trousers and lay down on his stomach and she shot him through the head. But he didn't die immediately so she shot him again.

Carol then began to stab him through the back and the buttocks. She would later say that she did this to make it look as if Jack had been attacked by a total psycho. It's more likely that she was venting her rage on him for all of the insults, the stolen money, the lies about leaving his wife and the broken dates.

She then realised that both the bullets in his head could be traced to her gun - so she cut his head off. It's likely that she also carried out this act to gain Doug's approval. After all, he had cut off Exxie's head. Carol left Jack's bloody torso in the van, where it swelled up horribly in the heat and became discoloured. It would be several days before it was found.

Meanwhile she proudly told Doug of what she'd done - but he reminded her that she'd left the shells in the van and that these could be traced to her. He told her that she wasn't bright enough to get away with murder without him. He now started to sleep with one of Jack's former girlfriends, pouring salt into Carol's emotional wounds.

Carol's mood deteriorated further, though when she was told of Jack's death she acted as if she were devastated, screaming and crying and wailing that it couldn't be true. Deciding that he'd had enough, Doug said that he was leaving her. Carol, who feared being alone, begged him not to go but he was adamant.

Carol's confession

Back at work, she started to arrive late and was unable to concentrate. Finally she blurted out to a colleague that Doug had killed several women and that she couldn't take any more. She verbally handed in her resignation and her terrified co-workers didn't exactly beg her to stay. Instead they rushed to the phone and called the police - but by the time they arrived at the hospital the killer was on her way home.

At home, Carol phoned the police herself and asked a detective to meet her that lunchtime for a coffee. It was clear that she wanted to control the way she turned herself in. And given Carol's level of emotional neediness she probably managed to convince herself it might turn into a romantic date.

The detective agreed - but the police who had been to the hospital arrived at her home just then. They arrested her as she put together a bag filled with evidence against her lover. This evidence included photographs of Doug in sexually compromising positions with eleven year old Theresa - Carol was about to make him pay for spurning her. She was immediately taken into custody, as was an outwardly calm Doug.

Carol's side of the story

Carol was edgy and over talkative but lucid when the police arrived and insisted on giving them the underwear that Doug had kept as trophies from his victims. She willingly admitted that she'd killed Jack and cut off his head, saying that he was 'an asshole who deserved to die.' She also told of the sex sessions Doug had had with Theresa, though it's unclear if at this stage she admitted her part in the child's abuse. Photos would be discovered of herself and Theresa together and the little girl would ultimately testify in court that Carol had been involved in many of the sexual acts. Doug Clark's supporters believe that Carol was given immunity against her paedophiliac crimes in return for testifying against Doug.

Even now, Carol was intent on finding herself a new man, openly propositioning one of the police officers. She talked in great detail about her sex life and said that killing was fun. When she was accompanied back to her apartment by police officers to gather further evidence she asked if they would have sex with her, explaining that it might be years before she had access to a man again. They declined.

Carol apparently found it difficult to orgasm and needed up to an hour of manual stimulation to get there, so it's clear that she wasn't a nymphomaniac. It seems that she wanted sex for what it represented to her - the chance to be held close, to feel as if she mattered to someone for a while. Both of her parents had constantly told her that she was fat and ugly but she could convince herself that she was desirable as she lay in a man's reassuring arms.

Doug's side of the story

Meanwhile, Doug denied that he'd committed any of the murders. Instead he said that Carol and Jack had committed them - but Jack's wife was able to give her dead husband an alibi for three of the homicides. Jack clearly hadn't cut off his own head, so Doug admitted that Carol had done that. Doug added that his only crime was to help her dispose of Jack's head in a dumpster. (It has never been found.)

A bloody footprint found at one murder scene matched Doug's boots and traces of blood in Doug's car were matched to other girls that had been killed - and the girl he had stabbed but failed to kill would identify him. Later this stabbing would be removed from Doug Clark's record as it transpired the girl had originally given a very different description of her assailant and had only been able to identify Doug Clark after being hypnotised by the authorities to supposedly recover her memory.

Carol in jail

In prison awaiting trial, Carol received a letter from a male prisoner who was in the same institute as Doug. She wrote back and was soon smearing her vaginal juices on the notepaper and telling him she'd done so. Even in jail she was desperate to hook a man.

Her attitude to Doug varied from one day to the next, so that sometimes she said she'd act insane and take the full blame for the murders. At other times she said that she'd act middle class so that no one would believe she was involved with the deaths. She wrote to him 'Remember I look innocent. Impression is worth as much as facts.' Carol the homicidal accomplice had transmogrified into Carol the jailhouse lawyer. When it came to a sense of her own identity she was in some ways a blank slate, ready to be written upon.

Ironically she stabilised in jail because, as her estranged sister Vicky would later put it, she no longer had to make any decisions. It's indicative of her lonely life that whilst she was awaiting trial she didn't have a single visitor.

The court case

Carol could have faced the gas chamber but instead plea bargained for a life sentence in return for testifying against Doug at his trial. There she said that he was the best lover she'd ever had and that 'Mr Clark had virtual total control over my personality and behaviour, my wants, my desires, my dreams.' She neglected to mention that she'd managed to break this hold the second he said that he was leaving her, the second she wanted revenge.

She spoke of how she'd watched him kill Cathy (but she, Carol, would be charged with Cathy's death) of how he'd brought her Exxie's head, of how he'd told her about the murders of Exxie's friend Karen Jones and the pretty prostitute Marnett and the half-sisters Cynthia and Gina. She added that he'd said he'd killed at least fifty times.

Her testimony - and that of Theresa, now fourteen, plus the forensic evidence - helped convict Doug and he was sentenced to die on all six counts of murder and was sent to San Quentin to start his inevitable appeals.

Meanwhile Carol sent the judge a Christmas card and a note that said it was a pity they couldn't meet for coffee some time.

She also got religion after being befriended by a religious volunteer. Carol had been ostracised by the other women because she had given evidence against Doug Clark and this is looked down upon in prison. She spent her time deciding on her defence, telling her volunteer that she wanted to 'appear ladylike and respectable, a middle-class housewife type.'

Carol's sentence

Carol had initially maintained that she was not guilty by reason of insanity. And, indeed, the jury at Doug Clark's trial saw her as a woman to be pitied, a sad woman who needed help. But she must have known that she'd acted rationally, wearing gloves to buy the chest that they planned to dump Exxie's head in, sending away her sons so that the apartment was free for paedophiliac sex and acts of cranial necrophilia. She'd also had the forethought to cut off Jack's head so that the bullets couldn't be traced to her gun.

Apparently realising that the insanity plea was unlikely to work, Carol burst into tears on the day of her trial (May 2nd, 1983) and withdrew it. Instead she pleaded guilty to killing Jack and to killing one of the girls.

The judge sentenced her to a minimum of twenty five years for the two murders, with the possibility of life imprisonment. She was given a further two years for the use of a firearm. Still intent on placating men, she sent him a thank you cartoon that she'd drawn and added that she was a decent woman and that's why she'd ultimately gone to the police.

She was sent to the California Institute For Women at Frontera, one of four women's prisons in California. A photograph of her taken in the yard there in 1990 shows a woman with a placating smile and with shoulders that are slightly rounded. She is still trying to please, sending her signature to those lost individuals who collect serial killers autographs.

Psychological profile

So what kind of woman watches her lover kill young girls, taking part in at least one of those murders? What kind of woman kills her former lover and cuts off his head?

Patricia Pearson, in her interesting overview about female killers *When She Was Bad*, suggests that Carol Bundy was a 'highly intelligent and remorseless psychopath.' The highly intelligent part is in doubt for Carol's IQ only tested at 109 in prison, slightly above average. She may well have been a psychopath, though, for she showed no compassion for her victims and even told the police that - although she initially disliked the fact that Doug came home covered in blood or that he wanted her to watch him shoot a prostitute - she ultimately found that killing was fun. Her psychiatrists said that she had woefully poor judgement and was unable to benefit from experience, the latter being a common psychopathic trait.

Many sources have suggested that Carol Bundy was totally insane, that she believed she was the secret wife of the serial killer Ted Bundy. She didn't - one of her sons once asked her if Ted was a relation and Carol looked horrified and said no. Ted went on to marry a woman called Carol, making her Carol Ann Bundy and Carol's full name was Carol Mary Bundy. Doug Clark must have noted this for later use.

It gave him yet another idea for his defence so he said in court that Carol was fixated on Ted Bundy and that she tried to commit a murder for every murder that Ted committed. Doug said that she ultimately planned to kill Theresa when she turned twelve because Ted had killed a girl who was twelve. Doug Clark's supporters say that Carol wrote to Ted Bundy. This may be true as she wrote to everyone she could think of from prison.

Two psychiatrists thought that Carol had been a volunteer in the murders, that she hadn't been coerced. This seems likely, given that Doug was often away from the house and she could have phoned the authorities to report him. They thought that she had deep reserves of hostility towards her father and towards Jack Murray. Given the way both men treated her, this also makes sense.

The psychiatrists didn't say so, but it may be that she also felt such hate towards her mother who had physically and emotionally abused her for fourteen years. Gladys had been pretty and slender - as were the girls who Carol helped Doug kill.

The psychiatrists noted that Carol liked to shock and that she would make increasingly outrageous statements until she got their attention. Her remarks were often highly sexual. Again, this isn't surprising given that her father and most of the subsequent men in her life only showed her love when they wanted sex. The desire to shock in this way can also be a form of sadism and Carol clearly had both a strong sadistic and masochistic streak.

Other victims

It's unclear just how many victims that Doug and Carol's sadism claimed - as we've seen, she was charged with two deaths and he was charged with six. Some of the internet crime sites have exaggerated this and state that they 'tortured fifty to death.'

The number fifty has arisen because Carol suggested it in court and because there were approximately this number of corpses found in the area during their 1980 crime spree. It's likely that they killed some of these Jane Does - but they'd have had competition from the many men and occasional other killing couples who take their violence out on highway prostitutes.

Aftermath

Grant Bundy, Carol's ex-husband, killed himself within days of Carol being found guilty, as he knew he had lung cancer. His death left their two sons effectively parentless. They were then sent from foster home to foster home and didn't see their mother again for several years. When one set of foster parents did take them to visit Carol in jail she didn't seem apologetic about sending them away or about beating them or about failing them. She didn't seem as pleased to see them as they'd thought she would be.

Carol continues to see herself as a basically good woman who was briefly in thrall to a bad man. She still says she likes Doug and has told psychiatrists that her father was a good guy with whom she had an intense rapport. She will be eligible for parole in 2012 when she is seventy years old.

12

IT'S MY TURN
Aileen Carol Wuornos strikes back

Aileen was born on 29th February 1956 to Diane Pitman, a seventeen-year-old single parent. Diane had been married to Aileen's father, Leo Pitman, since she was fifteen, but he had left her during the pregnancy. He would later be diagnosed as a paranoid schizophrenic and would become a convicted paedophile, serving time in mental hospitals for sodomising children as young as ten. He would ultimately commit suicide, and be found hanging in his prison cell.

Aileen never met him. She came into the world to find that she already had a year-old brother, Keith. Her young mother found it increasingly hard to cope so when the children were still infants she ran off, leaving them with her emotionally-distant parents, Lauri and Britta. They legally adopted the children and gave them their own surname of Wuornos. (Their parents had been Finnish, hence the unusual name.) The four of them lived in Rochester, Michigan, USA.

The older couple didn't tell Aileen and Keith that Diana was their real mum. Instead they described her as their sister - and this 'sister' figure soon lost touch.

Lauri Wuornos was a heavy drinker and a violent wife-battering man. He also beat the children with a belt and constantly told them that they were evil. He had been in the army and was obsessed with discipline. He was equally cold towards his wife, a timid woman who worked in a supermarket. She failed to intervene when her husband beat the kids. There was clearly a strong humiliation - and possible sexual - aspect to the punishments for he would make little Aileen strip.

The family had few outings and were miserable when couped up together in their poorly heated home. Lauri wouldn't let them open the curtains and the children weren't allowed to bring friends back to the gloomy and draughty house. A photo of Aileen taken at her elementary school shows her as a child with backcombed fair hair and a tensely smiling mouth.

With Lauri now drinking up to three bottles of wine a day and flying into wild rages, she had little to smile about. Britta, her pretend-mother was also drinking during Aileen's formative years but she did so in secret. She was made desperately unhappy by her domineering husband who only allowed her to make one phone call a week.

Aileen was often sent to school inadequately fed so she found concentration difficult. Her eyesight and her hearing were bad, which didn't help. Bored and broke, she and Keith began to start fires for fun, using lighter fuel. Unfortunately the flames set her on fire, badly burning her face. She would bear the scars for the rest of her life, and they would doubtless make her later prostitution more difficult. At the time of the accident she was only six years old.

Aileen Carol Wuornos' sad, loveless life continued. All that she had was her younger brother and the various animals that lived in their dilapidated backyard. She dreamed of being a singer or an actress and tried to block out the sessions of physical - and by now possibly sexual - abuse.

As she moved towards adolescence, she started to offer sexual favours in return for a lunchtime sandwich and a drink. By the time she was twelve she was offering the older boys sexual satisfaction in return for cigarettes and beer. She would also offer sex for mood-altering pills, anything that would take her mind off her real life. Lauri's attitude towards her remained brutal and he was always hitting her and locking her in her room.

Early motherhood

At thirteen or fourteen a male friend of her grandparent's drove her into the woods and raped her. By fourteen she was pregnant. Even today it isn't clear who the father was. Aileen at first claimed it was the rapist's baby, and said that Lauri wouldn't believe that she'd been assaulted and kept calling her a harlot. Then she blamed Lauri himself (his sex life with his wife had seemingly been abysmal) then she said that she'd been having an affair with her older brother, Keith. Whilst it's certainly true that abused siblings sometimes turn to each other for sexual comfort - Rose West used to masturbate one of her younger brothers - people who knew Keith didn't believe that he would have acted in this way.

Whoever the father was, he did not come forward to claim paternity and Aileen was sent to a home for unmarried mothers. There, on the 23rd March 1971, she gave birth to a boy who was immediately put up for adoption. Hopefully he had a better life than the physically and emotionally battered one that his mother had.

A few months later Britta died. The medical explanation was liver cancer, not an unusual death in heavy drinkers, but her daughter Diana suspected that Lauri might have killed her. He certainly threatened to kill Keith and Aileen if they weren't removed from his home.

Diane, Aileen and Keith's natural mother, now said that both teenagers could come and live with her in Texas, but they refused and briefly became wards of court. Aileen soon left, dropped out of school and became a prostitute. Because she had slept with all of the local boys for money she had a very bad reputation and no one wanted to date her so she was very much alone. Keith had also lost his way by this stage and was breaking into various premises and selling the goods he found there in order to feed his increasing dependence on drugs.

In the spring of 1976 their hated grandfather Lauri committed suicide by locking himself in his garage with the car engine running and inhaling the fumes. Aileen didn't attend his funeral. Four months later Keith died of throat cancer. He was only twenty one. Interestingly his father Leo's grandfather had also died of the same disease.

Aileen marries

Twenty-year-old Aileen now had only one remaining relative, her estranged mother Diane. But within weeks the lonely young prostitute would acquire an elderly husband, Lewis Fell. The sixty-nine-year old found her hitchhiking and fell hopelessly in love with her. Aileen at this time still had a good figure and nice hair. To the consternation of Lewis's acquaintances they swiftly married and he bought his new wife jewellery and a car.

But Aileen hadn't had the kind of childhood that makes for a stable marriage partner. She kept on drinking heavily and going out to parties without her elderly husband. She asked for more and more money and when he objected she hit him with his own walking stick. She alleges he hit her back. She also assaulted a bar room attendant, hitting him with a pool cue. She continued to drink and drive. Within weeks Lewis had a restraining order issued against her and she went back on the road as a hitchhiking prostitute.

Divorce and suicide

But by the time the divorce had come through she was financially secure again for her brother Keith had left her ten thousand dollars from a life insurance policy. Again, a more stable young woman would have spent it on a second hand mobile home - but Aileen spent it on a car and duly wrecked it. She spent the rest on drink and drugs and remained homeless, living in abandoned cars or sleeping on the beach.

Sometimes she got work in motels and at other times she waitressed. She kept on drinking with the guys at the biker bars, dressing in leather like they did so that she fitted in. When she couldn't make enough money from soliciting truck drivers she took to petty crime.

Aileen forged cheques and was arrested. She drunkenly breached the peace and was arrested. Then she upped the ante by hitching to Florida and holding up a convenience store. Caught again, she served just over a year in jail for armed robbery. When she was released she tried to commit suicide. A year after leaving prison she was arrested again for cheque forgery.

Various arrests followed over the ensuing months as she stole a car, stole a gun and was stopped for speeding. Officials found her loud and angry and determined to do exactly as she pleased. One man accused her of pointing her gun at him and demanding money, but she denied it and the case apparently didn't go to court.

Aileen acted as if she didn't give a damn about anyone - just as she'd ultimately tried not to show pain as her grandfather beat her. But deep down she wanted to be loved, to have a special person in her life.

The love object

In the summer of 1986, she went to a gay bar in Daytona and met Tyria Moore, who worked as a motel maid. Tyria was an athletic looking twenty-two-year old dressed in shorts and a baseball cap. Aileen was twenty seven and taller, and was looking impressive in one of her leather outfits. Both women had enjoyed previous lesbian relationships.

Tyria - soon shortened to Ty - was a religious woman who wasn't always comfortable with her own sexuality. Her mother had died when she was a toddler so she and Aileen each had lack of maternal love as an added bond. The two blondes talked and drank and had sex that first night. Soon they declared their undying love.

Within days they had rented an apartment together and repainted it. They hung around pool clubs and played the arcades and danced the night away. They drank in the Daytona bars and Aileen often did a few shifts there to bring in some more money. For the first year - as it is with most couples - the sex was particularly intense.

Tyria quit her job for a while. Some sources say this was because she preferred not to work whilst other criminologists suggest that it was at Aileen's insistence because she was jealous of Tyria having fun with her work colleagues. Whatever the reason, Ty stayed home and watched TV and the couple lived off Aileen's prostitution money for a while. She would go to truck stops or hitchhike and spin hard luck stories in order to get a few beers and much-needed dollars. Tyria would cook simple fried meals for them both when Aileen got home.

But the drink and hard life was taking its toll on Aileen - now shortened to Lee - and during the next four years she put on weight, her hair went lank and she became less and less attractive to the punters. The money she could bring in wasn't enough to feed one, far less two of them, so the couple often couldn't afford to rent a room in even the cheapest motel. Tyria was friendly and good at motel work so could have kept employment, but Aileen was sullen and jealous so the pair were often asked to move on.

In some ways this nomadic life suited Aileen as she wanted Tyria to be as rootless as she was. (Tyria had a sister and a father who she kept in touch with.) But at the same time she didn't want to lose her long-term relationship - and it was clear that Tyria wasn't coping well with sleeping in farm outbuildings or in the open air.

The couple constantly fought, sometimes coming to blows that again made them unpopular with motel keepers. Their sex life was over though they still cared deeply for each other. If only they could find enough cash to put a roof over their heads and keep them in much-craved beer.

184

Aileen began to look at the men she pleasured in a different way, noticing their watches and cars and radios. She was only making a few dollars from having sex with them but if she stole everything they had...

The first victim

At the end of November 1989 she got into conversation with Richard Mallory, a fifty one-year-old electrician who ran a Florida repair shop. He was a secretive man who had had numerous failed relationships. He had also served time for rape. He often took off on jaunts in which he visited porn theatres and topless bars so he wasn't reported missing when he didn't return from this latest trip. Mallory was a heavy drinker who was forever sacking his staff so he had many enemies.

He and Aileen drank and talked and drove the highways together for a few hours, then parked in the Daytona Beach woods for a sex party. But whilst they were sitting in the car drinking a bottle of vodka, Aileen shot him three times in the chest and once in the side with her .22 calibre pistol. She pulled him out of the vehicle and went through his pockets, soon emptying his wallet. Finally she covered his body with an old piece of rubber-backed carpet remnant that was conveniently lying on the ground.

She wouldn't have to do any more hooking or hitchhiking again tonight. Aileen swiftly drove away in Richard Mallory's beige Cadillac, taking his watch and camera and other goods with her. The next day she abandoned the vehicle in Volusia County, having wiped away any prints.

Aileen went home and told Tyria what she'd done. The new killer didn't seem upset and even hinted that she'd like to kill another man. Tyria apparently said she didn't want to hear any more.

Richard Mallory's body was found almost a fortnight later on Dec 13th 1989 still wrapped in the carpet. It was fully clothed.

The second victim

In May 1990 she was hitchhiking again when forty three-year old David Spears stopped his truck for her. The heavy equipment operator was heading towards Orlando to see his ex-wife and his daughter, a regular weekend trip. Aileen shot him six times with her .22 and left the body in the woods near Tampa. It wasn't identified until early June. She stole his truck but abandoned it soon afterwards, having ripped the licence plate off.

The third victim

The following month - on 6th June - Aileen flagged down forty-year-old Charles Carskaddon as he drove to Tampa to meet his fiancee. The part time rodeo worker had just landed a new job and was feeling good. At some stage in the journey they stopped and Charles took all of his clothes off. Aileen promptly shot him nine times.

This time she stole his .45 automatic, his money and his jewellery. She also took his car and drove it back to the motel where she and Ty were staying. The next day she dumped the car and it was immediately recovered by the authorities. But by the time Charles' body was found, close to Interstate 15 and just across the state line from Florida, it was badly decomposed.

The fourth victim

Peter Siems was driving towards New Jersey on 7th June to visit relatives. The sixty five year old was heavily involved in a religious organisation and had a stack of Bibles in the car. Aileen had also been interested in religion when she was younger (Britta had taken her to church when she was a child) and had sought out ministers to tell her life story to.

Peter stopped his Sunbird and picked the hitchhiker up. At some stage on the journey she shot him. His body has never been found but police believe it was most likely dumped in a swamp. Again, Aileen took his personal possessions and drove off in his car.

The car crash

On 4th July Aileen and Ty lost control of their vehicle - or, to be more precise, Ty lost control of the Pontiac Sunbird which Aileen had stolen from Peter Siems after shooting him. Both women staggered, bleeding, from the car and tried to put as much distance as possible between themselves and the wreck. A couple saw them running away but Aileen begged them not to call the police. She and Ty ran till they found a water spigot and used it to rinse the blood from their clothes and hair.

When a volunteer fireman stopped them and asked if they had anything to do with the car crash they denied it and said they were going to a fireworks display. Aileen did most of the talking whilst Ty stood holding a cooler filled with beer. The women disappeared into the darkness and were long gone by the time the car was identified as belonging to the missing Peter Siems.

The fifth victim

Eugene Troy Burress, a meat delivery driver aged fifty, was driving towards Daytona when he stopped to pick Aileen up. She shot him once in the back and once in the chest, then covered his body with leaves and stole his cash. Then she drove his truck away, abandoning it shortly afterwards. It was found the next day and his decomposing body was found after five days.

The sixth victim

On 10th or 11th September Richard (Dick) Humphreys, a married child abuse investigator picked Aileen up. The fifty-six-year old was a former police chief. Aileen shot him seven times and stole his car, abandoning it the following week. She also stole several of his personal effects, abandoning others some miles from the murder scene.

The seventh victim

A month later Walter Gino Antonio a sixty-year-old trucker picked her up and they parked in a quiet area to have a sex session. Aileen shot him three times in the back and once in the head with her pistol. The former reserve policeman was found nude except for his socks. She had stolen numerous possessions from his body and his vehicle, including his police badge, handcuffs and gold ring. She also stole his car, leaving it in Brevard County, the next state.

The men who were found nude had apparently prepared for sex - but the bodies showed no sign of sexual activity. Aileen must have shot them all before the act took place. In more than one instance they had been shot in the back, her gender ensuring that even the men with police experience turned away from her, not viewing her as a homicidal threat.

The net closes

Police now went to the papers with sketches of two women seen running from the wrecked car. Over three hundred readers responded. Several phoned in the names of Tyria Moore and her lover Lee (Lee was Alieen's nickname). People gave various surnames for Aileen Wuornos as she had used several aliases.

Meanwhile Aileen had started to pawn her victim's possessions using a false name. In early December 1990 she got cash for Mallory's radar detector and camera. In the same week, albeit in other pawn shops, she got money for Walter Antonio's ring and David Spears tools.

Increasingly anxious about the net closing in, Tyria packed her bags and went to relatives in Ohio whilst Aileen was out buying alcohol. Aileen was desolate. She'd have been even more desolate if she'd known that Ty had phoned the Florida police and told them what her former lover had done.

The police now traced some possessions of the dead man that Aileen had pawned. She'd left her prints on one of the cars that she'd stolen and on a pawn shop receipt - Florida pawn shops insist that you leave your finger or thumb print when pawning possessions. Those prints matched those of Aileen that the police had on file due to her earlier theft-related crimes.

The police began to keep her under surveillance, following her from bar to bar. She bedded down for the night in an old car seat outside the last bar she visited, fittingly called The Last Resort.

The next afternoon two undercover cops who had pretended to befriend her asked if she wanted to come back to their motel and freshen up. She said yes, at which stage she was arrested for an earlier outstanding charge. They didn't want to charge her with murder yet as they hadn't got the weapon or Tyria Moore.

The confession

On 14th January Aileen and Ty spoke on the phone. Police were taping the call to Aileen in prison. Aileen told Ty that she was only in jail for a weapons violation. Ty, in turn, said what the police had told her to say - that she, Ty, was being considered as the killer of the seven men. Ty and Aileen talked again on the phone the next day and the next. 'I'm not going to let you go to jail,' Aileen said, adding 'If I have to confess, I will.' She did so on the 16th of that month.

She said that all of the killings were self defense. She said this more than sixty times during her confession which was videotaped. 'I just got sick of it,' she said to the authorities, 'If I didn't kill all those guys I would have been raped a total of twenty times maybe. Or killed. You never know. But I got them first.' (Seven years later she would admit that this self defence claim was a lie.)

The trial

On 14th January 1992 Aileen went on trial in Florida for the murder of Richard Mallory. The jury comprised five men and seven women. The doctor who had autopsied Mallory said that he had taken up to twenty minutes to die.

Tyria Moore testified that Aileen hadn't seemed upset when she'd told her about killing the electrician. She also said that Aileen hadn't mentioned being assaulted by the man.

The prosecution said that Aileen was a predatory prostitute and added 'She killed out of greed. No longer satisfied with the ten, twenty, thirty dollars, she wanted it all. It wasn't enough to control his body, she wanted the ultimate - his car, his property, his life.'

A week and a half into the trial, Aileen took the stand in her own defence, stating that Mallory had raped, sodomised and tortured her. This contrasted strongly with her earlier taped statement, but she became angry when inconsistencies in her story were pointed out. Occasionally she cried.

The defense said that she was mentally ill, that she had a borderline personality disorder. Borderline adults have invariably been sexually - and usually physically - abused throughout their childhoods and as adults are filled with anxiety, depression and rage. With her nervous energy, suicide attempt and violent outbursts, Aileen perfectly fitted the bill.

Two hours after the summaries, the jury returned to find her guilty of first degree murder. She shouted that she was innocent, adding 'I hope you get raped, scumbags of America!'

The jury recommended that she be sentenced to die in the electric chair. Judge Blount accepted their recommendation on 31st January and she was put on Death Row in Broward County. As she was driven away in a police van, she called out that the cops were the guilty ones. It was a theme she would later return to again and again.

In April she was charged with killing Burress, Humphreys and Spears. The following month she was sentenced to death for those killings. This time she told the judge 'I'll go to heaven now and you will rot in hell.'

She offered to help police find Peter Siems body, but when they took her back to the area she was unable to do so. She has never been charged with his death.

Psychological profile

Aileen's entire life story explains her hostile thinking - abandoned by her mother, brutalised by her grandfather, raped by her grandparent's friend at thirteen and pregnant at fourteen, she had no reason to see the world as a benign place. Then her brother Keith died of throat cancer at a cruelly young age.

A prison psychologist who interviewed Aileen for several days described her as paranoid and said that she believed the world was out to get her. In truth, the little part of the world she knew as a child robbed her of love and trust and innocence - it *was* out to get her and it ruined her totally.

Her experiences of having sex for money for so many years must also have been incredibly destructive. Many men take all of their rage out on prostitutes and the words those girls hear most often are 'Suck it, bitch.'

She clearly didn't feel that she could elevate herself through work, marriage or education, and instead dreamed of becoming a singer or an actress - in other words she had fantasies rather than ambitions. Embryonic serial killers are big on fantasy but don't put in the hard work that actually makes events take place. They've usually been so harshly criticised when they were growing up that they don't feel, deep down, that they have the talent - or even the right - to succeed.

Yet Aileen could have made things happen with her voice, even if it was just as a nightclub singer. People who heard her sing in the Daytona bars said that she sounded good. When drunk, she would tell other drinkers that they'd read of her life story one day. Ironically she would achieve cinematic infamy rather than fame.

Not the first

The TV networks were quick to put the story on celluloid and soon Jean Smart was brilliantly portraying the nervy, fast-drinking Wuornos in the film *Overkill*. Jean Smart is equally believable in portraying Aileen's distress when her lover Ty leaves her. But she's much less ravaged looking than Aileen - and the supposed flashbacks to her childhood show a beautifully dressed little girl with perfect hair and graceful movements, a far cry from the neglected, underfed child she actually was.

The back of the video describes Aileen Wuornos as 'America's first female serial killer' - in truth, other American female serial killers that predate her include Amy Gilligan (who poisoned five husbands and several elderly patients) and Terri Rachels (who lethally injected nine patients) and Jane Toppan, who confessed to over thirty murders again using lethal injections. Some people believe Toppan may actually have caused over a hundred deaths.

Other US female serial killers who pre-date Aileen Wuornos are profiled in this book, namely Genene Jones, Martha Ann Johnson and Judith Neelley. And Carol Bundy (with Doug Clark) and Gwen Graham/Catherine Woods also qualify if you include female serial killers acting as part of a team.

The *Overkill* video description also rewrites history by saying that Aileen was 'deceptive in her elegance' - it seems that they've bought the classic femme fatale image. In reality, Aileen was a tall, tough-looking heavy drinker who hung out at Hell's Angels bars and whose swearing could put a ship's parrot to shame.

The eyes have it

Despite this, one born again Christian decided that Aileen wasn't capable of murder, that it was a set up. She came to this conclusion after seeing photos of the serial killer and allegedly reading her eyes. This woman said that she wished she could set the seven-times-killer free, but settled for formally adopting her.

At least one feminist writer suggested that Aileen was in jail for daring to be openly homosexual and said that she had only shot the seven men to defend herself. And an Aileen Wuornos Defense Group was formed, also claiming that she had been wrongly convicted, that each death she'd caused was indeed self defense. Websites told surfers how they could write to her and support her. Presumably these parties were embarrassed when she ultimately told the truth...

Update

Seven years after she was sentenced to death, Aileen Wuornos gave an interview from prison (broadcast on the internet via Court TV) in which she admitted that she'd made her self defense claim up. She said that Mallory, the first victim, had started talking to her as if she was a guy. He'd told her that he'd served time for rape - and hearing this had made her decide to kill him. 'It was situational insanity,' she said to the interviewer. The words sound wrong for her, like textbook psychology that she's read or been told by someone else.

She says, truthfully, 'I have been so stepped on,' and admits that she was a prostitute from the age of sixteen. She says that she went to churches for help but that they wouldn't assist her because she wasn't part of their congregation. She tried to become a police officer when she was twenty but they turned her down. The inference is that she had no option but to kill the seven men - but at one stage she'd had money from her brother's estate and she'd had a wealthy husband. She hadn't had many breaks, but she'd had some.

She says 'you can't rejuvenate me.' She probably means can't rehabilitate her. She alleges that at the time of the shootings she was drinking between six and twelve beers daily and that the victims 'just fell like a sack of potatoes.' At the time, she explains she was working eight to twelve hours a day on the highways, soliciting five days a week. Ty, her lover, would have two days off and Aileen would take the same days off to be with her. By the end of 1989 she wasn't making good money any more so shooting the victims gave her access to their belongings, which she pawned or sold.

'I'm extremely sorry this happened' she says rather than using the more direct and responsible 'I'm extremely sorry I did this.' But she doesn't look sorry - its clear that her grandfather beat all normal feeling out of her years ago.

Throughout the interview, she frequently repeats her claim that the police were trailing her for five months but didn't immediately arrest her because they were in the throes of organising a book and movie deal. She's been told that certain film producers were only interested in a female serial killer - so Wuornos believes the police wanted to make sure she murdered several times.

There's some truth in her story - Nick Broomfield, the documentary film maker produced a film on the subject called *The Selling Of A Serial Killer*. (Not seen by this author.) He found that the police planned to sell Hollywood exclusive rights to their investigations and that talks on the subject were held a month before her arrest. He also alleges that anyone who wants to interview Aileen has to pay various people who know her and others within the judiciary.

'You got some dangerous cops out there,' Aileen says in her Court TV interview. She also suggests, passing the buck, that 'law enforcement let me become a serial killer' and that 'they need to care about God and righteousness.'

Her religious conversion runs through much of her speech. 'I believe I'm totally saved and forgiven by Jesus Christ,' and 'I'm totally, totally into Jesus Christ.' She adds that there are angels waiting for her on the other side.

Meanwhile, life on Death Row is far from heavenly. She claims she's had 'sonic pressure running through my cell for like three years' and '4800 food trays tainted since 1994' and that love drove her to crime. In truth, hate drove her to crime.

She does not come over as likeable - but in fairness she has not been raised to believe she is likeable. Her speech is drawling, simplistic and often repetitive. Her Defense Attorney claims that Aileen has the emotional level of a child aged two to three. She is currently working her way through the appeals process but if her appeals fail she will probably go to the electric chair by 2007.

13

KARMA CHAMELEON

The public and private sides of Karla Leanne Homolka

Karla was born on the 4th May 1970 by Caesarean section, the first child of Karel and Dorothy Homolka. Karel was a Czech refugee who had been moved from school to school by his travelling farmworker father. His parents had fled from Czechoslovakia to Canada when he was seven to escape its communist regime. A handsome, small built man, he settled in Ontario with his wife Dorothy, a Canadian citizen. The couple - and many of their relatives - initially inhabited a trailer park.

The early years were financially uncertain ones as Mr Homolka originally ran a picture-framing business with his relatives. Dorothy had given up her secretarial job to be a full time mother to baby Karla. Dorothy was an excellent household manager as she had run her parent's household as a child after her mother became seriously ill.

Now she found that her beautiful blonde-haired and blue-eyed daughter Karla had asthma which tended to come on when she got over excited. As a result, she was often hospitalised at Christmas and other special events.

Mr Homolka had very little formal education and even after many years residing in Canada his grasp of spoken English remained volatile. His salary was equally variable so he and Dorothy had a financially unstable early marriage. But when he started selling velvet paintings and costume jewellery outside shopping malls his fortunes improved.

The increase in income allowed the couple to plan for another baby, so two years after Karla's birth they had a second blonde-haired daughter whom they called Lori. And three years after that they had a third equally blonde baby girl, Tammy Lyn. Lori and Tammy also had asthma but it didn't prevent them or their older sister Karla from taking part in numerous school activities. Tammy would eventually be one of three girls to die at Karla's hand...

When Karla was almost eight her parents moved the family to a small house with an outdoor pool in a nice area. She was given her own room to which she would occasionally bring a friend. The house and garden were often filled with the Homolka's neighbours who they got on well with. An animal lover, Karla soon acquired two cats, two rabbits and various hamsters. From an early age she was interested in being a vet.

Her father had now taken a job with a lighting company and was often away on the road selling lighting fixtures. When he was home he sometimes withdrew into himself and his daughter Lori would later suggest that he needed help. Karla certainly saw her mother as the stronger and more energised character - Dorothy arranged pool parties and cleaned and baked. Dorothy also confided to a friend that she was glad that her husband Karel was away a lot as he exhausted her with his frequent demands for sex.

School days

Karla was quiet at junior school and considered something of a loner. She favoured pretty frilly dresses and her contemporaries thought she had a princess-like, Alice In Wonderland look. She excelled at English and got over eighty percent for many subjects. She loved to play at - and draw - houses and adored her dolls. She had a stay-at-home mother during these years so clearly saw the house as the woman's domain.

Some of her peers remember her as being attention seeking, understandable in a family where all three daughters looked increasingly alike and had similar sporting interests. Several family photos show the blonde Homolka girls smiling for the camera but their faces look tense and Lori's nails were bitten to the quick.

Karla's teenage years

By senior school Karla enjoyed drama and skating, subjects which got her noticed. She also joined the French club and did well at the language as her IQ of circa 130 put her in the top two percent of the populace. Yet when she tried out for the choir she was so shy - or so determined to be noticed as different - that she made all her classmates turn their chairs to face the other way. Teachers would remember her as bright, non-conformist and intense and her fellow students would concur that she was different and slightly weird.

After twelve years at home, Dorothy went back to work, taking a job as a hospital administrator, work which brought home a regular paycheck. Unfortunately Karel made it clear to some of her co-workers that he fancied them and suggested he'd be willing to leave his wife. And according to a source in Stephen William's impressively detailed book on the case, *Invisible Darkness*, Dorothy suggested that a threesome - herself, the woman that Karel fancied and Karel - might save the Homolkas rocky relationship.

By now Karel's daughters were sometimes calling him names, perhaps safe in the knowledge that English wasn't his first language. Karla herself would later hint to psychiatrists that her father wasn't too bright - and in a letter she'd refer to both her parents as assholes. In general, she now talked too much and seemed even more obsessed with her appearance than other teenagers. She would spend hours talking dramatically on the telephone to her more conservative friends. The schoolgirl Karla's punk-dyed hair, monochrome clothes and multiple earrings gave the illusion of confidence - but there was increasing uncertainty at home.

Karla's father had always enjoyed a drink so the house was full of alcohol and friends were offered it on every occasion. But he increasingly went on drinking binges, many of which would last all day. Karla's schoolfriend Kevin would hear from Karla that the house was in a state of almost constant tension, with her father brooding or both parents arguing. Young Karla found the shouting matches distressing and often phoned Kevin in tears. She also told other friends that she wanted to leave home as soon as possible and spoke of university as a way out.

That said, Karla would go to her father if her mother refused her anything. But when he'd been drinking he'd misinterpret whatever she said and would become verbally abusive. At one stage she reported that he'd called her a whore - and his joking name for his own wife was 'the old bitch.' It's not known if Karla was physically chastened by either parent but after one argument with her father she tearfully phoned a friend and admitted she'd locked herself in her room.

A cry for help

When she was sixteen or seventeen she showed faint marks on her wrists to schoolfriends and admitted that she'd cut herself because sometimes she didn't want to live. Friends put this down to attention seeking - and psychiatrists would later describe her personality as histrionic, borderline. Karla had been brought up in a home where the lack of money was always a topic for discussion - so now she wanted to marry a rich man who would buy her a big house and many other material things. She and her sisters continued to suffer from asthma, and there's often an emotional component to this.

Beginning to rebel, Karla's favourite song became *Fight For Your Right To Party*, possibly because her parents preferred her to bring her friends home rather than for her to go out on the town where they couldn't keep an eye on her. Her father was protective towards all three of his beautiful daughters, referring to them as 'his girls.' But Karla was now a young woman who wore handcuffs on her jacket as a fashion statement and who toyed with the idea of becoming a detective. She needed an identity - and a man - of her own.

Meeting Paul

Whilst still a schoolgirl, Karla had taken part time work in a pet store and was very good at it. She seemed to love the animals she was selling, and made sure that they were properly exercised, watered and fed. Indeed, her boss was so impressed that he sent her to an out of town Pets Convention with a female friend.

The convention took place in October 1987 and involved an excited Karla staying in a hotel overnight. She wanted to make the most of this unusual freedom, so flirted heavily when she met tall, blonde and handsome Paul Barnardo and his friend in the hotel's coffee bar. The two men made a habit of cruising around and picking up girls and the charming Paul enjoyed far more conquests than the average male.

Karla was a seventeen-year-old schoolgirl who looked younger than her years, Paul a trainee accountant aged twenty three who liked very young teenagers. Karla and her friend and Paul and his friend talked, laughed and eventually went up to the girls' room. Someone put off the light and within moments Karla and Paul were having sex on top of her bed. The other couple lay there in embarrassed silence listening to over three hours of enthusiastic coupling sounds before everyone eventually fell asleep.

Paul was Karla's second lover and she fell hard, telling friends that she'd fallen in love with him the moment she set eyes on him. He was physically attractive and superficially charming and they were sexually very compatible and willing to experiment. They made a striking couple, both tanned and blonde and sometimes dressed in identical T-shirts. She was tiny and classically feminine-looking whilst he was broad shouldered and tall.

Beauty hides the beast

But behind Paul's handsome face and fit body lurked a hatred of women. It was a hatred that had been sculpted from years of abuse from his completely dysfunctional family. His parents wouldn't allow any of his childhood friends into the house - and his mother's idea of a family meal was to open a tin of macaroni. Yet the family were affluent, spending money on nice cars and a big house.

Ken, who Paul originally thought was his father, would veer between ignoring him and shouting at him. Ken hit all three of the children if they took a few seconds to respond to his commands and Marilyn screamed at them with the slightest provocation. She became increasingly hypochondriacal, though - unlike most toxic parents - she ultimately had the courage to seek psychiatric help. But one day in a fit of rage she told Paul than Ken wasn't his biological father, but the result of an affair she had had.

In some ways, Paul should have been glad as by now Ken had been exposed as a Peeping Tom and would later be convicted of sexually abusing a minor. But Paul had admired Ken's immaculate dress sense and his success in accountancy and was desolate to find out that a stranger was his real dad.

Ken often made derogatory remarks about women and Paul now began to do the same. By his late teens he was talking of how much he'd like to rape a girl and said he dreamed of setting up a 'Virgin Farm' where young girls would do whatever he desired.

He started making obscene phone calls to a friend's ex-girlfriend in 1986, the calls eventually being traced by the police. Paul then had a restraining order placed on him. Soon his activities would escalate into much more serious crimes. He committed his first rape, of a girlfriend, several months before meeting Karla, and would go on to rape many others, becoming known in the Canadian press as the Scarborough Rapist. He pounced on his victims as they walked home through Scarborough's darkened streets.

Paul and Karla's early relationship

At first Paul wooed the teenage Karla with flowers and cuddly toys. He also ingratiated himself with her family until they started referring to him as the son they had never had. Paul lived an almost two hour drive away from Karla's house and was soon exhausted by driving back and forward between the two houses, so her parents invited him to start sleeping over each weekend on the settee.

One source suggests that Karla couldn't talk to her mother about sex so Paul had to sneak into her bedroom when the rest of the family were sleeping. Another source says that Dorothy knew Paul stayed in Karla's room and would tap on the door to alert him each morning so that he was out of there before Mr Homolka came downstairs.

What is certain is that the couple were having increasingly adventurous sex. Karla had worn handcuffs on her jacket as a fashion statement and now invited Paul to use them on her. Later he asked her to buy a dog chain which he would tighten around her neck whilst they made love.

Karla clearly found this powerplay exciting and started to refer to Paul as her 'big, bad businessman' but when she told her school girl friends they were shocked. Like most teenagers they were somewhat puritanical and harsh in judging others, and decided that the couples roleplay was unnatural. But at this stage Karla and Paul's sexual games were consensual and they weren't hurting anyone else.

As the months passed, this was to change. Like most sadists, Paul was looking for his girlfriend's Achilles heel, finding out facts with which he could belittle her. He found it when Karla admitted that she wasn't a virgin, having had sex with a previous boyfriend after he'd left the area and she'd taken a plane to spend a weekend with him. Karla slept with this youth at the first opportunity, just as she did with Paul. When free of her parental home she was desperate to forge an early intimacy with any good-looking man.

Paul told Karla that her loss of virginity was a fault, something that she could literally rectify by offering him her virgin rectum. She did so, though she found it painful. Later she would lick his anus whilst masturbating him and would repeat the words that most aroused him. 'I'm your little cock-sucker. I'm your little slut. I'm your little cunt.'

Paul had also began to criticise other things about pretty and slender Karla. Leastways, she started to write herself demeaning self-improvement lists. Friends saw these lists and were horrified that the formerly outspoken teenager was becoming so self-conscious. One such list included the words 'Remember you're stupid. Remember you're ugly. Remember you're fat.'

She also wrote a reminder to herself to never let anyone know that the relationship was less than perfect. In this, she may have been mimicking her parents, for some people were only shown the Homolkas behaving like the perfect family, and mainly heard about the underlying discord second hand.

Karla's first goal in life was to get married, and she told all of her school-friends that she was desperate to become Mrs Barnardo. She seemed to see the state of matrimony as the most important thing in the world - rather than the quality of the marriage, the genuine love for each other that a couple can have.

That said, she did seem to love Paul in a typically over-the-top teenage way, sending him a note that said 'You're a dream come true.' Later in that same note she became sexually explicit: 'You know what I love? Having you stick it inside me and making me gasp for air when my parents are in the next room. I love it when you shoot it into my mouth. I want to swallow every drop and then some. The power you wield over me is indescribable... With you in my life I feel complete. Whole.'

The engagement

Whilst still at school she started dropping huge hints to Paul about want-ing an engagement ring. He obliged by buying a large expensive one which

Karla showed off at every opportunity. Needless to say, this gave her added status amongst her schoolfriends, most of whom thought that Paul was a fantastic catch. A few of the more mature girls realised that he was more talk than action - but the majority were impressed by his good looks, nice car and expensive clothes. Paul was an immature twenty-something who got on well with impressionable teenagers. Lori's teenage boyfriend would originally be impressed by Paul.

Karla now gave up her plans to go to university because Paul didn't want her to. That meant giving up her dream of leaving her parents home and studying to become a veterinary surgeon. For years she had spoken of university as a way out - but now her friends said she saw Paul as her means of escape. The little asthmatic girl who had loved drawing houses was now a shallow teenager who longed for a beautiful house of her own.

Ironically, she was letting less and less of her life remain her own. Early on in the relationship Paul had suggested she stop dying her multi-coloured hair, stop cutting it and let it return to its natural blonde. This she did, even though she tired of it being so long and unmanageable. He also disapproved of her punk-style clothes so soon she was wearing soft sweaters and adopting the preppy style she'd once mocked. Paul loathed overweight and badly dressed women like his mother, so Karla became extra careful about what she wore and ate. Later she would become a much stronger character but for now she was hellbent on pleasing her man, on maintaining the relationship.

Karla left school and found herself a job at a vetinary surgery. She loved the work and her employer was very impressed by her skills, noting she was equally good at working in every aspect of animal health care. But she had to get up early every day to take the bus to work because Paul didn't want her to learn to drive. Her fiance was showing increasing signs of being a control freak - and Karla was letting herself be controlled.

The next three years passed in this way with the couple enjoying lavish nights out with friends or sipping cocktails around the Homolka's poolside. There were many good times - invariably captured on video - but whenever they had an argument Karla would end up backing down and writing Paul an incredibly obsequious note. Like Carol Bundy, profiled earlier, Karla was determined to maintain her relationship against all the odds.

Sacrificing a sister

Like most embryonic serial killers, Paul had quickly tired of ordinary sex and found it increasingly difficult to maintain an erection with his by now twenty-year-old girlfriend, Karla. As such immature men often do, he turned his attention to increasingly young girls - and Karla's little sister Tammy fitted the bill.

Tammy, fifteen, had something of a crush on him, as did many of her school friends. After all, Paul was a six foot tall handsome man with an easy - if superficial - charm. Tammy, with her long blonde hair and wide smile looked very much like a younger Karla, a fact that Paul exploited by getting Karla to dress up in Tammy's clothes. Karla would murmur that her name was Tammy and that she was a virgin, an image that would stimulate Paul into having sex.

Paul also started standing beside Tammy's bed and masturbating whilst the teenager slept. Karla stood as look-out in the door, her main concern being that her parents didn't wake up and find out. She was showing what one psychiatrist would later term a 'moral vacuity' and didn't seem to see this as a violation of her sister's rights.

By late 1990 the couple had been dating for three years and Paul's interest in Karla seemed to have waned. It's possible that she tolerated Paul's interest in her younger sister because it allowed her to keep him in her home. There they raced around with the camcorder that Karla had purchased, videoing all of the Homolkas who were drinking cocktails and eating snacks. Paul was actually dating other women in his home town and having rough sex with them, something Karla probably suspected or even knew.

One day Paul took Tammy out with him to buy alcohol, a twenty minute journey. The pair didn't return for six hours and when they did Paul admitted that he'd been kissing the younger girl and fooling around.

It's likely that Karla was very jealous - though she would later deny that in court when challenged about her motivation for setting up her sister. Karla said that Paul kept badgering her to fix it so that he could take Tammy's virginity and that he nagged on and on until she agreed.

Because of Karla's work at the vets, she had access to animal pharmaceuticals. She read up on the subject and brought home Halcion tablets, which she and Paul ground into a powder. Then they asked Tammy if she wanted to stay up late with them and watch a horror video. Desperate to feel more grown-up, the girl agreed. It was Christmas Eve and Tammy's virginity was to be Karla's festive gift to Paul. The couple mixed cocktails for the entire family but only put the drug into the innocent teenager's drink.

Lori went to bed first, followed by Karla's parents. They saw that Tammy looked tired - and that her speech was slurred - and suggested she also retire for the night, but she mumbled that she wanted to stay up and watch the movie. Paul then gave her a further drink containing a sleeping draught and she slipped into a deep sleep or actual unconsciousness.

Karla then fetched a container of Halothane, a powerful animal anaesthetic that she'd also stolen from her boss. She soaked a rag with it and held it to her sister's nose and mouth. Halothane is normally inhaled with the careful use of monitoring equipment but Karla was just guessing the dose. Through the rape and sexual assault which followed, she would give her fifteen-year-old sister six times the amount used to knock out a large dog.

As a vet's assistant, Karla must also have known that animals - and people - musn't eat or drink before being given an anaesthetic as the risk of vomiting and choking are considerable. Moreover, one of Halothane's side effects was that it could cause nausea. Poor Tammy had been eating pasta and drinking alcohol so she was clearly at risk.

Paul got the camcorder, switched it on and put it on the floor next to the unconscious fifteen-year-old. 'Put on a condom,' Karla said, still holding the rag over her sister's face. Paul ignored her request and began to undress the helpless teenager. He began to rape the girl, with Karla - whose only concern seemed to be her parent's fury - constantly telling him to hurry up.

Paul then turned the girl over and sodomised her - the drugs had relaxed her sphincter muscles and made penetration easy. After he withdrew he told Karla to suck on Tammy's breasts, the camcorder capturing the entire assault. Paul then told her to perform oral sex on the teenager and when Karla refused because Tammy was menstruating he pushed her head down between Tammy's legs. The video continued, with Paul demanding that Karla digitally enter her sister. She did and he asked her how her blood-covered finger tasted. 'Fucking disgusting,' she says, pulling a face.

It's clear that Karla doesn't want to taste Tammy's menstrual blood yet she's indifferent to Paul raping and sodomising the younger girl.

Karla now held the camera whilst Paul raped and sodomised the teenager a second time. He then withdrew saying that he thought something was wrong, that she'd stopped breathing. When they turned Tammy over her face had turned blue. 'Oh my God, I think I just killed my sister,' Karla shrieked.

The couple tried to resuscitate the girl, dressed her, moved her to another room and called the emergency services. They - and others - noticed a red mark around Tammy's nostrils, her mouth and even on her left shoulder, as if she'd vomited some caustic agent up. When asked, Karla and Paul said that it must be a rug burn because they'd dragged her into another room where the light was better in order to resuscitate her. This made no sense as they wouldn't have dragged her face down.

Dorothy, Karel and Lori got up when the police and ambulance arrived and were told that Tammy had stopped breathing. Medics worked hard to get her heart started again. In shock, the Homolkas followed their comatose youngest daughter to the hospital.

Meanwhile a policeman stopped Karla from putting a comforter that Tammy had been lying on, and which might be needed as evidence, into the washing machine. The couple gave statements - which said that they'd been watching a movie and suddenly noticed Tammy had stopped breathing - then they were allowed to go.

Tammy died the next day. In the interim period, Karla didn't tell the medics that she'd given the teenager powerful veterinary drugs. Perhaps this knowledge would have enabled the hospital staff to save her. The subsequent autopsy ruled that the death was accidental, that Tammy Lyn had choked on her own vomit. The fact that she'd been drugged and menstruating presumably hid the telltale signs that she'd been raped anally and vaginally by twenty-six-year old Paul.

Strangely, the autopsy didn't show anything untoward, though the red burn mark on Tammy's face, neck and shoulder remained inexplicable. Death was put down to Tammy choking on her own vomit after imbibing a little alcohol. Despite the makeup skills of the morticians, the mark was still visible when she lay in her open casket on her burial day. The fact that Karla, her big sister, had been present the entire time that Paul and Tammy were together presumably stopped the authorities from suspecting foul play.

Home sweet home

After Tammy's death, the Homolkas wanted their home to themselves in order to complete their grieving. Karel Homolka had taken the death especially badly and was unable to go to work. And Lori, who had told Karla and Paul not to give Tammy any more alcohol that night, no longer wanted Paul in the house.

The Homolkas asked Paul to go back to his parents, a place he hated. He agreed to leave but then Karla said she was leaving too. Later she'd say that she only went to stop Paul telling her parents the truth about Tammy's death - but this doesn't make sense as he was enjoying life with his various girlfriends and had no wish to confess and go to jail.

The Homolkas also suggested that Karla and Paul postpone their wedding, as they could no longer afford it. They similarly went around telling everyone that they couldn't afford Tammy's funeral - but within weeks Dorothy had got herself a new car and Karel purchased a new van. But a determined Karla had spent the last three years dreaming of her wedding day, and refused to cancel it.

In late January they moved into their new house, a palatial residence that they got for a reasonable rent because the owner's didn't want it left vacant. Karla would write to a friend at length about the house's decor, a letter which was in turns vain and superficial or filled with rage at the fact that she and Paul were now paying for their wedding by themselves.

Yet she and Paul weren't totally oblivious to the horror that they'd caused. Both lost weight after Tammy's death and Paul behaved very strangely at the funeral, stroking the dead girl's hair and crooning how much he'd loved her. Karla would later say that she knew she could never leave Paul now because they shared this terrible secret between them - and if he told her parents they might never speak to her again.

Not that, to friends, it looked as if she wanted to leave her attractive fiance. She continually wrote to them about how brilliant Paul was, conveniently forgetting that he often chatted up other women in her presence and that he was increasingly calling her names. He even called her a bitch in front of her parents - but his tone was light and no one remarked on it.

If appearances were indeed everything to Karla, you'd have expected her to leave now that Paul had started to belittle her in public. Instead, she seemed to blame herself for each supposed fault that he found in her and wrote him notes of apology almost every day. She would tell him again and again that she loved him and that he was her master, he was the king.

But the king soon failed his accountancy exams because he partied when he should have been studying. Paul then gave up work rather than resit the exams, telling anyone who would listen that he was going to become a rap singer instead. He was showing the classic serial killer traits; an underachiever with majestic plans. Karla seems to have bought into her fiance's latest boast, so that it became a shared delusion, and began telling friends that he'd soon top the charts.

Paul now made his money solely from smuggling cheap American cigarettes into Canada, something he'd done part time for several years. He often took Karla with him so that they looked like two young people crossing to the states for a special evening's romance. He also went smuggling with a male friend and kept the authorities from becoming suspicious by constantly changing their vehicle's number plates.

Paul would go out late at night and steal new plates, peeping into girl's windows on these journeys and watching them undressing. (Just as Ken, the man he'd originally thought of as his father, had done.) He told Karla about some of these escapades, but she didn't seem to mind. At least one writer has suggested that she was happy as long as he stayed with her, sharing his erotic fantasies rather than acting them out alone. On the surface, Karla had what she desired - a good looking man and a pretty house in an excellent neighbourhood.

Paul was bringing lots of smuggling money to the relationship but he spent as freely as he made, often picking up the restaurant tab when they went out for expensive meals with other couples. He bought designer clothes and state of the art stereo equipment, went on exotic holidays and enjoyed fine wines. Eventually he ran up such huge bills on all of his credit cards that he had to declare himself bankrupt. Now the only official income they had was Karla's wage. Her upwardly mobile accountant had become an unemployed bankrupt smuggler, yet still she stayed by him and made increasingly lavish wedding plans.

Three weeks after Tammy's death, the couple videoed themselves naked in Karla's house and Karla was heard to say 'I loved it when you fucked my little sister.' She added that she felt proud and happy when he raped Tammy, that they could abduct a girl every weekend. Karla had discovered that she enjoyed lesbian sex with an unconscious victim and knew that it made her daring - and hopefully irresistible - in Paul's eyes.

The second rape victim

In the summer of 1991 Karla delivered another virgin to Paul in the form of a fifteen-year-old girl whom she'd known when she worked at the pet store. Tammy had died after being drugged by Karla - yet Karla was prepared to drug this unsuspecting teenager for Paul to rape and for herself to enjoy. She gave their visitor the same drugs and anaesthetic that she'd given her little sister, knowing that one of the side effects was vomiting as described in her work's animal compendium. The unconscious girl was then raped by Paul and sexually assaulted by Karla, the camcorder recording the entire event.

Karla is seen to finger the girl, a virgin - and was later to clean the blood off her before she woke up. When the girl awoke she hurt all over and thought she had flu. She had no reason to suspect her older friend Karla, a fellow animal lover, who treated her in a sisterly way.

Just prior to staging this rape, Karla had found out that Paul was dating another woman and he'd admitted he was thinking of breaking off their engagement. It's possible that she brought him this new virgin to keep him close to home.

But another video shows her drugging a young girl by herself at a time when the courts would later determine Paul wasn't present. Karla holds the cloth drenched with anaesthetic over the already drugged teenager's face and is seen to reapply it frequently. She caresses the teenager's body and inserts the unconscious fingers into her own vagina. She clearly enjoys having a helpless girl to use as a masturbatory aid.

The second murder victim

Paul would procure the next teenager for himself whilst Karla slept - but she would take part in various assaults on the terrified fourteen-year-old. Paul found the girl by chance when he went driving in a different area, planning to steal yet another set of car number plates.

He parked and started wandering around a nice housing estate. It was around 3 am so he was surprised to find a schoolgirl, Leslie Mahaffy, sitting outside her house in the darkness. They got chatting and she admitted that her parents had locked her out for not keeping to her curfew and that she was too scared to wake them up.

After a few minutes she asked for a cigarette and Paul said he had some in his car. She followed the handsome man back to his vehicle, but was cautious when he invited her to sit inside. She sat on the front seat but kept her legs on the ground outside. It was then that Paul produced the knife and told her to get into the vehicle properly if she didn't want to die. (She'd have been more likely to survive if she'd screamed loudly and struggled hard at this moment rather than risk being driven to a quiet place of the abductor's choice.)

Leslie immediately complied with her abductor's demands and was driven to the pretty home that Paul shared with Karla. He went upstairs, woke his fiancee and told her of his new trophy, Karla's main comment was 'Did anybody see you?' She would later admit that she soon went back to sleep. Again and again Karla's behaviour would show that her conscience was completely missing. She lacked the ability to empathise, a classic psychopathic trait.

Later Karla joined Paul in the room where he was keeping the terrified teen. The constantly-blindfolded Leslie, who had by now been raped by Paul multiple times, was glad at first to hear a female voice and asked Karla to help her. But Karla merely held the camcorder whilst the teenager was sodomised.

Karla also helped Lesley into position so that the kidnapped teenager could give Paul analingus. A few minutes after that, with Paul still directing, Karla performed oral sex on the naked child. She would later say that the younger girl was acting on automatic pilot, clearly trying to distance her mind from the ordeal.

Leslie repeatedly asked to go home, saying that she missed her baby brother. She swore that she hadn't seen what they looked like and said she couldn't remember anything about the car that had brought her to their home.

As she couldn't identify Karla and had only seen Paul for a few moments, they could, in theory, have let her go - but at this moment (Karla would later say) Paul confessed to her that he was the man known as the Scarborough Rapist. This rapist had been responsible for vaginally and anally raping numerous women. One woman had seen Paul's face and as a result a police artist had produced a good likeness which was reproduced in all the local papers. Some people who knew Paul - and had heard him talk misogynistically on many occasions - had then anonymously phoned the police suggesting it was him. Paul had been taken in for questioning and had given body samples. He knew the net was closing in.

By sheer chance it would take police two years to test all of the samples they'd taken from potential suspects, so Paul was to remain free for that period. But ultimately if the same DNA was found in semen in Leslie's body it would point to him.

Paul wanted to keep Leslie as a teenage sex slave for as long as possible as he was enjoying himself. But Karla's parents were due at their house for dinner forty-eight-hours after the kidnapping so Karla wanted the girl out of the way before then.

Left alone with Karla whilst Paul was out buying them all a takeaway, Leslie pleaded for her life, saying that the two of them could escape together. She added that she'd tell the police that only Paul was responsible, that he'd forced Karla to participate.

As a supposed mercy act, Karla gave Leslie two sedatives and handed her a teddy bear to hold. When the teenager was suitably drugged, Paul allegedly returned and entered the room holding an electric cord. Leslie's actual murder wasn't recorded on the camcorder so the details aren't fully known and are still a source of discord. What is certain is that Lesley died that day at either Paul or Karla's hand.

Karla would say that Paul strangled the girl, that she revived and that he re-strangled her, but the body would show few signs of pressure on the neck to confirm this. Paul would claim that he came back from buying the takeaway to find that Karla had murdered Leslie, claiming that the girl had tried to run away. Bruising found in the deep tissue would suggest that someone of approximately Karla's size could have knelt on the girl's back, pushing her head into a cushion to suffocate her.

The corpse would remain in the basement whilst everyone enjoyed a home cooked meal at Paul and Karla's house. The young couple chatted happily to Karla's parents and gave no sign that anything was amiss.

Dismemberment

Two days after Leslie's death Karla and Paul dismembered the teenager's body. She would deny taking part in this - but she had attended animal autopsies and knew how to cut up a cadaver. Karla had written to a friend saying how 'neat' it was to amputate puppies tails without anaesthetic and she later cut up their pet iguana after Paul killed it, barbecued it and ate it with him and her friends.

One or both of the couple cut up Leslie's corpse with an electric saw, then put each section into a box which Paul filled with concrete. The hair was sticking out of the concrete block containing the head so he painted it black to make it look less conspicuous. Finding he had some unused concrete left over, he took it back to the store and got a refund then realised that the concrete - and its bloody cargo - might be traced back to him.

That night he and Karla drove to a stretch of water and threw the blocks over the bridge. They assumed that they'd sink forever. But within a few weeks the water at that particular point would become shallow and fisherman would make a very grisly find...

Till death us do part

On 17th June 1991 Karla married Paul in an expensive and showy white wedding. As they celebrated, a concrete block containing the torso of Leslie Mahaffy was found by a fisherman. The police rushed to pull other blocks containing her head and butchered limbs from the lake. They knew that carrying the blocks would have required two people, but presumed the killers were both men.

Karla looked beautiful on her wedding day and Paul looked composed and handsome. Her father, in contrast, was clearly still grief stricken over Tammy's death and mentioned her during his speech. Paul's mother caused a scene about the menu and Paul told her to fuck off.

Some friends of Karla's would later state that she had a bruised left arm at the ceremony - and that they'd seen other bruises on her back when she was fitted for her wedding dress. But Karla would shrug these off as injuries sustained at the vets whilst trying to control large dogs.

The couple set off on their honeymoon, taking the inevitable camcorder with them. Karla would later state that she was beaten during this period - but videos show her dressed in a bikini without visible marks and on her return she told friends that the honeymoon had been brilliant. On the videotapes she looks happy and relaxed and not at all afraid of Paul, at one stage telling him she's bored with being filmed. She appears in another video whilst he's out of the room declaring her undying love for him.

The third murder

After their return, boredom soon set in. Karla would work and Paul would lie around the house thinking up rap lyrics that suggested he was superior to the rest of the planet. The couple bought themselves a Rottweiler puppy - but Karla really wanted a baby and told friends she'd get pregnant as soon as Paul earned more cash. Both of them seemed to see him as a top ten recording artiste but he didn't even contact any record companies and would later admit that the songs were mainly in his head. The couple told neighbours that Paul was still an accountant, so many assumed he was free-lance as he was so clearly homebased.

Karla would smile at the neighbours as she walked Buddy, the loveable puppy. She was always beautifully dressed, with her hair immaculate. Paul wasn't seen in the neighbourhood so often but when he was he'd be talking ostentatiously into his mobile phone.

The couple's sex life continued to go downhill, with Paul finding it harder and harder to maintain an erection and achieve orgasm. They consequently decided to kidnap another sex slave for them both to enjoy. For several weeks they drove around looking for a likely suspect. Then one rainswept afternoon - 16th April 1992 - they saw a schoolgirl walking home on her own.

Karla called the girl over to the car. She was fifteen and her name was Kristen French. She had long hair and a wide smile, just like Leslie Mahaffy and like Karla. She was a bright and athletic teenager from a loving home.

Kristen walked over to the vehicle and Karla used the pre-arranged ploy of asking for directions. Karla then stepped out of the car and spread a map across the roof. As the fifteen-year-old stepped closer to the vehicle. Paul rushed round and tried to bundle her inside. Karla helped.

The girl fought valiantly - a woman driving past thought that she saw three people pretending to fight - but was no match for two strong adults. When she was in the front seat, Karla grabbed her hair from the backseat and held it firmly as Paul drove to their home.

They dragged their victim into the house and Karla went around hiding all the phones so that Kristen couldn't call anyone. The teenager was then raped and sodomised by Paul.

Later Karla joined in the abuse which they, as usual, captured on video. Karla can be seen undressing Kristen and performing cunnilingus on her. She runs her hands over the girl as if inspecting her. When she says 'You're a pretty girl' her voice is hoarse with desire - a desire that intensifies when Kristen is made to go down on her. She can also be heard telling the fifteen-year-old when to suck Paul, how to move her hand up and down his penis and so on.

This sexual assault was to continue for the next three days, with the violence intensifying. The teenager was punched in the back by Paul and had her hair pulled when she didn't fulfil his every command. He was trying to live out his fantasies word for word and became enraged if she said some of the right words in the wrong order. Drugged and bound each night and assaulted each day, Kristen must have become increasingly ill.

Karla is seen to perform enthusiastically in the sex sessions, and even complied when Paul told her to insert the neck of a wine bottle into Kristen's anus. But she hesitates when Kristen winces and doesn't want to push it in further. Paul then takes over the abuse.

The three days passed in a bizarre mix of rape and lesbian assault, interspersed with watching ordinary videos and listening to Paul's rap music. At one stage when Paul asked Kristen what she wanted to eat she named a takeaway outlet far away from the house. The intelligent teenager obviously knew that separating Paul from Karla was her only chance.

Whilst he was out, she begged Karla to let her go. Karla said that she daren't. What happened next differs according to who is telling the story. Paul would say that he returned with the takeaway to find Karla crying and saying that Kristen had tried to escape and that she'd had to hit her and mistakenly killed her. Paul had left Karla in charge, holding a rubber mallet, and Paul would say that Karla had used it to bludgeon the girl about the head and face. Whatever the true story, there were deep bruises below Kristen's eyes when her body was found and her mouth and nose had filled with her own blood.

Karla's version would be that Paul strangled Kristen with a cord for a full seven minutes. As with Lesley's murder, a forensic authority would later dispute this, saying there wasn't enough damage to the throat to suggest ligature force.

Whatever the modus operandi, Kristen was killed. Karla then showered and blow dried her hair in order to look nice for going to the Homolkas. Again, she sat through the family meal and no one noticed anything amiss. Her parents even mentioned how sad it was that Kristen was missing and commented on the massive search.

Back home, Karla douched Kristen's vagina and anus to make sure that she got rid of any semen samples. She also cut off the girl's hair so that any carpet fibres caught in her locks wouldn't be traced to them.

Paul couldn't bear to help dismember another corpse so they left her body intact, driving it to a lonely country road. Karla then helped Paul carry it to a dump. Because the means of disposal was so different to Leslie's, police didn't initially link the two deaths.

Four months later the couple went to Disneyworld with their beloved camcorder. At one stage Paul trains the video on a tanned Karla and asks her what she likes to do. 'Showing off, licking little girls, making my man happy,' she replies.

Hiring a prostitute

The next week they drove up to a prostitute and Karla asked her to accompany them to a hotel. At first the working girl said no as she didn't want to have sex with a couple, but they approached her several times. Eventually Karla persuaded the older woman, whom they secretly filmed, to go to bed with them.

The sex video shows Karla looking fulfilled and calm, a more pampered version of the blonde call girl. The girl says on tape that the pair of them clearly like rough sex. Paul loses his erection during the threesome and is clearly out of his depth when talking to a streetwise woman, but Karla looks confident and relaxed.

After the marriage it was Paul who increasingly went to pieces. He didn't try to find another job after failing his accountancy exams, relying instead on his cigarette smuggling money. But it was becoming increasingly risky and at one stage he had to abandon the contraband that he'd paid for, a significant financial loss. Though he talked of becoming a bestselling rap artiste he merely played at this, recording his voice over another record and scribbling a few banal lyrics down.

He sat around drinking most days, watching videos and reading books like *American Psycho* in which a man very like himself treats women with appalling savagery. Karla also enjoyed such books, borrowing several from the library every week and reading out sections to her co-workers at the veterinary clinic.

Karla as victim

Throughout most of Karla's relationship with Paul she made it clear to friends, family and camcorder alike that she was having a brilliant time. She told Paul that he was her king, her big bad businessman, the only person that she had ever loved. She wrote him letters telling him how wonderful he was.

But she called a former friend one day, asked her out to lunch and admitted that Paul was verbally abusing her, criticising everything she did and calling her stupid. She admitted that he still didn't want her to learn to drive or to go to university. When asked, she denied being physically abused.

Karla was also distraught during this conversation because the animal clinic she worked for had noticed drugs missing and was mounting an investigation so she feared she'd be under suspicion. She didn't add that she'd stolen the drugs to knock out her sister Tammy and subsequent teenage girls.

How much violence there had been between the couple prior to the horrific beating that led to their breakup is open to dispute. The Homolkas saw Karla and Paul every week but didn't see any signs of violence on their smiling daughter. And there isn't bruising on show in the videotapes that she appears in. But John Douglas states in *The Anatomy Of Motive* that some relatives and friends had seen evidence of abuse.

It's true that Karla was treated in hospital for a cracked rib and a broken finger, and co-workers said that she was sometimes in such pain that she found it difficult to do her job. She also had a bad leg wound that became infected, a wound she would later attribute to Paul.

It's clear that Paul's grandiose plans were crashing down around this time. Karla had lured two more teenage girls to the house and made it clear that she was happy for them to sleep with Paul, but both had spurned him. He was still out of work and apparently hated spending any time on his own.

Whatever had transpired before, one thing is certain. Just after Christmas 1992 they were having an argument when he grabbed a flashlight and battered it into her face, leaving her with the two blackest eyes imaginable. In photos taken several days after the assault she looks like a racoon. She called in sick for a few days then went into work with her face still brutally disfigured. She was also walking with difficulty as she'd been kicked in the legs.

A friend anonymously phoned Karla's mother twice and said to come and get her daughter as she was being badly beaten. Dorothy did and was horrified at what she saw. Though Karla made light of her injuries and refused to implicate Paul, it was obvious that she'd been battered. Dorothy went home and told her husband and the pair of them went round to remove Karla from the house.

But Karla refused to leave - either because she still loved Paul or because she feared that he'd implicate her in the deaths, including that of her little sister. In the end Karel Homolka physically dragged her from the house. They drove her to the hospital where she was treated for her injuries. The hospital then informed the police that she'd been abused.

A place of safety

The Homolkas now arranged for Karla to go and stay with relatives in another part of Canada where she'd be safe from Paul's pleas for her to return or his unexpected violence. They visited her there frequently bringing her bottles of red wine. Karla would drink these throughout the day and sleep a lot, but she often refused to eat. To her aunt and uncle, she alternated between saying that she loved Paul and calling him names.

But as soon as her bruises began to heal she went out to a club with her aunt. She immediately saw a man she liked and made approaches to him. They danced and kissed - then Karla asked her aunt if she could bring the man home to her bed. Shocked, the aunt said no.

The next night Karla persuaded her aunt to go out with her again. Feeling sorry for the battered wife, the aunt did so. Again, Karla zeroed in on the man she liked and spent the evening kissing him. That night she went home with him, not returning to her aunt's house till the next day. Most people need solitude after a break up but Karla seemed to feel lost unless she was in an intense sexual relationship with a successful-looking man.

The evidence increases

Meanwhile the police were finalising their tests to determine who the Scarborough Rapist was - with the answer Paul Barnardo. When they realised this they questioned Karla about him and she wrongly assumed they knew about her part in Leslie and Kristen's deaths. She was cold and unhelpful throughout the police visit, but broke down in tears after they'd left. She cried and cried and her aunt asked her what had happened. At this stage Karla admitted that she and Paul had kept the teenagers captive and that she'd helped dispose of their corpses after their death.

Her aunt asked why she hadn't gone to her parents when Paul first assaulted her, and she said that they might have blamed her for having been beaten. Presumably the truth is that the first assault was the one where he gave her the black eyes. Prior to that she'd enjoyed having sex slaves as much as he did, and she had no reason to want to go back to her parent's tension filled home.

Luckily for Karla, she had looked after the dalmatian of a top lawyer when she was a vet's assistant. She now contacted him for legal representation and he agreed to help, assuming she had a history of being a battered wife. Karla was downplaying her part in the murders and he didn't realise she had actively taken part in the sexual assaults on Leslie and Kristen and had carried their bodies to the river and a dump respectively.

Karla now booked herself into a psychiatric unit and took every sedative available and asked for more. Again, she talked to people on the phone every day, something which doesn't fit the pattern of the withdrawn abused woman. She wandered around in tiny baby doll nighties, wrote letters to friends about how misunderstood she was and started to read books on victimhood and repressed memory. Her parents visited, and it was then that she handed them a note which admitted her part in her sister Tammy's death.

The plea bargain

It's a well known fact that whoever squeals first gets the lightest sentence. Karla's legal reps presented her as a victim who had been forced to participate in Kristen's abduction by Paul Barnardo. She accepted a plea bargain of twelve years if she testified against her husband in court.

Some time after this the tapes were discovered - and they showed Karla instructing the girls how to sexually satisfy Paul and herself. They also showed her performing oral sex on them and making them perform it on her. She did not look at all victim-like in any of the films, saying to Paul 'I got some good mouth shots there' when directing the fellatio part of the videos. And when Kristen was licking Karla, Karla instructed 'A little deeper, please.' She would also show a complete lack of empathy with the terrified girl, telling Paul that Kristen was getting off on it.

Kristen, clearly trying to form a bond with her captors, at one stage says that Karla is experienced in 'this', meaning lesbian activities. Karla denies it, but it was, of course, true. Paul thought only of his pleasure in bed so it was easier for Karla to find sexual satisfaction with other women - and as she was a psychopath she didn't care if the other women consented or not.

The judge ordered that Canadians couldn't legally read of Karla's crimes until Paul had also been tried. This sent many Canadians into a frenzy. Thousands crossed the American border to buy American newspapers covering the story. Others found information on the internet.

Court

The Homolkas now told friends and co-workers that they didn't know where they'd find the money to buy Karla's temporary freedom, but her father eventually put up their house as bail. Her friends were equally loyal. But as the facts leaked out the Canadian public were understandably incensed and she was spat upon in the street. She would write to a friend that the public were wrong to hate her, that she was as much Paul's victim as anyone else.

The police and certain psychiatrists had initially assumed that Karla was a compliant victim - and had thus unwittingly given her a defense. By the time she went to court Karla had become a lay expert on post traumatic stress disorder and was presenting herself as Paul's helpless pawn.

During the trial she showed little emotion, only dabbing theatrically at her eyes with a handkerchief when the mothers of the dead girls made statements. She smiled when she heard about the local news ban. So many indignities had been carried out on the young victims that it took almost half an hour to read the charges out.

The trial was attended by Mr and Mrs Homolka. Witnesses report that Karel wore a look of resigned despair and Dorothy tried to maintain a detached expression. Karla's remaining sister, Lori, continued to support her but often wept.

When asked why she'd brought one teenager to the house and drugged her, she said she hoped that if she got another girl involved with Paul he would leave her, Karla, alone. She proved again and again that she cared nothing for anyone else.

The videos of herself and Paul with the victims weren't shown, but the court did see videos of Karla having enthusiastic sex with two other women. It was clear that she wasn't just doing whatever Paul desired. She had also written to a friend, saying 'take as much as you can while you can.'

At first Karla was softly spoken and in full victim mode, but this facade soon slipped and at times she became cold and angry. Like most of the Team Killer females in this book, she attempted to blame the deaths entirely on the man.

On the 6th July 1993 Karla was charged with manslaughter, and given twelve years on each charge to run concurrently. She was given two extra years for her part in Tammy's death.

Prison

She was sent to Canada's Kingston Prison For Women and soon segregated with other 'at risk' prisoners. There she still earns a few dollars daily doing prison work. She told a friend that prison wasn't so bad, that it gave her a chance to catch up on reading books and that she also had access to the internet.

She's gone on to take a correspondence degree course in women's studies and psychology, continues to read about victimology and presents herself as the battered wife. Incredibly, she suggested to friends that, when freed, she might like to counsel abused women. She's apparently forgotten she abused women herself.

Karla obtained a divorce from Paul (who is serving a life sentence of at least twenty five years) in 1994. One of their victims tried to sue them and Karla seemed amazed, writing to a friend that 'Paul and I are broke.' She still seems unaware of the enormity of her crimes, telling everyone that she intends to make herself into a better person than she was before she met him. Most of this betterment seems to involve styling her hair, playing badminton in the gym and doing her nails.

Psychological profile

So what kind of person lives inside Karla Homolka's head? Burnside and Cairns, who wrote a book about the case, *Deadly Innocence*, state that 'Karla had a pitiful, pathetic needy obsession with Paul. Its genus seemed to lie more within her own troubled psyche than solely in Paul's charm or magnetism.' This is true of the females from most killing teams - the man sees some weakness in them and exploits it. But the fact that he manipulates her doesn't rob her of responsibility for her actions - she still makes the decision to help him kill.

Stephen William's book on the case, *Invisible Darkness*, suggests that Karla might have been a hybristophilic, someone who is only turned on by a partner who is a rapist or similar criminal. It's certainly clear that Karla was one of the dominant five percent of women - and she wanted an even more dominant male partner. Given that she had no empathy with other young women, the thought of Paul raping them might well have been exciting to her. This is partly borne out by the tape that Paul made after Karla left him, in which he says that he tried to be larger than life because that is what she wanted him to be.

The third book on the case, *Lethal Marriage* by Nick Pron, states, rightly, that Karla wanted her pretty house and garden so badly that she wasn't prepared to let anything get in the way. Nick Pron quotes what she said in court about how she felt after she left Paul. It perfectly sums up her selfish state of mind. 'I forgot about Tammy. I forgot about Leslie. I forgot about Kristen. I forgot about everything and went out and had a great time.'

Psychological tests presented by Karla Homolka's defense said that she was captivated by Paul at a young age, that she was desperate to be in a romantic relationship with a dominant male. They would add that Paul offered her a much wanted lifestyle (she believed he would become a millionaire) and that she feared abandonment.

For Paul Barnardo's trial both the crown and defence hired various psychiatrists to examine Karla, expecting them all to come up with the abused and brainwashed woman explanation, but Patricia Pearson (in the landmark text *When She Was Bad*) explains they didn't. Instead, the reports used terms like a 'degree of callousness and insensitivity of major proportions' and 'an immature, moody, shallow, rigid, hostile individual, preoccupied with themes of violence and victimisation.' Karla was angry at her parents for creating a tense household, had been angry at Tammy, her love rival, and was now vengeful towards Paul.

She simply doesn't fit the Battered Wife Syndrome profile. (I have worked with battered women who, as shellshocked survivors, were a million miles removed from the dancing, flirting Karla.) Yes, Paul Barnardo hit her badly at least once, but she wasn't originally in the isolated position most battered wives find themselves in. Karla was living with her family when she met him and she continued to visit them throughout the relationship.

Battered wives who go on to inflict violence on others have invariably had abused childhoods, but we simply don't know enough about Karla Homolka's childhood to infer this. She may have been *someone's* victim, however, as she hinted to friends at school that something bad had happened to her and she talked of suicide.

The most likely explanation is that Karla was a shallow psychopathic woman from an unhappy home who had been brought up to see marriage as the most important goal. How things *looked* were more important to her than how things actually *were* so whilst she had a large engagement ring on her finger and Paul calling her his Princess she was happy. He was the only person she'd ever loved, and to keep this crumbling facade of love she was willing to let innocent girls die.

She also had a high libido and enjoyed having the girls perform sex acts on her - and she had a dramatic side so enjoyed videotaping the experiences to replay afterwards.

It's hard to build up a full picture of her thought processes during the rapes and killings. Her family said that she never looked depressed when with Paul - so presumably most of her letters to friends about being happy were genuine. Her parents saw her at least once a week and didn't notice any bruises. They approved of her marriage to Paul.

One police investigator would tell her 'You're innocent, you're the victim,' clearly finding it hard to believe that this well spoken attractive woman would willingly take part in such atrocities. And a prison psychiatrist would suggest she should quickly be let out. To an extent, the legal system would help bolster this false picture of Karla's innocence, for the tapes of Lesley and Kristen's abuse were not played at Karla's trial but were played at Paul's.

Karla continued to have an emotionless viewpoint of the deaths, telling friends she might write a book on the subject in which she herself was profiled as the victim. And Dorothy told colleagues that Karla would be very rich when she got out of prison because she could write a book about the crimes.

A psychopath

Some crime books have suggested that Karla can't be a psychopath because she loved animals and psychopaths don't usually care for anyone, far less so-called inferior creatures. But a closer look at Karla's love for pets shows something is awry.

First, as a child she taught one of her cats to perform tricks - something that got *Karla* attention rather than something which was good for the cat. Second, when working as a vet's assistant, she sent a friend a puppy's tale and a note which said it was 'neat' that they removed the tails without an anaesthetic. A true animal lover would be shocked by this.

Similarly, when Karla wanted a dog she spent ages pouring over breeding books before choosing an expensive pedigree Rottweiler puppy. Again, this was about attention and the way things looked to others – rather than rescuing a mongrel Karla chose a breed that is impressive and possibly dangerous. Less impressively, the Rottweiler would urinate copiously each time someone entered the house so it's not clear that it felt secure and loved.

Finally, she brought home a sick iguana, another designer pet, and nursed it back to health. But it bit Paul and he cut off its head in front of friends - at which point a genuine animal lover would surely have become very emotional. Instead, Karla autopsied the three foot lizard for her friends and then they barbecued it and Karla ate a little bit.

Psychopaths use people for their own ends - and it seems that Karla used animals in the same way, seeing them as designer objects. Chillingly, after she got the iguana and the Rottweiler she started telling friends that she wanted a child...

An outcry

Three hundred thousand people signed petitions against Karla getting out, but the judiciary said that it couldn't go back on its plea bargain. Soon her lawyers were trying to get her out of prison and into a halfway house though the authorities - at the time of writing in 2000 - have so far refused. But by 2001 she is eligible for parole and by 2004 she must be released.

Her family are allowed to visit her every six weeks, staying in a little trailer in the grounds. Mr Homolka sometimes stays at home to look after the Rottweiler. Karla has told them that she wants to return to the area where she briefly lived with her aunt after having her eyes blackened by Paul. She continues to celebrate Christmas, explaining that Tammy wouldn't want her to be miserable during a time of year that she herself always enjoyed.

Update

In July 2000 Court TV broadcast a programme on the internet about Karla Homolka as part of their *Mugshots* series. There, psychologists from both standpoints put forward their assessment, with one seeing her as a 'vulnerable young woman... terrorised' whilst another had real doubts about the Battered Wife Syndrome defence.

Some of her friends were interviewed and they described her as 'strong willed, independent' and 'a leader, not a follower.'

It emerged that Karla had told psychologists that within the first six to seven months Paul subjected her to intense psychological abuse and advised her that she was worthless. Again, her friends disagreed saying that Karla and Paul were totally in love, totally into each other. The programme broadcast photos of them together looking exuberant.

Karla would initially tell police that her first three years with Paul were happy - but by the time she spoke to psychologists and to the courts she had decided that they were bad years, and that fear of him had led her to drug and sexually assault her sister Tammy. She said that Paul hadn't told her that he was the Scarborough Rapist until they were on their honeymoon.

But Lesley was killed before they married - and Karla suggested in court that they couldn't let Lesley go because they'd find Paul's sperm in her and link it to the sperm they'd taken from him as a rape suspect. This suggests that she knew of his rapes before she married him.

Karla relayed most of the information about the crimes without showing undue emotion - and the police said she was matter of fact when talking about Lesley's death.

At one stage they took her back to the house she'd shared with Paul, the house that Lesley and Kristen had been murdered in. Karla asked what would happen to her furniture and asked if she could have some of the perfume in the bathroom for her sister. She seemed completely oblivious to the fact that this had been a house where young women had been forcibly held, raped, sodomised and ultimately killed.

The prosecutor said that when he got tough in court that Karla got tougher and that her claim of being a subjugated woman clearly wasn't true.

Stephen Williams, the author of *Invisible Darkness*, was asked by the programme makers what he thought the motive for the deaths was. He said that it was to conceal the sexual crimes. He added that Paul didn't kill any of the women he raped in the street, so why would he start killing those he'd blindfolded and brought home to rape? It was *Karla* who was terrified of being caught, of going to jail - therefore Lesley and Kristen, whose bodies contained Paul's sperm, had to die.

The programme makers explained that Karla had been given her deal before the hellish videotapes had come to light, but that the tapes showed her part in the atrocities was much bigger than originally suggested. They added that the prison sees her as 'a model prisoner... no danger to the public' who will be released in 2004.

14

WE ARE FAMILY
Classifying female serial killers

As the profiles in this book have shown, women can kill multiple times and kill brutally. Yet the reality of the female serial killer has never entered popular consciousness in the way that the male serial killer has. Indeed, many newspapers wrongly dubbed Aileen Wuornos - who killed between 1989 and 1990 - as the first ever American woman to fall into this category.

Though the FBI doesn't fully classify such multiple murderesses - putting them all into the inadequate category of *compliant victims* - other criminologists and true crime writers have defined specific motivations for such female crimes.

The much respected author Brian Lane identified seven motives in his *Encyclopedia Of Women Killers*. That is, Gain, Jealousy, Revenge, Elimination, Lust, Conviction and Thrill. He believed that Thrill Killers were distinct from Lust Killers in that the main motivation was the taking-of-a-life thrill, though they might engage in sexual abuse as a secondary stimulus. The Gwen Graham & Catherine Wood team fit into this category.

More recently (1999) Michael and C.L. Kelleher have outlined various categories in *Murder Most Rare*. The classifications they offer are Question Of Sanity, Black Widow, Revenge, Angel Of Death, Team Killers, Profit Or Crime, Sexual Predator, Unexplained and Unsolved. Some killers fit into more than one category.

Brian Lane's motive of Conviction is similar to the Kelleher's classification of Question Of Sanity in that conviction usually involves the woman hearing voices or having religious delusions that urge her to kill.

The following paragraphs give my interpretation of various female serial killer typologies.

Question Of Sanity

Such Question Of Sanity murderesses kill in a seemingly haphazard way and as a result their mental health becomes suspect. This insanity may be episodic: for example, women can become temporarily unbalanced following childbirth as huge hormonal surges and falls cause them to behave in uncharacteristic ways. Question Of Sanity cases are thankfully rare - of the women profiled here, only child killer Jeanne Weber fits into that camp and even then I suspects Weber only drifted towards insanity at the end of her killing spree.

Black Widow

The Black Widow, who murders mainly family members, usually does so for financial gain. She will often poison her victims over an extended period and nurse them conscientiously till their deaths, which then look like the result of long term illness. She gains the insurance money or their legacy, moves to another part of the country and remarries. Soon her second husband becomes ill and dies, then her third... Providing she remains mobile and manages to conceal her earlier identity, it may be years before she's suspected of any crime.

Anna Zwanziger has some of the Black Widow characteristics in that she used poison and used her nursing skills to confuse witnesses. She killed a woman in order to steal the woman's husband. But she also killed a man who refused to marry her, which puts her partly in the next category, that of *Revenge*.

Revenge

The Revenge Killer annihilates a lover who has scorned her or she kills a rival. These women often operate under a strong level of neurosis so will see treachery and rivalry when there isn't any. Their rage can cause them to kill again and again.

Martha Ann Johnson was a Revenge Killer, murdering her children because of the heartache it would cause Earl Bowen who had jilted her. Unlike most serial killers she had a low IQ, but she still knew exactly what she was doing and took four young lives in the hope of hurting her ex-lover or forcing him to return to her.

Babykilling nurse Genene Jones also partially fits into the *Revenge* typology because she killed children who were being cared for by certain other nurses that she hated. She then tried to put the blame on to them.

Angel Of Death

Genene Jones also fits into the *Angel Of Death* category. Women like her often work in an outwardly caring capacity, especially with vulnerable groups like babies or the elderly. They enjoy the drama of life and death situations and may go to supposedly heroic efforts in order to try to save - or pretend to save - the dying child.

Angels Of Death like to be in control of everything so it gives them enormous emotional satisfaction to be able to decide when a person lives or dies. They often have a history of failed relationships with other adults - killing their young or elderly charges is something at which they can succeed again and again.

The *Angel Of Death* feels no guilt at her own actions for she is able to convince herself that these people would have died anyway, or that they have gone to a better place, so she believes she has done nothing wrong.

Most *Angels Of Death* operate alone - but Gwen Graham and Catherine Wood operated as a pair and also fit into the category of *Team Killers*. Such couples are usually heterosexual, but Graham and Wood were lesbian lovers though both had had heterosexual relationships in the past.

Team Killers

Team Killers often have a dominant individual who plays a greater part in the killings than his partner, such as in the Moors Murderers case. Ian Brady was very much the mastermind behind the children's abductions, with Myra providing the reassuring female presence and the car. Similarly,

Catherine Birnie drove the abduction vehicle and asked women if they wanted a lift, then David Birnie raped them again and again.

But the initially compliant partner often participates in the sexual assaults more and more as time goes by, and may enjoy looking at the victims videoed ordeal or moments of torture captured by photographs. The aforementioned Catherine Birnie later joined her common law husband in assaulting their young victims, and she took photographs of them both alive and dead. Similarly, Charlene Gallego allegedly bit the nipples of her victims and forced them to perform oral sex on her. Karla Homolka was captured on video fondling her teenage victims and instructing them how to please her and her husband, Paul.

Myra Hindley told a ten-year-old child to put a gag in her mouth and to stop complaining. Her fingerprints would later be found on photos of the girl in pornographic poses. Rose West assaulted young girls with dildos and with her fingers - and may have participated in far worse excesses with the girls that Fred actually abducted. It's known that she enjoyed blindfolding her consensual lovers, placing a pillow over their heads and terrorising them.

Profit Or Crime

The Profit Or Crime murderess has a very different slant on life. She kills alone in order to enhance her income - but unlike the *Black Widow* she often kills strangers. Aileen Wuornos fits into this category - and as her profile has shown she also fits into the typology of *Revenge*, as she got her own back on the male sex.

Profit Killers carefully weigh up potential victims, working out how much they are worth and how easy it will be to kill them. In Wuornos' case she got the short term use of their cars and also managed to steal their possessions which she pawned to make money to keep her female lover by her side. She even hired a garage in which to keep the stolen goods.

Wuornos followed the classic *Profit Or Crime* approach of isolating her victims so that she could murder them and then rob them at her leisure before putting distance between herself and the crime.

Sexual Predator

Some crime writers erroneously classified Aileen Wuornos as a *Sexual Predator* but her motivation wasn't sexual. Far from it - the last thing a worn out highway prostitute wants is yet more sex. In most of the killings, Wuornos shot her victims before any sexual activity took place, as evidenced by the unused condoms left at the crime scenes. She wanted their money and she wanted the pleasure of watching them die. Sex just didn't enter into the equation - even her initially lustful relationship with her lover Tyria had subsided into a sisterly one.

I cannot think of any female sexual predators - although killers like Rose West and Carol Bundy undressed and molested their victims, the sex was a secondary stimulus. The primary motive was dominance and power.

Thrill Killer

So Sexual Predators are rare amongst females - as opposed to *Thrill Killers*, usually half of a team, who have been portrayed extensively in this book. Myra Hindley, Judith Neelley, Rose West, Charlene Gallego and Karla Homolka and their male partners all fit into this category. They killed partly for kicks, to enliven their otherwise dull world and bolster their flagging relationships.

Unexplained

Unexplained murders by women are those in which a clear motive hasn't been found but where there is no question of the killer's sanity. As most students of human behaviour know, there will always be a reason for the crime though it may be very obscure to someone who isn't following the same internal script. None of the murders in this book are Unexplained - though the reasons that some of the women committed the murders may seem ludicrous to readers who have had less traumatic lives.

Unsolved

Finally, the *Unsolved* category pertains to crimes which are widely believed to have been caused by a female or females - perhaps because the victims wouldn't have opened their doors to a male caller. Antonio Mendoza suggests in *Killers On The Loose* that some unsolved deaths may be the result of female killers. It is easier for a woman to get away with murder as our society sees her as loving and unthreatening.

15

EVERYBODY WANTS TO RULE THE WORLD
Fabrications of femininity

Society tends to see the female killer as totally at the mercy of her emotions, a mentally-frail being who acts on impulse to please a bullying lover. But none of the women in this book acted on impulse. Rather, they carefully planned their crimes so that they could spend as long as possible with their terrified victims and avoid being traced.

Karla Homolka went round her pretty pink house hiding the phones so that her captives couldn't contact anyone. Catherine Birnie, conversely, made her victims phone their friends - or write to their parents - and say they were fine so that the police wouldn't search for them. Rose West terrified her children so that they wouldn't tell of their physical and sexual abuse at her hands. She pretended to both civilians and police that she'd never met one of her missing lodgers and made up a story about another having emigrated, whereas in truth their remains were buried beneath her house.

Myra Hindley drove to a relative's home and ensured that her elderly gran remained there. This was vital as she and Ian Brady were holding a ten-year-old girl hostage at her gran's house. She bought a wig and a headscarf so that she could talk to children and remain disguised.

Charlene Gallego drove for miles to abduct girls from county fairs and rejected one potential victim when she found that the girl's uncle was nearby and was a security guard. Aileen Wuornos hitched the highways so that she could kill her punters at lonely woodside spots. These weren't hysterical or spontaneous acts.

Jeanne Weber waited until her relatives were out of the way before she assaulted their children - and when a relative returned suddenly, Jeanne pretended she was trying to revive the half-strangled child.

Judith Neelley drove her victims to quiet woods to kill them and leave their bodies. She drove Lisa to a remote canyon and tortured her there before throwing her into a ravine.

Genene Jones also planned her attacks on babies carefully, turning up at the pharmacy with prescriptions for strong drugs and pretending they were for her workplace. She took little Chelsea from her mother's arms and said she'd take her to the play area, but instead used the time alone with the child to make her violently ill.

Carol Bundy would go out driving with her partner Doug Clark in her old car, looking for hitchhikers and prostitutes to rape and murder - in other words, victims that might not be reported missing. She laundered bloody clothes and wore gloves to avoid leaving fingerprints and even decapitated a man she'd shot, taking the head away so that her bullets wouldn't be found.

This careful planning by female serial killers isn't a modern trend. When the nineteenth century housekeeper Anna Zwanziger was dismissed by one employer, she carefully plotted her revenge, putting white poison in the sugar and salt canisters which she knew would be used by everyone. And she gave a little baby a poisoned sweet or biscuit as she left the house for good.

Cherchez la femme

Nurses like Genene Jones are the last people that hospital personnel suspect when the death toll heightens. Similarly, kindly babysitters such as Jeanne Weber and concerned housekeepers such as Anna Zwanziger aren't high on the list of suspects when the very young or the very old suddenly expire. Society's romanticised view of motherhood means that women like Martha Ann Johnson can get away with murder multiple times.

But even when a woman operates in tandem with a man her very presence tends to throw law enforcement off the scent. After all, the traditional view of the serial killer is that he's a lone operator who prowls the highways. A man with a girlfriend or wife and children looks respectable, so he just doesn't fit the bill.

Police had visited Paul Barnardo when they were investigating the Scarborough rapes. He was guilty - but the picture of him and his beautiful blonde wife Karla Homolka initially convinced detectives that he wasn't their rapist. And when two young women were abducted and murdered,

Karla's parents talked to her about it, never thinking for a moment that she was to blame.

One of Karla's other victims was a teenager identified as Jane by the courts who Karla drugged and sexually assaulted. Paul also raped and sodomised the unconscious teenager. Jane's mum was suspicious of Paul's motivation - but Karla's presence in the house initially helped allay her fears.

Later Jane's mother's anxieties resurfaced - just what did this twenty-something couple want with her fifteen year old daughter? She suggested to Jane that her visits weren't a good idea - but the young girl loved Karla and didn't connect her subsequent illness with her friend. After all, why would a teenager suspect a young married woman of doing her sexual harm?

Leslie Mahaffy - soon to be strangled or suffocated in Karla's home - was initially relieved to hear that the second person she was expected to sat-isfy sexually was a female. She would soon learn that Karla was as compassionless as any psychotic male...

Rose West, usually weighed down by shopping, was also an unlikely murderess on the surface - which is why no one searched her and her husband Fred's home for years whilst lodgers, babysitters and even her own children went missing. And blonde twenty-three-year old Myra Hindley talked to her neighbours about the young people who were disappearing from the Manchester streets and no one suspected she was involved.

Police also looked for a male killer when men began to turn up dead in wooded areas around Florida and there were several deaths before they issued Aileen Wuornos description. Hospitals spent a great deal of time checking their equipment and medical supplies when babies fell ill rather than suspect the hardworking nurse Genene Jones.

Many such killers have, like Genene, adopted the caring and benevolent persona of a nurse. Others are outwardly good mothers or devoted housekeepers. We tend to have a healthy respect for men, to spend time getting to know them before trusting them. But we are mainly brought up to believe and trust women, to see them as at best loving and at worse benign. This allows the female serial killer to continue on her homicidal path long after a male would be taken in for questioning. (The male serial killer is statistically caught after four years, his female equivalent after eight.)

Martha Ann Johnson took child after child to the emergency room but the deaths were regarded as natural, despite the fact that the children were outside the normal age range for Sudden Infant Death Syndrome. Even when her eleven-year-old daughter Jennyann told social workers that she feared for her life, little was done - and Jennyann became the last victim to die.

Jeanne Weber was alone with her own children and those of her relatives when they suddenly died - yet no one suspected her and even when she was brought to court she was originally found not guilty. And when one of Judith Neelley's victims, John Hancock, staggered into a hospital emergency room and said that a strange woman had shot him, the medics initially thought he was making it up. They had seen their share of violent or self defending wives wounding their husbands and they'd seen abused daughters wounding their fathers, but the notion of a woman shooting a male stranger just for thrills didn't strike a chord.

The police, too, initially suspected that John Hancock had killed his girlfriend Janice then deliberately injured himself to make his story of a female killer look more believable.

The kindly courts

Even when she's convicted of premeditated murders the female serial killer is often given a more lenient sentence than her male cohort, Myra Hindley, Britain's longest serving prisoner being one of the rare exceptions.

Paul Barnardo got life - whilst his partner Karla who provided the drugs and anaesthetic to knock the girls out, and who was adamant that Paul couldn't let them go, was sentenced to twelve years. Gerald Gallego got the death penalty but Charlene Gallego served almost seventeen years and is now free, despite the fact that she was the one who lured the female victims into her van. They responded to the tiny blonde girl with the high IQ and the cute voice, whereas they would have been very suspicious of her burly ill-educated spouse.

The overweight and under educated Alvin Neelley was sentenced to life despite the fact that law personnel thought he was the most unlikely serial killer they'd ever seen - but tall and strong Judith, who originally got

235

the death penalty, later had it commuted to life imprisonment. Some people fear she will be paroled, especially as she is fighting to get her children back.

Doug Clark got the death penalty but his partner Carol Bundy, who talked some of the prostitutes into their car and who killed at least two out of the known six victims, was given a life sentence that can potentially lead to parole.

If a man killed his four children one at a time over several years he would ultimately get the death penalty or a life sentence. Yet Martha Ann Johnson had her death sentence quashed and may ultimately be paroled.

Folie a deux

Many of the team killing cases are considered to be results of what was once called *folie a deux* but is now known as *shared paranoia*. It tends to occur when the most charismatic partner, who ironically is also the most disturbed, persuades the other that the outside world is in some way threatening or lacking and that this gives them carte blanche to live by their own cruel script.

Catherine Wood found that several of her lesbian colleagues were attracted to her and that she got promoted at work despite breaking various rules there. She started to believe that she could do anything and get away with it - and persuaded her lover Gwen Graham that they wouldn't get caught if they killed.

Karla and Paul were physically beautiful and impeccably groomed young people. They got away with the unintentional murder of Karla's sister during a drugged rape - and went on, feeling invincible, to abduct and kill two more girls and to drug and rape more.

Similarly, Rose West got away with killing her stepchild - and Fred West got away with killing his former wife and a girlfriend. Together they abused and killed at least ten women and buried most of them beneath their feet.

Judith was simply an angry and unloved young girl who despised her prostitute mother - until she met Alvin Neelley who already had a prison record. Together they held people at gunpoint and committed various theft and fraud crimes before abducting young girls for Alvin to rape and for Judith to terrorise and ultimately kill. Apart they were misfits, but together they felt special and invincible.

Carol Bundy was a lonely and unstable woman lurching from one relationship to the next until she met Doug Clark and became enthralled by his talk of capturing sex slaves that they could eventually murder. She bought them both guns at his behest and put makeup on a prostitute's decapitated head so that the necrophile Doug could have sexual fun with it.

Alone, these women were bad news. Catherine Wood completely failed to nurture her young daughter. Gwen Graham hit her lovers during drunken arguments. Karla Homolka was so shallow and lacking in empathy that she would have spent her entire life hurting those she came into contact with. Rose West would have been a brutal single parent - indeed, she terrorised her children when Fred, her husband, was away in jail.

Judith Neelley threatened other girls who were in care with her and may well have ended up being jailed for crimes against property if she'd remained on her own. Charlene Gallego had abused drink and drugs and had two failed marriages behind her by the time she was twenty. As a teenager Catherine Birnie had already committed various burglaries.

However it's doubtful that they would have *killed* if they had remained on their own. They were filled with anger and hostility, but would probably have just taken it out on their children and lovers. It took the arrival of an equally enraged partner to act as a catalyst.

The exception, again, is Myra Hindley who showed no violence towards children prior to meeting Ian Brady - indeed she was a caring and respected babysitter. She also loved animals and continued to pay for her remaining dog's keep after she was sent to jail. She wasn't even promiscuous in the way that the other killers in this book were - indeed, she wouldn't bathe or undress in front of her less bashful younger sister, Maureen. Most of the women profiled experimented by having consensual sex with same-sex partners, one of the signs of a dominant personality, but Myra didn't do this prior to imprisonment.

237

Your love is king

When the woman has acted in partnership with a man he is often portrayed by her legal defence as a Svengali figure who swept an otherwise good woman into his web of corruption. And it's true that some women are hugely influenced by the person they fall in love with. But this is often a psychological flaw in the woman's psyche, a desperate neediness, rather than any particular charisma on the part of the man.

Ann Rule delineates this perfectly in one of the true cases at the back of her book *The End Of A Dream*. The case is called *The Girl Who Fell In Love With Her Killer* and looks at a fifteen-year-old who wasn't wanted by her mother and who set off hitchhiking in the vain hope of finding her absent father. She was picked up by a hitchhiker who chatted to her as he drove to an isolated spot. There he raped her multiple times, battered her over the head with his gun, waited till she regained consciousness then laughed at her pleas and shot her in the head, only driving away when he believed she was dead.

The teenager crawled some distance for help despite her massive injuries and later underwent operations to remove a bullet from her jaw. Once out of hospital she visited her assailant in prison and, incredibly, married him. She chose to remember the fact that he'd given her a lift and chatted nicely to her rather than recall his murderous act. Ann Rule points out that, not surprisingly, the marriage to this violent convict with previous convictions didn't last.

Charlene Gallego felt this need to make her man, Gerald, seem extra special, calling him Daddy because she knew it excited him. She told him again and again that he was the best and didn't intervene when he had incestuous relations with his own underage child. Instead, she helped him flee from these same incest charges and ultimately helped him to lure girl after girl for them to use as their sexual slaves.

Karla Homolka also pandered to husband Paul Barnardo's skewed ego, telling him that he was the king, that he was her big bad businessman, that she would do anything for him. She drugged teenage girls for him (and for her) and held the video camera whilst he raped them. She performed with these same girls - and with others - whilst he directed her as if she was a porn movie star. She wrote him hundreds of notes telling him how special he was.

Judith Neelley also imbued her marriage to Alvin with a magical quality, giving the impression that they could read each others minds. Rose and Fred West said something similar. Ironically, both Judith and Rose would turn against their magical men when being tried in court.

These men were not gods - Gerald Gallego had been married six times, had done time in prison, had rarely held down a job. And Paul Barnardo had given up work, declared himself bankrupt and was making an illegal living from smuggling cigarettes. Fred West was so animalistic that he rarely showered, ate food out of the kitchen bin and lied incessantly. Hardly 'one day my Prince will come'. But these men were made to feel invincible by their psychologically-disturbed female partners, and that perception made it easier for them to rape and to kill.

The exception to this rule is probably Myra Hindley and Ian Brady for he was indeed brighter than she. He had more life experience, having lived in both Scotland and England. He had been to borstal whereas she had only moved between her mother and grandmother's house, a few doors away.

Brady read de Sade and Dostoievsky and Myra had read little more than a fashion magazine. Brady could speak German whilst Myra had the restricted speech patterns of her class. She was square jawed and heavy boned whereas he was tall and slim and had the handsome features of an Elvis or a James Dean, both heroes of the day.

Charlene Gallego and Karla Homolka were as attractive as their partners and Charlene had a much higher IQ and better education than her untutored husband Gerald - but both were sufficiently damaged that they felt the need to make these men feel brighter and more important. Myra was less bright and less attractive than her partner so she fell heavily for him, gave in to his murderous plans, and ultimately paid a very heavy price.

The forgotten killers

When the courts convict a female team killer, society quickly forgets about her. (Again, Myra Hindley is the notable exception.) At the time of writing, summer 2000, Gerald Gallego is still in the news - but his killing accomplice Charlene simply isn't mentioned in many of these contemporary news flashes. Instead, they refer solely to 'serial killer Gerald Gallego.' She has been released and as far as younger members of the public are concerned, she never existed to lure young females to her van of death. Yet those of us who are familiar with the case know that Gerald Gallego didn't kill before he met her - and she had a higher IQ and more access to money and a vehicle than he ever did.

The same is true of Doug Clark and Carol Bundy. Some of the serial killing sites on the internet mention her almost as an afterthought - yet she killed her lover Jack when Doug Clark wasn't present and she was also convicted of killing a young girl that she and Doug picked up for that very purpose. She has admitted that if she is ever freed she will probably kill again.

Catherine Birnie gets less press coverage than David Birnie, and Rose West would probably have been given less prominence than Fred West if he hadn't hanged himself in jail. Admittedly, Fred West himself contributed to this state of affairs by telling everyone that Rose was innocent and that he'd acted alone when she and the children were in bed.

Judith Neelley is probably exceptional in gaining more publicity than her husband, Alvin, but that's only because at age eighteen she was the youngest woman ever sentenced to Death Row. Even she is being portrayed by some religious groups as a victim rather than a sadistic murderess - and these groups exhort strangers to write to 'poor Judy' because she doesn't get many letters in jail.

Men only

It's clear, then, that the female *accomplice* is quickly forgotten. But even when the female killer acts alone, potential witnesses often refuse to believe that she has killed. It's an attitude which allowed Genene Jones to inject baby after baby with potentially lethal medication. Even when one hospital became very suspicious it preferred to sack *all* its nurses and give Genene a reference rather than contact the authorities.

Similarly, the French medical profession stood behind Jeanne Weber twice and swore that the dead children in her care had died of natural causes. Their mistaken faith in female goodness and mother love allowed her to kill again and again.

Anna Zwanziger was dismissed by at least one employer after he became suspicious of the weight of illness the new housekeeper left in her wake but he, too, chose not to go to the authorities. Zwanziger's trail of death and suffering continued. She vehemently denied the poisonings throughout her extended trial and only admitted to the deaths when new forensic tests proved that there was arsenic in the exhumed bodies of her former employers.

When Martha Ann Johnson lost three formerly healthy children she still was allowed to keep in touch with the fourth and so few checks were made that the child was ultimately returned to her, whereupon she killed her too. Hospital authorities did not feel that they had enough evidence to accuse this mother and it was a determined investigative journalist who reopened the case.

Some female killers have even dropped huge hints about their crimes yet still encountered no response from society. Gwen Graham and Catherine Wood separately hinted to many of their co-workers that they were killing helpless patients but the co-workers decided the pair must have a macabre sense of humour. When one supervisor went to the authorities and suggested that Wood and Graham shouldn't work together because they were acting inappropriately, she was ignored.

Even when the elderly people themselves said that they'd been threatened by staff they were merely considered delusional. A loving relative of one patient noticed that she was terrified when a washcloth was produced - it would later be explained in court that the patients were partially suffocated by a washcloth. But it simply didn't occur to anyone that Cathy and/or Gwen might be remorseless killers. After all, we aren't taught to view women in this way.

The dominant five percent

Although perceptions of women have changed markedly since Victorian times, they are still largely viewed as the gentler and more nurturing gender. Many women have careers, mortgages, cars and sporting interests - but are also expected to have children, to care for their elderly parents and to be less aggressive than the male.

Two of the women profiled here were dominated by their murderous male partners - notably Myra Hindley and Catherine Birnie. And the child killer Martha Ann Johnson, with her lack of ambition and her fear of being alone, wasn't a dominant woman. But the others fall into the category of the dominant five percent.

The dominant five percent of the population comprises go-getters, natural leaders. They are strong willed - and if they are female they want a male partner who is even more dominant than themselves. If the couple isn't criminally minded then this can make for an exciting, intelligent and adventurous partnership. But if they are of a criminal bent then these energetic and driven people can do a great deal of harm.

Such women are usually highly sexed. Rose West certainly was, having intercourse with up to five men during an average day of prostitution. On other mornings she had lesbian sex with a neighbour or she went out in the van at night to pick up other paying customers. Afterwards she posed pornographically for her husband Fred. Rose made lesbian advances to her children's nannies, had sex with her male lodgers and took part in the sexual abuse of her stepdaughter Anne Marie.

Karla Homolka was equally highly sexed, taking a plane ride in her teens to give her virginity to a former boyfriend. She had sex with Paul Barnardo the night she met him. She drugged and sexually assaulted various young girls and also had sex with Leslie and Kristen who she or Paul would go on to kill. Shortly after she left Paul, Karla picked up a man in a nightclub and went back to his house for intercourse. Even when she was awaiting trial she found the enthusiasm to send him bare breasted photographs of herself.

Charlene Gallego similarly had many sexual experiences behind her and one of her ex-husbands would say that her sexual demands were outlandish. As a schoolgirl she had boasted of having a black lover, later had a married white lover and had sex with other women whilst living with her third husband, Gerald.

Gwen Graham was an aggressive lover, who had extensive experience of lesbian sex in her teens. Gwen's preference was for lesbian relationships, whereas many other high dominance women simply try lesbianism in the way that they try out many sexual options. Most wouldn't classify themselves as lesbian.

The dominant woman often has more than one lover at a time - especially if they are medium dominance males who she soon tires of. Carol Bundy had multiple affairs whilst living with the writer Richard who loved her. She would experiment with male and female lovers and, later, with a child. Whilst in custody Carol suggested that the policemen have sex with her and she later wrote an inappropriate note suggesting a date with the judge.

Aileen Wuornos' preference was for women and she went to bed with Tyria on the first night they met. Judith Neelley handcuffed her female victims to the bed or to the inside of her car and sexually assaulted them again and again.

Genene Jones was said to go into a near-orgasmic frenzy when around dying children and her first ex-husband hinted to an investigative journalist that there was something unusual about her sexuality.

Anna Zwanziger tried to lure men into bed when she was over fifty, despite the fact that the years had not been kind to her. Both she and Jeanne Weber turned to prostitution towards the end of their murderous lives, though this was probably for economic rather than sexual gain.

The dominant woman is sexually-driven, but there's no reason why she shouldn't be. It's her body to do with as she desires.

She also wants a partner that has status in the *outside world* in financial or career terms. It's no accident that Karla Homolka nicknamed Paul Barnardo her 'big, bad businessman.' Paul's fantasy was that his teenage wife would fellate him as soon as he walked in the door with his briefcase - and Karla was happy to oblige. Though a strong, self-opinionated young woman in many ways, she wrote him notes saying that she was 'his little whore, his little cocksucker'. Ironically this sent his already misogynistic viewpoint of women spiralling further downhill.

Rose West was a loud mouthed, hard hitting mother who made aggressive sexual passes at lodgers and nannies. But when Fred came home he took over and the already strained atmosphere got even more tense. Rose would write Fred slave contracts in which she promised to do whatever he wanted and Fred would later tell the police that he'd 'gotten Rosie young' and had trained her to obey.

Charlene Gallego had travelled on planes and boats with her successful father and she later travelled the country in her own right as part of her work for a food processing firm. But she also wanted a strong man - and quickly ended her two marriages to men who were less dominant than she.

Charlene opted to make the outwardly strong looking but emotionally weak Gerald Gallego her husband and was determined to remain his leading lady, to the extent of helping him to procure teenage sex slaves. Her father had been a hugely strong presence in her life and she told the courts that she would never tell the man what to do.

Actions speak louder

Many of these women have lied to the police, to the courts, to their relatives and even to themselves, as do male criminals. It is people's *actions* more often than their pretty appearance or honeyed words which show the type of person that they are - or that they are trying to be. Thus Myra Hindley posed for photographs over children's moorland graves, showing her lover Ian Brady that she was as nonchalant as he about his crimes. And Catherine Wood told her ex-husband about the murders because they implicated her lesbian ex-lover and she wanted revenge.

Anna Zwanziger also craved revenge and enjoyed watching the upper classes die in poisoned agony. She should have been part of this class but life had robbed her of her station - and now she would gloat over the dying, content in the knowledge that she still had her life and her health.

Charlene Gallego wanted to keep Gerald at all costs and was willing to lure girls to her van to provide him and herself with youthful sex objects. Karla Homolka had a very similar motivation. These young women were willing to snuff out human lives so that they could keep their lover's interest and enjoy better sex.

Similarly, Genene Jones made helpless infants suffer so that she could intervene and appear like a heroine in a medical soap opera. She was also willing to put the parents through the hell of bereavement whenever her intervention didn't work in time. Most of us have a natural urge to protect children and animals or anyone else who is more frail than we are - but in Jones this urge was subverted so that she put her own false image first.

Rose West would paint herself as Fred's victim - but she was the one who killed Charmaine when he was in prison. She was the one who sat on Anne Marie's face whilst Fred raped her. She was the one who phoned Stephen's school and asked them to send him home, whereupon she beat him with her belt until he was hysterical with fear and pain. Rose also sexually assaulted Caroline Owens and frightened her consensual lesbian lovers. She was in control of her life at least part of the time.

Judith Neelley would try to tell the world that Alvin terrorised her, but law enforcement said they'd rarely seen such an ineffectual male prisoner. She claimed that she was totally under his influence twenty-four hours a day - but they had separate cars and sometimes he was in prison for fraud whilst she was free. And the victim who lived, John Hancock, would testify that it was Judith who mocked him and shot him whilst Alvin was out of sight.

Carol Bundy also chose to portray herself as a nice respectable woman in court, trying to put all of the blame onto Doug Clark, her accomplice. But it was clear that she'd killed her ex-lover Jack Murray by herself, so she then opted to plead not guilty by reason of insanity. Ultimately she admitted having shot and stabbed Jack whilst sane and similarly shot dead at least one female prostitute. There were also at least two photographs showing her behaving inappropriately with Theresa, an eleven-year-old child.

Paint it black

Some women commit terrible deeds then are treated leniently by the legal system. But occasionally, female killers are wrongly made out to be more cruel than they actually were during their criminal life. For example, some internet crime sites say that Myra Hindley tortured her young victims to death. In truth, she didn't actually kill any of them herself - her partner Ian Brady did. And even the detective who reopened the case, Peter Topping, admits in his biography that torture wasn't involved.

In a recent Mori poll of 2004 adults, 83% thought that Myra Hindley should stay in prison - and 26% of them said 'because she is a woman who has killed a child.' Surely people should remain locked up, or not, on account of their crimes, not because of their sex?

Some people think that she has met the grounds necessary to be granted parole. That is, she has admitted the crimes and shown remorse for them. She has served a long sentence. She has improved herself whilst in prison by taking a degree and she is not considered a danger to the public since being freed of Ian Brady's influence.

Punishment in prison

We've seen that female serial killers tend to serve shorter sentences than their male cohorts, but is their experience of prison qualitatively different? Former prison officer Robert Adams suspects that it is. Talking of female offenders in general, he told me that 'women's physique and biological function - when menstruating, giving birth, etc - puts them in a different situation to men and their needs.' This may mean that they suffer more.

He also notes that 'women offenders tend to be seen more than men as mad not bad. This leads to many being viewed as being in need of medical treatment. Female offenders tend to be prescribed psychotropic drugs more than men.'

Being imprisoned, the removal of freedom, is supposed to be the sole punishment meted out to prisoners but it seems that female prisoners also suffer by being penalised for failing their gender - some prison officers have apparently told new violent prisoners about Myra Hindley's crimes, knowing that this will encourage the new prisoners to attack her. One prison officer put a decapitated angel in Carol Bundy's prison block at Christmas and helped ensure that Bundy was ostracised. Aileen Wuornos claims that her meals are constantly adulterated.

You can argue that these women have caused intense suffering - but it's equally true that they themselves suffered appallingly throughout their childhoods and that this contributed to their criminality. Do we really want to create a society where, for some people, suffering never ends?

Several hundred enlightened charities and pressure groups have advised that it needn't be this way, that we can create a non-violent society by changing the way we treat our children. The latter part of the next chapter will explore their hugely encouraging research.

16

DO YOU REALLY WANT TO HURT ME?

Theories about why women kill

Because women make up such a small percentage of killers - even in America which boasts the largest number of female serial killers, only 1.5% of the Death Row population is female - most of the research that has been done has focused on men. The few theories about women have centred around their passivity, seeing them as the compliant victims of their murderous male partners. As the profiles in this book have shown, this is rarely true.

Not compliant victims

Many of these women couldn't have been 'compliant victims' of murderous males because they acted alone - namely Anna Zwanziger, Martha Ann Johnson, Genene Jones and Aileen Wuornos. They were all single or separated at the time of their solo killing sprees. Jeanne Weber was married when she suffocated and strangled children but her husband wasn't present. Convinced of her guilt, he left her after her first trial - and she went on to kill again and again. These solo killers were all in the dominant five percent of the population, hardly the weaklings that the authorities would have us believe.

The female half of the Team Killers were also often part of the dominant five percent. Wealthy Charlene Gallego had an IQ of 160 and travelled the country as part of her work whereas her husband Gerald was a barely educated bartender from an impoverished family. She simply doesn't fit the pattern of a passive victim. The police were called to some of their fights and their reports showed that Charlene gave as good as she got. (According to author Eric van Hoffmann, Charlene's mother hit Gerald across the face with a gun to break up one of her daughter's fights.) Authorities would later determine that Charlene was controlling and manipulative, that she liked to subtly pull the strings of any relationship.

Similarly, Karla Homolka wasn't a compliant victim. She had a high IQ and an assertive bent. Her friends described her as aggressive, pushy, a leader and a non-conformist. Karla drugged and sexually assaulted one young girl when Paul, her husband, wasn't even present and was clearly enjoying herself on the videotape she made of the event. She was equally cool when dealing with the police, her lawyers and the courts.

Judith Neelley drove her own car, carried out teenage robberies on her own and had a much higher IQ than her husband Alvin. There were times when he was in prison and she was not, but she chose to wait for him. And the one living witness testified that it was Judith who had marched him about at gunpoint, refused to let him speak and callously shot him whilst Alvin wasn't even in sight.

Rose West donned a soft voice and a new timidity for her court appearances and tried to blame everything on Fred, her dead husband. But living witnesses testified that she had physically and sexually assaulted them and it was found that little Charmaine had died in her care whilst Fred was in prison. Moreover, Rose assaulted one of the officers who came to arrest her - and she was tape recorded at the station shouting and swearing at the police.

Carol Bundy didn't score as highly as her co-killer Doug Clark in the IQ stakes, but she was still very controlling. She tried to buy his time, his clothes, and even his sexual favours by providing him with an eleven-year-old girl they could have threesomes with. She shot and killed her ex-lover Jack when Doug wasn't around and mutilated his corpse with a knife. Psychologists suspected that she was in competition with her necrophiliac lover Doug - he decapitated one of his victims, Exxie, and then Carol decapitated Jack.

These were all high dominance, if very damaged, women who knew what they wanted - dangerous sex that would help them to keep a roving partner, that would make them the aggressors rather than the victims they had been as children, that would temporarily make them feel incredibly strong.

Lower dominance women team killers

But not all female serial killers are in the dominant five percent. Myra Hindley was medium dominance and therefore something of a traditionalist - she was religious and romantic and looked forward to marriage and children. Then she met the more dominant Brady and was gradually ensnared into his self-serving world. The medium dominance woman finds the high dominance man both frightening and compelling - and as we've seen Myra had a similar relationship with her own violent and distant father, making her especially needy and eager to please.

As Colin Wilson has written, whilst in no way excusing her actions, 'she was literally brainwashed,' by this soft voiced and opinionated man.

Catherine Birnie was also submissive towards her common law husband David. She would express this in physical ways, regularly licking around his anus. She had decided to make him her entire life and remained constant to this viewpoint even after they were both sent to prison, writing him numerous letters and arguing that it was unjust that they should not be allowed to see each other again. Catherine told detectives that she had been everywhere that David had been and was determined to be sentenced with him, to put herself firmly in the frame.

Of the lesbian Team Killers Cathy Wood and Gwen Graham, it was Gwen who was sexually dominant. She had been the aggressor from her early teens, enjoying a power in her sexual relationships that had been denied her during her abusive childhood. Cathy at first presented herself as medium or low dominance to the world, but as her profile shows, she was more than capable of pulling the strings. Cathy dominated at home in a passive way - refusing to do housework so that her husband had to do it. She often refused to cook so her child would go out and bring home takeaway food.

Cathy's dominance came to the fore when she found that she could inspire both love and fear in her new workplace - and she took that power to its limit by helping Gwen to terrorise their elderly charges. As her need for power intensified, those patients began to die.

Not bad seeds

Killing, as we've seen, is about regaining control, about having total dominance over others. Criminologists who believe in the genetic theory would have us believe that these women were born with such control issues, that they inherited specific genes that made them cruel and amoral and murderous. Those writers who believe this often cite murderer Gerald Gallego as a prime example - he never knew his violent father yet went on to kill multiple times, just like dad.

In truth, baby Gerald was raised by his violent teenage mother, who had herself been abused throughout her childhood. She took to prostitution and Gerald was then violated by her many clients. His crimes weren't due to nature but to nurture - or rather the lack of it. As former prison officer and Professor of Human Services Development Robert Adams told me during my research 'You never forget your experiences of being abused as a child.'

Sexual explorers

One of the traits that the women profiled here share is promiscuity, a common symptom of women who have been abused. The exception is Myra Hindley who was a virgin prior to meeting Ian Brady and so self conscious that she wouldn't even bathe or undress in front of her younger sister Maureen. She also objected when others used what she thought of as bad language - yet within months of meeting the hugely influential Brady she was swearing and posing pornographically for his camera.

Several of the women profiled also had lesbian experiences though only Aileen Wuornos and Gwen Graham wholly identified themselves as lesbian. The others were sexually experimental, as the dominant five percent of the population tend to be.

Most of these women lied compulsively, tried to manipulate their coworkers and were sadly lacking in empathy.

Schooled in sadism

But the most crucial thing that these female serial killers have in common is that they weren't raised in loving or stable homes. Anna Zwanziger and Catherine Birnie both had mothers who died when they were young and they were then passed from one relative to another, with Catherine's grandparents being controlling and abusive. Aileen Wuornos mother deserted her and left her at the mercy of her violent grandfather. Myra Hindley's parents gave her to her lonely grandmother - and when she did see her dad he often hit her or her mum.

Judith Neelley's father died and her mother started sleeping with men whom she'd picked up via her CB radio. Judith soon ended up in a home for teenagers and claims that she was sexually abused there. (Such establishments are magnets for paedophiles.) Gwen Graham and Cathy Wood both came from families where they were physically abused and shown little love.

Rose West's father was a violent and controlling man, at times a madman. And though Charlene Gallego's father doted on her she was forced to grow up incredibly quickly to take her mother's place after Mercedes automobile accident. We know very little about this family unit - but Charlene was sufficiently lost that she turned to drink and drugs and sex by age thirteen. Like Catherine Birnie she thought that women didn't matter - so she devoted her third marriage to a violent man.

Even less is known about Jeanne Weber's early life, but the fact that she left her home village at fourteen and quickly became an alcoholic may speak volumes. It's very common for parental alcohol abuse to be copied by a daughter or a son.

Carol Bundy was physically abused by both her parents and after her mother's early death she was sexually abused by her father. Karla Homolka's father went on drinking binges and her parents were always arguing. She told a friend after a family argument that she was afraid and had locked her bedroom door.

Abuse is still seriously under reported. I was told by leading British social worker that when they hold training courses for employees, they find that a third of the females and slightly less of the males come forward to talk about their childhood experiences of being abused.

Violentization

But many people are abused by their parents yet still go on to become compassionate adults who abhor violence. So was there some extra component in those killer's lives which propelled them towards homicidal acts?

Criminologist Lonnie Athens, himself the survivor of a violent working class home, has identified this extra component. (Lonnie's life and theories are the subject of *Why They Kill* by Richard Rhodes.) Lonnie believes that very violent people are literally 'violentized', that is socialised into very aggressive ways. Lonnie has worked mainly with violent males so uses the term 'he' throughout his work. But when I studied his results I found that most of what he said is equally applicable to violent women, so for the purposes of this chapter the prefix 'she' is used.

In the first stage of violentization, the child is forced to submit to an aggressor, usually a parent, carer or someone from her peer group. Most of the women in this book were brutalised in this fashion. She also sees others close to her, often siblings or her mother, being struck and belittled. Again, this is applicable in our profiles. She notes that violence is used to settle arguments.

In the second stage, known as *belligerency*, she mentally promises herself that next time there is a fight she'll join in and be violent too. Myra Hindley grabbed at her father's legs in a vain bid to stop him hitting her mother. Judith Neelley stood up to her mother's dirty and drunken clients. Gwen Graham physically fought with her violent mother and by seventeen was also coming to blows with the woman she was living with.

The girl then enters the third stage of violent performance and notes how - perhaps for the first time - the person she has beaten and any witnesses to her violence respect or fear her. Rose West turned from a cry baby into a tough girl who would even fight the older boys. Myra Hindley took up judo, and wouldn't release competitors from holds until they screamed. Aileen Wuornos became so harsh that she was given a wide berth by all of the other girls in her class.

The fourth stage of virulency can now take place in which she decides to use violence to settle all other disputes. She now sees herself as a violent woman - or at least as a woman who, as Rose West put it, 'isn't a soft chair to be sat upon.' Such damaged women now see potential enemies everywhere - Judith Neelley originally said that her husband was the only person in the world who she trusted and psychologists said that Karla Homolka was obsessed with themes of victimisation and hostility.

Coached to kill

Lonnie Athens notes that violentization can also involve coaching, where the aggressive party encourages the more submissive one to display aggression or cruelty towards others. This coaching can probably occur up to the age of around twenty-five as psychiatrists estimate that until then the ego is still developing. Many of the young women profiled here have had such coaching experiences prior to age twenty-five.

For example, the teenage Myra Hindley was taken to war atrocity films and given books about torture and existential philosophy by her older lover, Ian Brady. He also persuaded her to join a gun club and to indulge in painful sodomy sessions. He told her that most people were worthless, that they should crush them like ants. When she was totally convinced by his philosophy, a process that took several years, he asked her to procure the first teenager for him to kill.

Seventeen-year-old Karla Homolka was happy to initiate sadomasochistic games with her lover, Paul. She bought and wore a dog collar, offered him her anal virginity and handcuffed herself for his sexual pleasure. But Paul, unlike most harmless erotic-power-exchange players, wasn't content with the consensual aspect. He started to humiliate her in their day to day existence and by the end of the relationship he gave her two of the blackest eyes that the local hospital had ever seen.

Paul also coached Karla in violent ways, bringing home books about killers and their victims. He would later coach Leslie and Kristen, who he abducted, on what to sexually do and say. Later Karla borrowed such books from the library and insisted on reading the most brutal passages out to her offended co-workers. It was part of her increasing sadism, a desire to shock.

Charlene was similarly coached by her older husband Gerald Gallego and was persuaded to act like his young daughter who he was having an incestuous relationship with. He encouraged Charlene to call him Daddy and to dress in outfits like those his daughter wore. She bought a gun and ammunition for him - and, according to author Eric van Hoffmann, she enjoyed biting and having lesbian sex with the bondaged girls. This would certainly explain why the Gallegos often abducted a pair of victims at a time - one each - rather that the more usual one.

Gwen Graham was coached by her father on how to kill animals on their farm - including farm animals that she loved and pets that she had grown up with. She was taught how to use a gun at an early age.

This 'violent training' explains why so few women become seriously violent, for a violent father is more likely to coach his son to emulate him than he is his daughter. The women in this book were exceptional in that a man did coach them in vicious ways.

Sometimes we don't know how many different forms the violence took. Carol Bundy was battered and emotionally abused by both parents and sexually molested by her father. Genene Jones had a troubled and increasingly hypochondriacal childhood (an ongoing cry for help or a desperate means of seeking affection) and has said it included abuse. Presumably Martha Ann Johnson did too, given that her low IQ would have made her a target for anyone irritated by mental sluggishness. We know that Martha feared being alone and married for the first time at age fourteen.

It's hard to know after so many years exactly what happened to Bavarian poisoner Anna Zwanziger during her childhood but she was passed from relative to relative after her father died and such a history increases the likelihood of physical cruelty. Step-parents are statistically more likely to abuse stepchildren than they are their natural born. Anna's first suicide attempts were made as a very young woman so she'd clearly suffered during her early life.

Violence can be lost in the midst of time - one crime book suggested Anna had a good stable childhood in her father's inn, whereas more detailed research shows that her father died when she was five leaving her doubly orphaned and spending the next five years being shunted from one foster home to the next.

Similarly, a recent television programme on Peter Sutcliffe suggested that his childhood was unremarkable - yet a close reading of his life shows that as a child he was terrified of his father and used to pop his head around the door to make sure that the man wasn't home before he entered the house.

Other sources have suggested that Ted Bundy had a good upbringing, whereas in truth his religious unmarried mother was ashamed of him and his violent and bigoted grandfather became his role model for his formative years.

Cruel and controlling families

Alice Miller wrote in *Banished Knowledge* that 'It is absolutely unthinkable that a human being who, from the start, is given love, tenderness, closeness, orientation, respect, honesty, and protection by adults should later become a murderer.' As we've seen, the women in this book weren't given most of the necessities she describes.

Further proof that violence comes from within the family is found in Oliver James impressively detailed *Juvenile Violence In A Winner-Loser Culture*. The book shows that the children who ended up being labelled as aggressive had been hit hard and long by their parents. This was true of studies carried out in places as culturally diverse as England, Sweden and New York. Moreover, the violent parents rarely praised their children and were unenthusiastic about the good things their offspring did. Carol Bundy's hyper-critical and vicious parents fit the bill.

Oliver James also looked at the impact a depressed mother had on her children. Small children (under the age of five) in her care were particularly at risk. He notes that 'Murder of children is the only violent offence that women are more likely to commit than men.' Quadruple child killer Martha Ann Johnson, depressed but determined to get her ex-husband back, and the alcoholic Jeanne Weber slot into this category.

He describes depressed mothers who rejected their babies. By age one the child became equally rejecting, refusing to acknowledge the mother when she came into the room. These neglected children also avoided eye contact and seemed to retreat into their own little world.

This account squares with Gwen Graham's comments that as a baby she didn't like to be held. She'd been ignored by her youthful and isolated mother so didn't bond with her. The mother then became violent towards Gwen as she grew up. Gwen was doubly unfortunate in that her father beat her too.

Self hatred

Sociologists, psychologists and women's studies specialists have all identified the self harm that women from such high conflict families experience.

As these abused girls grow up they harm themselves by starvation, overeating or heavy drinking. Others cut their arms or burn themselves with cigarettes and there may be several attempts at suicide.

This is true of the killers in this text - Anna Zwanziger, Jeanne Weber, Catherine Birnie, Charlene Gallego and Aileen Wuornos all had drink and/or drug problems. Martha Ann Johnson, Catherine Wood, Rose West, Myra Hindley and Carol Bundy were overeaters. Gwen Graham had cut and burnt herself, Genene Jones abused prescription medication whilst Judith Neelley lived off a diet of junk food and neglected herself physically to the point where she and her clothes were unclean.

Karla Homolka, though slim and beautiful, became obsessed with her diet and thought she was fat. She also turned up at school talking of suicide and showed faint marks on her wrists. She came from a family of heavy drinkers and in the days before her trial was sometimes drunk by the afternoon.

It's true that many criminals don't accept responsibility for their own actions, blaming the crimes on bad luck or pornography or hearing voices - and some might say the same is true of those who cry abused childhood. But there are independent witnesses to many of the cases in this book who testify that the children were indeed abused.

Some of these girls were so isolated and brainwashed by their abusive families that they thought the beatings and excessive rules were normal. Rose West, who continued to have an unhealthy relationship with her incestuous father when she was a married woman, conforms to this pattern. Carol Bundy also talked about the good times like family outings - and it was through talking to relatives that they uncovered the physical beatings and emotional humiliation that had actually occurred in her childhood home.

Parents in denial

Many of these punitive parents knew that the neighbours were talking about them, and in some cases their children were fostered because of the abuse, but the parents still didn't seek help for their violence or change their behaviour. There is a rigidity amongst some parents that prevents them from acknowledging the pain they can create.

John Douglas, in *The Anatomy Of Motive*, tells the story of mass murder-er Charles Whitman, who was frequently hit by his father. His father also beat his mother. Young Charles was often bruised and was almost drowned by his father for coming home drunk when he was eighteen.

Charles Whitman eventually took this hatred out on the world, killing his wife and his mother then taking refuge in a Texas tower. He shot thir-teen strangers before being shot dead by police.

After the massacre, his father admitted that he had made his children call him 'sir' throughout their brutalised childhoods - but rather than regretting his harsh treatment of them, he felt he hadn't punished them enough.

Life after life

Charles Whitman isn't alone as a beaten child who grew up to take revenge on the world. Again and again, prison authorities note that today's prison-ers were yesterday's abused children. As we've seen, many of the killers profiled here were regularly hit by their parents or grandparents when they were growing up. As adult prisoners, such men and women often remain distressed or dangerous. Most institutions opt for a policy of just locking such prisoners up but Grendon Prison in Buckinghamshire, England, has opted for a more constructive approach.

This prison offers group therapy to some of the country's most violent male prisoners. Eric Cullen, former head of the prison's psychology unit, spoke of Grendon's work in the BBC2 documentary *Behind Bars*. He said that prisoners had to come to terms with what they'd done to others, that they had to understand how they'd become the person that they now wanted to change.

Dr Joseph Marr, one of Grendon's psychotherapists added 'If we were showing abused children, people would want to rescue them. The inmates are these children grown up.'

The talking - and listening - cure seems to do some good, though we're not talking miracles. Most prisons have a recidivism rate of sixty percent whereas Grendon has forty-five percent, the lowest reoffending rate of any British prison.

At group therapy sessions the men talk of their childhoods - being beaten by their parents and/or sexually abused in children's homes is revealed in their stories again and again.

Ironically, the public often opts for even more punitive measures when abused children become criminally abusive adults. Readers of crime magazines sometimes suggest that we should put killers in the stocks and publicly humiliate them. The awful reality is that these men and women have already been humiliated and hit by their supposed carers throughout their childhoods and are now passing the violence on.

Robert Adams, who I interviewed in the summer of 2000, agrees that there's often a link between being a victim and becoming a victimiser. 'There is evidence that people who have been physically or sexually abused in their childhood, *and who haven't coped with this*, go on to abuse others or be violent towards them,' says the former prison officer. (My italics.) He adds that some people don't pass the abuse on. 'The major problem is how to predict who will and who won't. By and large, criminologists can't help with this one, though they do have lots of theories.'

As this book has shown, Lonnie Athens four-step theory of violentization (being brutalised, resolving to return the violence, being violent, realising that this violence pays off) is one of the theories that makes sense.

The perils of punishment

Extensive data has shown that children who are frequently smacked have more behavioural problems, show more aggression or depression and have more problems with their mental and emotional health than children from less punitive families. Carol Bundy, Judith Neelley, Catherine Birnie, Cathy Wood, Gwen Graham, Rose West and Aileen Wuornos all showed these aggressive or depressive traits during their violent and dysfunctional childhoods. The others would show their aggression later - but the seeds were sown when they were young.

Three large American studies conducted in the 1990's showed that children who were spanked regularly showed a marked rise in anti-social behaviour over a two year period. Conversely, those children who were rarely or never hit showed no increase in anti-social behaviour over the same period. (Research found in Barnardo's National Children's Bureau Highlight newsletter number 166)

Other countries - including Austria, Cyprus, Denmark, Finland, Norway - have taken notice of the data and have made it illegal for adults to hit children. Sweden banned such punishment in 1979, which means that an entire generation has now grown up largely without being physically humiliated.

Granted, most of us who are regularly hit by angry adults don't go on to become serial killers - but many such children grow up to develop drink problems and eating disorders. Others go on to hit their partners or their children or just live very unhappy and damaged lives.

Many parents think that if they stop hitting their children that they will spoil them - but Elie Godsi, author of the compassionate and knowledgeable *Violence In Society*, writes that it is love rather than hate which saves people from criminality and from ongoing personal distress. To quote from Walter Parsons, a former Chairman of Leeds Juvenile Court 'You can whip vice into a boy but you can't whip it out.'

Poisonous parents

So how does society make such abusive parents change? Hard-hitting mothers and fathers somehow manage to blank their actions out, to rewrite history in their heads.

Many people saw Rose West striking her children in the street. Other neighbours thought that she was too severe when it came to discipline. Yet her oldest son Stephen says, truthfully, 'I think Mum has forgotten the beatings she gave us as a child and how she treated us. She would deny it ever happened in court. I know she would.'

There was also a form of denial in Daisy, Rose's mother, who seemed surprised that her terrorised children grew into adults who couldn't cope with life. But how could they be expected to cope when they'd had no praise, no fun, and had been regularly brutalised by their hate-filled father?

Society often makes excuses for spiteful and inadequate parenting or - in the absence of full information - puts a benign slant on child cruelty. The original reports of the West household described it as a disciplined but loving home.

The press also said that Myra Hindley came from a loving respectable home - yet observers said that Myra's parents had nothing in common and that her father was reclusive and violent. He himself admitted he never had any feelings for the child. One of the websites about Carol Bundy states that her parents did their best for her - their best being to physically, emotionally and sexually abuse her so badly that she made her first suicide attempt at the age of twelve or thirteen.

Elie Godsi has worked with offenders in Rampton, a maximum security hospital for offenders detained under the Mental Health Act. He writes eloquently of his experiences in *Violence In Society*. Again and again he found that such prisoners had been repeatedly abused by their parents or carers. He's all too aware of the fact that 'various levels of hitting, shaking, shoving, and pulling children is for much of the population an acceptable method of child rearing' and that there is a fine 'transition between physical punishment and physical abuse.'

Over ninety percent of parents at some time hit their children - and some people hit them several times a week - so there is a great deal of emotional hurt, fear and physical pain in the world today. Small wonder that violent crime rates are so frighteningly high.

So-called legitimate punishment often turns into abuse. The parents of the serial killers in this book mocked and hit their helpless offspring again and again - but they believed that they had the law on their side so they continued their attacks.

Not just a smack

Many parents refuse to see their own actions as abusive. Catherine Wood's mother admitted that her husband was 'difficult' but was adamant that she wouldn't have let him abuse Cathy or her siblings. A relative believed otherwise. Rose West's father moved his family to a different area, rather than change his violent ways, when the neighbours gossiped about his frightened children's screams.

Other research has backed this up, finding that parents trivialised hitting their children, saying that it was 'just a tap.' But when the children themselves were asked they said 'It feels like someone banged you with a hammer,' and 'It's like breaking your bones.' Aileen Wuornos grandfather kept the curtains closed so that passers by couldn't hear her crying as he hit her and Gwen Graham bore the marks of childhood punishments into adulthood.

Many other children are also given more than minor smacks. Dr Susan Forward, author of *Toxic Parents*, states honestly that 'any behaviour that inflicts significant physical pain on a child, regardless of whether it leaves marks' is physical abuse.

Over the past few years many children's charities have become aware that legal punishments in the home constitute abuse and lead to increased violence in society. In a bid to both educate and legislate, the charity EPOCH was formed in 1989.

EPOCH, which stands for *End Physical Punishment Of Children* later linked to the *Association For The Protection Of All Children*, generally known as APPROACH. Many religious groups have joined the campaign to stop parents hitting their children, pointing out that though 'spare the rod and spoil the child' appears in some holy books it does not constitute doctrinal text.

EPOCH have produced a range of leaflets, booklets and posters which show the dangers of hitting children and which emphasise the use of positive discipline. As they say 'rewards such as praise, approval and hugs work much better' than smacks and 'the more politeness, consideration and co-operation children get, the more they'll give.' The organisation also reports that 'parents who try alternatives report success.'

Most of the female killers in this book suffered parental shouts and blows rather than the deserved love and hugs and approval. The others were coached by violent men who had once suffered at the hands of *their* violent parents. The results were ultimately disastrous.

As Alice Miller writes in *Banished Knowledge*, 'When one day the ignorance arising from childhood repression is eliminated and humanity has awakened, an end can be put to this production of evil.' She's describing the repressed memories of being hit and humiliated as a child.

Almost all of the profiled female killers gave birth to children who are now in the homes of foster families or relatives. If the law was changed to make physical punishment illegal then these children would assuredly suffer less than their mothers did.

261

Select Bibliography

Adams, Robert *The Abuses Of Punishment* Macmillan Press, 1998

Biondi, Ray and Hecox, Walt *All His Father's Sins* Pocket Books, 1988

Burn, Gordon *Happy Like Murderers* Faber and Faber, 1998

Burnside, Scott and Cairns, Alan *Deadly Innocence* Warner Books, 1995

Canter, David *Criminal Shadows: Inside The Mind Of The Serial Killer* Harper Collins, 1995

Cauffiel, Lowell *Forever And Five Days* Pinnacle Books, 1992

Clark, Steve and Morley, Mike *Murder In Mind* Central/Boxtree Publishing, 1993

Cook, Thomas H. *Early Graves* Signet/Onyx, 1992

Douglas, John and Olshaker, Mark *The Anatomy Of Motive* Simon and Schuster, 2000

Douglas, John and Olshaker, Mark *Journey Into Darkness* Heinemann, 1997

Farr, Louise *The Sunset Murders* Pocket Books, 1992

Forward, Dr Susan *Toxic Parents: Overcoming The Legacy Of Parental Abuse* Bantam Press, 1990

Godsi, Elie *Violence In Society: The Reality Behind Violent Crime* Constable, 1999

Goodman, Jonathan (edited) *The Lady Killers: Famous Women Murderers* Piatkus, 1990

Goodman, Jonathan (edited) *True Crime* Parragon, 1999

Hare, Dr Robert D *Without Conscience: The Disturbing World Of The Psychopaths Among Us* Warner, 1994

Hoffmann, Eric van *A Venom In The Blood* Pinnacle Books, 1990

James, Oliver *Juvenile Violence In A Winner-Loser Culture* Free Association Books, 1995

Jones, Richard Glyn *Couples Who Kill* Virgin Publishing, 1993

Kelleher, Michael and Kelleher, C.L. *Murder Most Rare* Dell Publishing, 1999

Kendall, Philip C and Hammen, Constance *Abnormal Psychology* Houghton Mifflin Company, 1995

Lane, Brian *The Encyclopaedia Of Women Killers* Hodder Headline, 1994

Manners, Terry *Deadlier Than The Male: Stories Of Female Serial Killers* Pan, 1995

Masters, Brian *She Must Have Known* Corgi reprint, 1998

Mendoza, Antonio *Killers On The Loose* Virgin Publishing, 2000

Miller, Alice *Banished Knowledge: Facing Childhood Injuries* Virago, 1990

Moir, Ann and Jessel, David *A Mind To Crime* Michael Joseph, 1995

Moore, Kelly and Reed, Dan *Deadly Medicine* St Martin's Press, 1988

Norris, Joel *Serial Killers: The Growing Menace* Arrow Books, 1988

Nash, Jay Robert *Compendium Of World Crime* Harrap Ltd, 1983

Pron, Nick *Lethal Marriage* Ballantine Books, 1995

Rhodes, Richard *Why They Kill: The Discoveries Of A Maverick Criminologist* Alfred and Knopf, 1999 (The maverick criminologist is Lonnie Athens)

Ritchie, Jean *Myra Hindley: Inside The Mind Of A Murderess* Angus and Robertson, 1988

Rule, Ann *The End Of The Dream And Other True Cases* Warner Books, 1999

Stevens, Serita Deborah with Klarner, Anne *Deadly Doses: A Writer's Guide To Poisons* Writer's Digest Books, 1990

Sounes, Howard *Fred And Rose* Warner Books, 1995

Sparrow, Gerald *Women Who Murder* Arthur Barker Ltd, 1970

Topping, Peter *Topping: The Autobiography Of The Police Chief In The Moors Murders Case* Angus and Robertson, 1989

Weber, Don and Bosworth, Charles *Precious Victims* Virgin Publishing, 1992

West, Stephen and West, Mae *Inside 25 Cromwell Street* Peter Grose Publishing, 1995

Williams, Emlyn *Beyond Belief* Pan Books, 1960

Williams, Stephen *Invisible Darkness* Bantam edition (USA), 1998

Wilson, Colin *The Corpse Garden* True Crime Library, 1998

Wilson, Colin *A Plague Of Murder* Robinson Publishing, 1995

Wilson, Colin and Seaman, Donald *Encyclopaedia Of Modern Murder* Pan Books, 1986

Wilson, Colin and Seaman, Donald *The Serial Killers* W.H. Allen, 1990

Magazines

True Crime Monthly, *True Detective Monthly* and *Master Detective Monthly* have all given useful updates on the cases of Myra Hindley, Rose West and mothers who kill over the years.

Leaflets and booklets

Children & Violence Report The Gulbbenkian Foundation, 1995

Hitting People Is Wrong - And Children Are People Too EPOCH Worldwide/APPROACH

The No Smacking Guide To Good Behaviour by Penelope Leach, APPROACH

Think Before You Smack APPROACH

Towards A Non-Violent Society: Checkpoints For Early Years by Sue Finch, National Children's Bureau

For EPOCH subscription details send an sae to APPROACH Ltd, 77 Holloway Road, London, N7 8JZ.

Webography

The True Crime Library http://crimelibrary.com A regularly updated website which profiles many serial killers and offers up to date reportage on other serious crimes.
Court TV http://www.courttv.com A first class American site which broadcasts its true crime television programmes on the internet.

Filmography

Behind Bars (Grendon Prison) BBC2 documentary broadcast in the UK, 2000
Lambs To The Slaughter/The Investigation/The Web Of Evil Three part series on the Moors Murders by Chameleon Television broadcast on Channel 5 in the UK, 2000
Modern Times: Myra Hindley BBC2 documentary broadcast in the UK, 2000
Overkill: The Aileen Wuornos Story Republic Pictures Television, 1992. Released as an Odyssey video, 1993
Interview With Aileen Wuornos Court TV web premiere, 4th May 2000
Mugshots Documentary: Karla Homolka Court TV web broadcast, 4th July 2000

Index